THE

OF

Anne Askew

WOMEN WRITERS IN ENGLISH
1350–1850

GENERAL EDITORS
Susanne Woods and Elizabeth H. Hageman

MANAGING EDITOR
Elizabeth Terzakis

SECTION EDITORS
Carol Barash
Patricia Caldwell
Stuart Curran
Margaret J. M. Ezell
Elizabeth H. Hageman
Sara Jayne Steen

WOMEN WRITERS PROJECT
Brown University

THE EXAMINATIONS
OF
Anne Askew

EDITED BY

Elaine V. Beilin

New York   Oxford

OXFORD UNIVERSITY PRESS

1996

OXFORD UNIVERSITY PRESS

Oxford   New York

Athens   Auckland   Bangkok   Bogota   Bombay
Buenos Aires   Calcutta   Cape Town   Dar es Salaam
Delhi   Florence   Hong Kong   Istanbul   Karachi
Kuala Lumpur   Madras   Madrid   Melbourne
Mexico City   Nairobi   Paris   Singapore
Taipei   Tokyo   Toronto

and associated companies in

Berlin   Ibadan

Copyright © 1996 by Oxford University Press, Inc.

Published by Oxford University Press, Inc.,
198 Madison Avenue, New York, New York 10016

Oxford is a registered trademark of Oxford University Press.

All rights reserved. No part of this publication may be reproduced,
stored in a retrieval system, or transmitted, in any form or by any means,
electronic, mechanical, photocopying, recording, or otherwise,
without the prior written permission of Oxford University Press.

Library of Congress Cataloging-in-Publication Data
Askew, Anne, 1521–1546.
The examinations of Anne Askew / edited by Elaine V. Beilin.
p.   cm. — (Women writers in English 1350–1850)
Includes bibliographical references
ISBN 0-19-510848-5 (cloth). — ISBN 0-19-510849-3 (pbk.)
1. Askew, Anne, 1521–1546.   2. Protestant women—England—
Biography.   3. Christian martyrs—England—Biography.
4. Persecution—England—History—16th century.   5. England—Church
history—16th century.   I. Beilin, Elaine V., 1948–   .   II. Title.
III. Series.
BR350.A75A3   1996
272—dc20   95-47245
[B]

This volume was supported in part by the National Endowment
for the Humanities, an independent federal agency.

3 5 7 9 8 6 4 2

Printed in the United States of America
on acid-free paper

For Carolyn Collette

CONTENTS

FOREWORD

Women Writers in English 1350–1850 presents texts of cultural and literary interest in the English-speaking tradition, often for the first time since their original publication. Most of the writers represented in the series were well known and highly regarded until the professionalization of English studies in the later nineteenth century coincided with their excision from canonical status and from the majority of literary histories.

The purpose of this series is to make available a wide range of unfamiliar texts by women, thus challenging the common assumption that women wrote little of real value before the Victorian period. While no one can doubt the relative difficulty women experienced in writing for an audience before that time, or indeed have encountered since, this series shows that women nonetheless had been writing from early on and in a variety of genres, that they maintained a clear eye to readers, and that they experimented with an interesting array of literary strategies for claiming their authorial voices. Despite the tendency to treat the powerful fictions of Virginia Woolf's *A Room of One's Own* (1928) as if they were fact, we now know, against her suggestion to the contrary, that there were many "Judith Shakespeares," and that not all of them died lamentable deaths before fulfilling their literary ambitions.

This series is unique in at least two ways. It offers, for the first time, concrete evidence of a rich and lively heritage of women writing in English before the mid-nineteenth century, and it is based on one of the most sophisticated and forward-looking electronic resources in the world: the Brown University Women Writers Project textbase (full text database) of works by early women writers. The Brown University Women Writers Project (WWP) was established in 1988 with a grant from the National Endowment for the Humanities, which continues to assist in its development.

Women Writers in English 1350–1850 is a print publication project derived from the WWP. It offers lightly annotated versions based on single good copies or, in some cases, collated versions of texts with more complex editorial histories, normally in their original spelling. The editions are aimed at a wide audience, from the informed under-graduate through professional students of literature, and they attempt to include the general reader who is interested in exploring a fuller tra-dition of early texts in English than has been available through the almost exclusively male canonical tradition.

SUSANNE WOODS
ELIZABETH H. HAGEMAN
General Editors

ACKNOWLEDGMENTS

The collaborative effort that is the Women Writers Project thrives on the contributions of all its members. Ongoing thanks are due to Brown University and its administrators, especially President Vartan Gregorian, Provost Frank Rothman, Dean of the Faculty Bryan Shepp, and Vice President Brian Hawkins. Members of the Brown English Department, particularly Elizabeth Kirk, Stephen Foley, and William Keach, have provided indispensable advice; many thanks to Marilyn Netter for her help in finding the WWP a new director. Gratitude is also owed to Don Wolfe, of Brown's Computing and Information Services. At Brown's Scholarly Technology Group, Geoffrey Bilder and Elli Mylonas are unfailingly resourceful and obliging in all matters, and Allen Renear is a rare source of energy and inspiration.

Working with Oxford University Press is always a pleasure; many thanks to Elizabeth Maguire for making the Series possible and to Claude Conyers for his unlimited patience, his unfailing sense of humor, and the laugh that goes with both.

A more committed set of colleagues than the WWP staff is hard to imagine. Project Coordinator Maria Fish facilitates all contacts with the outside world with her unerring knowledge of protocol and her considerable diplomatic skills. The computer textbase from which this volume was drawn approaches perfection largely through the efforts of Carole Mah and Syd Bauman. I thank Julia Flanders for defining the position of managing editor and easing me into the very big shoes she left behind. New Director Carol DeBoer-Langworthy deserves thanks for bringing a hearty serving of Midwestern pragmatism into the office. Others who have made this series possible include Elizabeth Adams, Anthony Arnove, Rebecca Bailey, Kim Bordner, Susie Castellanos, Paul Caton, Nick Daly, Cathleen Drake, Faye Halpern, Loren Noveck, Anastasia Porter, Kasturi Ray, Caleb Rounds, and Kristen Whissel.

ELIZABETH TERZAKIS
Managing Editor

ACKNOWLEDGMENTS

Throughout this project, I have relied on the scholarship and advice of many people. I owe a great debt to Elizabeth Hageman for overseeing the edition; her careful reading, research, and expert advice have been essential from beginning to end. I also thank the editors of texts published earlier in this series for their pathbreaking work. Scholars whose published work has consistently informed and guided my research on the early Reformation in England include Janel Mueller, John N. King, Susan Brigden, and John Guy. I am particularly grateful to Janel Mueller for commenting so helpfully on the Introduction. I thank Susan Brigden for graciously answering my questions. My work on Askew has benefited from hard questions asked by Janis Butler Holm. Margaret P. Hannay first gave me the opportunity to write about Askew in the anthology, *Silent But for the Word: Tudor Women as Patrons, Translators, and Writers of Religious Works* (1985), from which time I date a friendship and many productive conversations. Thomas S. Freeman has generously shared his research on Foxe's sources for the *Actes and Monuments* and has kindly given me permission to cite his unpublished work. Discussions with Lynn Staley, especially about religious dissent, have always been enlightening; as a friend and colleague, Lynn is a continuing inspiration.

Students and colleagues at Framingham State College have given much support. The experience of teaching women's texts with Helen Heineman will always influence my work. Students Laura Beals, Lisa Zagami, and John Riley took the time to read and comment helpfully on the Introduction.

I am grateful to Professor Philippa Goold of the Classics Department, Mount Holyoke College, for her kind interest; and to G. P. Goold, Lampson Professor Emeritus of Latin, Yale University, for translating John Foxe's "Epitaph in Sapphic Verse" especially for this volume.

I am grateful for the assistance of the staff at the Bodleian Library; the British Library; the Guildhall Library; Cambridge University Library; Lincoln Cathedral Library; the Language and Literature

Library of the Central Library, Manchester, England; the Folger Shakespeare Library; the Huntington Library; the Houghton Library, Harvard University; and the Pierpont Morgan Library. I particularly thank Hugh Amory, Senior Rare Book Cataloguer at the Houghton Library, Harvard University, for his assistance with bibliographic scholarship.

As founding editor of Women Writers in English, Susanne Woods has fostered a vigorous community of scholars committed to the Women Writers Project. The staff at Brown University has been a pleasure to work with: I thank the original managing editor, Elaine Brennan, and her successors, Julia Flanders and Elizabeth Terzakis, for all their expertise and support.

Dr. Margaret Tatham's generous hospitality in London has most materially helped this project. I greatly appreciate Sheila Pulver's assistance with proofreading.

To my family, as always, my great gratitude for their sustaining presence. My husband, Bob Brown, and my daughters, Hannah and Rachel, are a constant source of strength and delight.

Carolyn Collette, to whom I dedicate this book, is the beloved friend and wise colleague who has made all the difference.

ELAINE V. BEILIN

INTRODUCTION

Anne Askew (ca. 1521–1546) could have lived a prosperous, conventional life as a gentlewoman in Lincolnshire. Instead, she broke the law and defied the rules of her society: converting to the "heretical" Protestant faith, she sought a divorce from her Catholic husband and went to London, apparently to join other Protestant Reformers and to participate in current debates on controversial questions of belief.[1] Perhaps through her connections to the Protestant women surrounding Queen Katherine Parr, she came to the attention of Henry VIII's bishops and councillors who were actively persecuting Reformers in the city and at court. Askew was arraigned for heresy, imprisoned, and tortured; on 16 July 1546, when she was about twenty-five, she was brought to Smithfield, the place for executions just outside London Wall, and suffered a heretic's punishment of death by fire.

In her *Examinations,* Askew creates her own record of her interrogations for heresy, representing herself as the worthy opponent of numerous officials of church, city, and state.[2] Askew's text continually exposes their attempts to suppress a woman's voice raised in religious controversy, and she never falters in articulating her right to read and interpret Scripture, to examine religious doctrine, and to debate religious practice. Part spiritual autobiography, part dramatic dialogue, her work is also an extraordinary history of political and religious life in midsixteenth-century London, written by a woman with an unflinching and often ironic gaze. Besides her *Examinations,* Askew also wrote "The voyce of Anne Askewe out of the 54. Psalme of David" (page 72) and "The Balade whych Anne Askewe made and sange whan she was in

---

1. One of Askew's early admirers, John Foxe the martyrologist, believed that "she might have lyved in great wealth and prosperitie, if she wold rather have folowed the world than Christ..." (page 191 in the present edition).

2. Although the title of the present volume, *The Examinations,* is in modern spelling, the spelling of the first edition has been retained when *The first examinacyon* and *The lattre examinacyon* appear in a sixteenth-century context.

Newgate" (page 149); her name also survives in "A Ballad of Anne
Askew, Intituled: I Am a Woman poore and Blind" (page 195).

The Examinations are essentially Askew's chronological account of
her interrogations for heresy and her imprisonments, interspersed with
the supporting statements and letters she wrote during the course of her
conflict with civil and religious authorities. *The first examinacyon* begins
with a "quest," an official commission appointed to hold a heresy hear-
ing, and continues with Askew's interrogations by the lord mayor of
London and by the bishop's chancellor, the bishop of London's chief
deputy.[3] Askew records her imprisonment in the Counter, a prison
under the jurisdiction of the City of London, where she stays for twelve
days until her cousin, Christopher Brittayn, comes to bail her. Askew is
again interrogated, this time by Edmund Bonner, the bishop of London, and his archdeacon, John Wymesley, who charge her with sub-
scribing to specific Reformed beliefs. Askew describes both how Bishop
Bonner pressures her to sign a confession and recantation and how she
avoids doing so, thus arousing the bishop's fury. Eventually, after several
influential friends intercede, Askew is released.

Her subsequent re-arrest is recorded in *The lattre examinacyon*, which
begins with her two-day examination in June 1546 by the king's council
at Greenwich; again she is confined, this time in the London prison of
Newgate. She is accused of heresy and apparently condemned without a
quest, contrary to the law.[4] In her letters to Lord Chancellor Wriothesley and Henry VIII, she asks for justice; instead, one of the king's councillors, Sir Richard Rich, sends her to the Tower of London, where he
and Wriothesley interrogate her about her court connections and torture her on the rack to extract information. Askew's silence and her
refusal to recant ensure that she will be burned as a heretic. She concludes her history with her own detailed confession of faith in the
Reformed religion.

---

3. Askew dates *The first examinacyon* in March 1545. See the discussion of this date on pages
xx–xxii.

4. For analysis of Askew's legal position, see Paula McQuade, "'Except that they had offended
the Lawe': Gender and Jurisprudence in *The Examinations of Anne Askew.*" *Literature & History*,
3d. ser. 3 (1994): 1–14.

During the course of her narrative, Askew provides almost no details about her family background. John Bale, who first edited and published Askew's *Examinations,* gathered some information from unnamed sources and pointedly identifies Askew in the title of her text as "the yonger doughter of Sir Wyllyam Askewe knyght of Lyncolne shyre." In his preface to *The first examinacyon,* Bale tells us that Askew's two examinations by the authorities occurred when she was about twenty-five (page 7), so that she was probably born around 1520-1. Her father was Sir William Askew or Ayscough (1489-1541) of Stallingborough in Lincolnshire, and her mother was Elizabeth Wrottesley, daughter of William Wrottesley of Reading in Berkshire; they were married some time before 1512.[5] Sir William Askew was knighted in 1513 by Henry VIII at Touraine and attended the king at the Field of the Cloth of Gold in 1520; he was high sheriff of Lincolnshire in 1521 and a member of Parliament.[6] Askew's mother died and her father married Elizabeth Hutton Hansard, the widow of Sir William Hansard of South Kelsey.[7] The marriage increased the already substantial Askew lands and brought the family to live in South Kelsey, closer to Lincoln. Askew had two sisters, Martha and Jane, two brothers, and two half-brothers— Francis, Edward, Christopher and Thomas.[8] Askew's brother Francis (d. 1563), who was head of the family after Sir William's death, was knighted at the siege of Boulogne in 1544, and married the Hansard heiress, Elizabeth Hansard, his stepmother's granddaughter. Her brother Christopher (d. 1543) was a gentleman of the king's Privy Chamber. Her brother Edward (d. 1558) was a member of Archbishop Cranmer's household and cupbearer to Henry VIII. Her sister Jane mar-

---

5. In his will of 1512, William Wrottesley left bequests to his daughter Elizabeth and "his sonne-in-lawe Escue." Cecil G. S. Foljambe, "Anne Askew," *Lincolnshire Notes and Queries* 3 (1893): 177.

6. W. D. Pink, "Ayscough of South Kelsey," *Lincolnshire Notes and Queries* 3 (1893): 118.

7. Derek Wilson dates Elizabeth Wrottesley Askew's death in 1521, but provides no documentation. Dating Sir William Hansard's death on 11 January 1522, he implies that William Askew and Elizabeth Hansard married in 1523. *A Tudor Tapestry: Men, Women, and Society in Reformation England* (London: William Heineman, 1972), 21–24.

8. A. R. Maddison, ed., *Lincolnshire Pedigrees* (London: Harleian Society, 1902), 58.

ried first the Protestant George St. Paul (d. 1558), steward of the duke and duchess of Suffolk's Lincolnshire estates, and then Richard Disney, later a well-known Protestant.

Anne's open conversion, her brother Edward's service to Cranmer, and her sister Jane's marriages suggest a familial commitment to the Reformed faith. As in all families of that time, however, her grandparents' generation was Roman Catholic. William Wrottesley, her maternal grandfather, had requested that his body "be buried within the Parish Church of Saint Olaf in Silver-strete of London, before the image of Our Blessed Lady." He also left bequests to his sisters, one of whom was a nun at Dartford in Kent.[9] Askew's father also asked that his body be buried "in our lady's choir within the parish church of St Peter before the image of our lady in Stallingborough."[10]

In the years when Askew was growing up, religious and political unrest occurred in Lincolnshire, primarily in response to Henry VIII's establishment of an English church. As a landowner and county administrator, her father was involved in several conflicts between the king and his subjects. The most overt expression of the generally conservative and Catholic nature of the county was the Lincolnshire rising in October 1536, a clerical and popular protest over the suppression of religious houses, the collection of new royal subsidies, and proposed changes in ancient church practices.[11] As one of the commissioners of the subsidy, Sir William Askew, along with other officials, was taken prisoner by the rebels and forced to write a letter to the king asking for a general pardon. The king threatened dire punishment to both the rebels and the mediators until the commissioners escaped and the commoners dispersed.[12] In the next few years, Sir William's name also appears in let-

---

9. Foljambe, 177.

10. Wilson, 162.

11. Margaret Bowker judges that "too much innovatory action was taking place" in a very small area. *The Henrician Reformation: The Diocese of Lincoln Under John Longland 1521–1547* (Cambridge: Cambridge Univ. Press, 1981), 149. Her account of the rising and of the religious climate in Lincoln provides insight into the county when Askew lived there.

12. *Letters and Papers, Foreign and Domestic of the Reign of Henry VIII*, vol. 11 (London, 1888), nos. 533, 568, 569, 587, 616, 665, 706, 728.

ters to Henry's chief minister, Thomas Cromwell, for refusing to accuse
a heretic in one case and for too harshly punishing a priest in another
case.[13] Perhaps these activities indicate his Protestant sympathies.

Bale provides a few details about Anne Askew's marriage, his purpose
apparently to justify her eventual departure from her home. Bale's
unnamed sources informed him that she was "compelled agaynst her
wyll, or fre consent," to marry Master Kyme after the death of his fian-
cée, her older sister Martha. Anne apparently had two children, but her
conversion and conflict with the priests of Lincoln led Kyme to drive
her "vyolently" away. Citing St. Paul, Bale approves her separation from
her husband, implying that Kyme was later responsible for her examination by the Privy Council (page 93). Kyme's identity is unclear since
complete genealogies for his family have not survived. He might be the
Thomas Kyme of Friskney, born around 1517, who later married Alice
Tournay or the Thomas Kyme of Friskney who married Eleanor
Whichcot and was buried in 1590. In her writings, Askew never refers
to herself as "Kyme," but always signs her name as "Anne Askew," an act
that attracted the attention of both her supporters and detractors. Bale
also heard from his sources that Askew sought a divorce. Although there
appear to be no extant supporting documents, it is possible that she
went first to the bishop's court at Lincoln, and failing to win her case
there, to the Court of Chancery in London.[14] The likelihood of her
succeeding in Lincoln was slim, given Bishop John Longland's conservatism and active hostility to Protestantism.[15] Askew's own behavior
was confrontational, for by her later account, when she heard that the
priests of Lincoln would "put me to great trouble," she went to Lincoln
for six days to hear what they might say to her (page 56).[16]

With Askew's arrival in London, her activities begin to appear in

---

13. *Letters and Papers, Foreign and Domestic of the Reign of Henry VIII*, vol. 13 (London, 1893),
no. 245; vol. 15 (London, 1896), no. 601.

14. Wilson, 166; Susan Brigden, *London and the Reformation* (Oxford: Clarendon Press,
1991), 371.

15. Bowker, 156.

16. In the first edition, the length of her stay is six days, but in later editions and in Foxe, the
duration is said to be nine days.

a variety of documents that attest to her position as both heretic and martyr and that also provide something of a historical record. But while these documents may give us a sense of the reality of people and events, they also raise interesting and difficult questions of provenance and interpretation. For example, Askew's arraignments appear in *A Chronicle of England,* a contemporary record by Charles Wriothesley, the Windsor Herald. Wriothesley records the arraignment on 13 June 1545 in the Guildhall of Robert Lukine, a servant; Anne Askew, a gentlewoman; and Joan Sawtery, all "endyted for sacramentaries by the Acte of the 6 Articles for certeine wordes by them spoken against the sacrament." But after their examination, no witnesses came against Askew and Sawtery, and only a false witness against Lukine, so that the three were found not guilty by "12 honest and substantiall men of the citye of London." They were discharged and paid their fines.[17] Askew does not mention this arraignment, firmly dating her first examination, "in the yeare of oure Lorde M.D. xlv and in the moneth of Marche" (page 19). Is it possible that Askew was arrested again in June but did not record that examination? Bale does refer to "her other knowne handelynges" (page 13).

Some ambiguity surrounds the March 1545 date that appears at the beginning of *The first examinacyon.* According to the old-style dating customarily used in official documents in England before 1751, the year began on 25 March, so that dates between 1 January and 24 March were part of the previous year; thus, Askew's first examination might actually have occurred in March 1546. She specifically dates the arrival of her cousin Brittayne to bail her on 23 March (page 36), so that when she was finally bailed after a four-day delay, the date was 27 March. If she dated her work old-style, Brittayne visited her on 23 March 1545/6 and she was bailed on 27 March 1546. If she dated her work new-style, the first examination occurred in 1545 and the latter examination

---

17. Charles Wriothesley, *A Chronicle of England During the Reigns of the Tudors. From A. D. 1485 to 1559,* ed. William Douglas Hamilton (London: Camden Society, 1875), 1: 155–56. The *Chronicle* was transcribed in the early seventeenth century.

occurred a year later in 1546.[18] Even a copy of Askew's purported confession in Bishop Bonner's Register does not resolve the issue. Although the entry is dated 20 March 1544 (that is, new-style 1545), and refers to her first examination, it appears after an entry for Nicholas Shaxton's submission in June 1546 and mentions Askew's condemnation which occurred in that month.[19] Foxe noticed the discrepancy in the dates and assumed it derived from the bishop's rigging a case against Askew (page 177). However, Foxe's own dating is not precise. In the *Actes and Monuments* of 1563, on the page where the *Examinations* begin, Foxe refers to the death of "George Wizarde" (George Wishart) in 1546, and then tells "the story of one William Crosbow maker...who a little before" had been punished for speaking too freely. He then introduces Askew's work: "Here next foloweth the same yeare the true examinations of Anne Askew...," apparently implying that both examinations occurred in one year (page 165). Four pages later, in a marginal gloss, Foxe dates *The latter examination* in 1546. In the edition of 1570 and in subsequent editions, however, Foxe dates *The first examination* "an. 1545." [20]

Another dating clue would be the identity of the lord mayor of London who interrogated Askew, since the lord mayor was elected every October. Although Askew herself does not name him in *The first examinacyon* (page 27), some years later, Archdeacon John Louth identified the interrogator as Martin Bowes; Bowes was mayor from October

---

18. A note in the *Short Title Catalogue* indicates that "most citizens, including authors and printers, were heavily influenced by the host of almanacs beginning the year with January; consequently for ordinary publications old-style dating should not be assumed without corroborative evidence." *A Short Title Catalogue of Books Printed in England, Scotland and Ireland and of English Books Printed Abroad 1475–1640*, 2nd ed., revised and enlarged, ed. W. A. Jackson, F. S. Ferguson, and Katharine F. Pantzer from materials compiled by A. W. Pollard and G. R. Redgrave (London: Bibliographical Society, 1976), xxxviii (hereafter cited as *STC*).

19. Guildhall MS 9531/12, fol. 109r.

20. In editions after 1563, the *Examinations* are preceded by the account of Dr. Crome. The date December 1545 is noted, and "the next Lent folowyng" (that is, March-April 1546) Dr. Crome preaches and then recants at Easter (25 April). Foxe then refers to the burning of "Anne Askew and her felowes, in the moneth of July the yeare folowing," meaning the year following December 1545.

1545 to October 1546. Unfortunately, some of Louth's details are suspect: he appears to confuse the first and second examinations by locat-
ing the first examination in the Tower, not in the Guildhall, and by
placing the mayor with the Privy Council; thus, Bowes may not have
been the lord mayor participating in the first examination, but in office
only during the second.[21]

The most likely chronology to emerge from contemporary records,
including Askew's own account, is that she was arrested in March 1545,
June 1545, and June 1546.[22] City of London records confirm that
Askew was detained on 10 March 1545 "for certeyn matters con-
cernyng the vi Articles."[23] She could have written her account of her
two examinations in two separate installments, or perhaps she wrote the
whole work early in July after her condemnation on 28 June and her
racking on 29 June and before her execution on 16 July.

Wriothesley's *Chronicle* records Askew's arraignment at the Guildhall
in June 1546 with Nicholas Shaxton, the former bishop of Salisbury;
Nicholas White; and John Hadlam. He notes their confessions of heresy
"without any triall of a jurie" and their condemnation to be burned.
The justices are named as Sir Martin Bowes, the lord mayor; the duke
of Norfolk; the bishop of London; the bishop of Worcester; the two
chief justices of the King's Bench; the lord chief baron of the exchequer;
the master of the rolls; the recorder of London; and the bishop of London's archdeacon, chancellor, and commissary.[24] Wriothesley also
records Askew's imprisonments in Newgate and the Tower, her torture,
and, finally, her execution. Askew; John Lassells; John Hemley, a priest;

---

21. *Reminiscences of John Louth.* In *Narratives of the Days of the Reformation, Chiefly from the Manuscripts of John Foxe, the Martyrologist,* ed. John Gough Nichols (London: Camden Society, 1859), 40–41. See the discussion of Louth on pages xxxvi–xxxvii. Robert Parsons clearly dates the first examination in March 1545, and notes the second arrest in June 1545; see page xxxviii.

22. Wilson, however, argues for the chronology of June 1545, March 1546, and June 1546 (188 n.).

23. C.L.R.O. Repertory 11, fol. 174v. For a discussion of related events in 1546, see Susan Brigen, "Henry Howard, Earl of Surrey, and the 'Conjured League.'" *Historical Journal* 37 (1994): 523. I am grateful to Susan Bridgen for her advice on the dating of Askew's examinations.

24. *Chronicle,* 1: 167–68.

and John Hadlam, a tailor, were burned at Smithfield, "which fower persons were before condempned by the kinges lawes of heresie against the sacrament of the alter." He also names the chief witnesses at Smithfield as the lord mayor, the lord chancellor, the duke of Norfolk, "with the most part of the lordes, noblemen, and the kinges Councell, with the aldermen of the cittie of London." Having recanted his Reformist beliefs, Nicholas Shaxton preached, "but theise fower persons died in their said erronious opynions."[25]

The events leading up to Askew's condemnation and burning are also documented in the proceedings of the Privy Council. On 24 May 1546, "two yeomen of the Chamber, sent to apprehend Sir Robert Wesdom, priest, had with them letters to one Kyme and his wife to appear within 14 days."[26] On 19 June, the record shows that Kyme was "called hither" with "his wiffe, who refused him to be her hosbande—without any honeste allegacion." He was sent home but Askew was detained: "and for that she was very obstynate and headdy in reasonyng of matters of relygeone, wherein she shewed herselfe to be of a naughty oppinyon, seeinge no perswasione of good reason could take place, she was sent to Newgate, to remaine there to answere to the lawe..."[27] Askew more fully records her examinations by the Council over two days (pages 91–98), the first of which she says lasted over five hours, and the last of which ended with her being sent "in my extremyte of syckenesse to Newgate prison. Another contemporary account of Askew's burning "for grett herrysy" is that of an anonymous Franciscan friar in the *Chronicle of the Grey Friars of London*. He names the heretics as an Observant friar of Richmond named Hemmysley; Askew, "otherwyse callyd Anne Kyme by hare husband"; John Lassells, identified as a lawyer of Furnivalls Inn; and a tailor of Colchester.[28] Like Wriothesley, he

---

25. *Chronicle*, 1: 169–70.

26. *Letters and Papers, Foreign and Domestic of the Reign of Henry VIII*, vol. 21, pt. 1 (London, 1908), no. 898.

27. *Narratives of the Days of the Reformation, Chiefly from the Manuscripts of John Foxe the Martyrologist*, ed. John Gough Nichols (London: Camden Society, 1859), Appendix, 301.

28. Wriothesley's *Chronicle*, this *Chronicle of the Grey Friars*, and Bale all agree on the names of the three men burned with Askew; however, Foxe names the priest as Nicolas Belenian.

also notes that Shaxton preached, "and there satt on a scaffold that was made for the nonse" the lord chancellor, the duke of Norfolk, other councillors, the lord mayor, aldermen, sheriffs, and the judges.[29]

To understand why the execution of Askew and her three companions should be attended by so many powerful officials of the city and the state, it is necessary to remember how thoroughly matters of church and state were intertwined in the sixteenth century. Askew's story is anchored in the complications of Reformation religion, politics, and culture in both Lincoln and London. By 1536, a series of statutes had separated the English church from Rome and established the king as the supreme head of the English church. Religion, political power, and social policy were inextricably linked; thus, Askew's writing can be seen in the context of evolving Protestant doctrine, Henry VIII's religious conservatism, court politics, and cultural attitudes to women.

By the late 1530s, the Reformation had brought the redistribution of Church lands and the printing of 8,500 English Bibles for distribution to every parish church, but a powerful resistance to Reformed doctrine resulted in the passage of the Act of the Six Articles in 1539.[30] The Act essentially stopped the legal spread of the Reformation until 1547 when Henry VIII died and his son, Edward VI, succeeded to the throne. Crucial differences between the Roman Catholic and Reformed faiths involved the sacrament of the Eucharist, communion in both kinds, celibacy of the priesthood, private masses, and auricular confession; in each case the Act made Roman Catholic doctrine the law of the land. Accordingly, until 1547, to deny the Catholic doctrine of transubstantiation was to risk a charge of heresy and a horrible death by fire. Transubstantiation, the doctrine that at every Mass the whole substance of the consecrated elements of bread and wine converts into the real body and blood of Christ, became the most controversial theological issue of the day. Many Reformers, often known as "sacramentaries," categorically denied this doctrine, affirming that the sacrament of the altar was

---

29. *Chronicle of the Grey Friars of London*, ed. John Gough Nichols (London: Camden Society, 1852), 51.

30. See John Guy, *Tudor England* (Oxford: Oxford Univ. Press, 1988; rpt. 1990), 182.

either symbolic or a remembrance and that Christ was not really present. When Askew asserts that the bread is "an onlye sygne or sacrament" or that "the breade is but a remembraunce of hys death" (pages 103–4), she attests to Reformist beliefs long influenced by John Wycliffe's writings. In *Wyclyffes wycket,* for instance, sacraments are explained as "myndes," or remembrances, "of the body of Chryst for a sacrament is no more to say, but a sygne of mynde of a thynge passed or a thyng to come…"[31] Askew's belief that Christ cannot be taken "for the materyall thynge he is sygnyfyed by" also resembles the seminal Reformist writings of John Frith, who argued that Christ's words about bread and wine "were spyritually to be understonde…even as he called hym selfe a very vyne, and hys dyscyples very vyne braunches, and as he called hym selfe a dore."[32] Her repeated insistence that Scripture is the ultimate authority on all matters of faith, including the sacraments, was a central tenet of the Reformation, taught in England by scholars such as William Tyndale and Hugh Latimer (page 49).

Under the Six Articles of 1539 any persons who "publishe preache teach saye affirme declare dispute argue or hold any opynion" against transubstantiation would be "demed and adjudged heriticke" and would suffer the "paynes of death by waye of burninge." Only two witnesses were needed to accuse a suspect before special commissions in every shire, although accusations could also come from the usual twelve-member panels of inquiry; all local officials were ordered to enforce the Act.[33] In 1543, *The King's Book or A Necessary Doctrine and Erudition for Any Christen Man* (STC 5168) reiterated as official belief the Catholic doctrine of the Six Articles concerning the Creed, seven sacraments, Ten Commandments, and the Lord's Prayer. The Act for the Advancement of True Religion in the same year reaffirmed the Act of the Six Articles, but mitigated somewhat the punishments for heresy, for the accused would be allowed to recant their heresies twice; and the

---

31. *Wyclyffes wycket* (London, 1546), sigs. A8v–Br. STC 25590.

32. *A boke made by John Frith…answerynge unto M. Mores letter.* 1533 (London, 1546), 22v. STC 11382. See Askew's interview with Paget in *The lattre examinacyon* (pages 99–101).

33. Acte abolishing diversity in Opynions, 1539, *Statutes of the Realm,* 31 Hen. 8, c. 14.

sentence of burning could be ordered only after a third episode or in the case of an "obstinate" heretic. The accused could call their own witnesses in a "tryall by witnes."[34] A statute of 1544 further modified the Act of the Six Articles by requiring that a "presentment" or statement be sworn by twelve men before any person could be arrested, imprisoned, or brought to trial for heresy.[35] In accordance with this law, Askew was first examined by a "quest," a grand jury of twelve men appointed to hold an inquiry; after her second examination, however, she remarks that she and her fellow prisoners were "condempned without a quest" (page 112). A clause in the statute of 1544 did allow suspected heretics to be arrested on a warrant from one of the King's Council or from two justices or commissioners, but the absence of a grand jury suggests that the authorities were moving swiftly against her as a relapsed heretic.

Just as relevant to Askew's case is the section of the Act for the Advancement of True Religion that sought to control reading of the Bible in English. Drawing distinctions along class and gender lines, the Act allowed "no woomen nor artificers prentises journeymen serving men of the degrees of yeomen or undre, husbandemen nor laborers" to read the English Bible "pryvatelie or openlie." Those above these ranks could read the Bible privately for their own edification, and "everye noble wooman and gentlewooman maie reade to themselves alone and not to others."[36] It is likely that this statute was a response to Reformed emphasis on the Bible which was now available in every parish church in England. The cathedral in Lincoln, for example, had acquired two English Bibles by September 1541.[37] If her trip to Lincoln occurred after the passage of this Act, as is probable, Askew was deliberately defying the law when she read the Bible so publicly in Lincoln minster (page 56).

---

34. Acte for thadvauncement of true Religion and for thabbolisshment of the contrarie, 1542-3, *Statutes of the Realm*, 34 and 35 Hen. 8, c. 1.

35. A Bill concerning the vi Articles, 1543–4, *Statutes of the Realm*, 35 Hen. 8, c. 5.

36. *Statutes of the Realm*, 34 and 35 Hen. 8, c.1. See also John Guy, 194, and Susan Brigden, 346–47.

37. Bowker, 101.

When Askew was arraigned in June 1546, Henry VIII had only six months to live, and his evident poor health had raised the stakes in the struggle for power between the conservative Catholic and Protestant factions. Henry's heir, Prince Edward, was a minor, and the two groups struggled for the guardianship of the boy and the kingdom. The conservatives included Stephen Gardiner, bishop of Winchester; Thomas Wriothesley, the lord chancellor; Thomas Howard, duke of Norfolk; and Sir Richard Rich, a member of the king's council. Against them were ranged Edward Seymour, earl of Hertford; John Dudley, viscount Lisle; and courtiers and councillors associated with Queen Katherine Parr, including her brother, William Parr, who was marquis of Northampton and earl of Essex. Sir William Paget and Sir Anthony Denny, the king's closest advisors, eventually sided with the Hertford-Lisle faction, which in fact assumed control of the Privy Council on Henry VIII's death in January 1547. Askew was apparently connected to Katherine Parr's circle, for her last examination concluded with Richard Rich's asking for names of other sacramentaries at court; he suggested the queen's close friend, the duchess of Suffolk, as well as the countess of Sussex, the countess of Hertford, Lady Denny, and Lady FitzWilliam (page 122).[38] The conservatives clearly hoped that Askew's confession would bring down major pillars of the court opposition, but since Askew did not confess, Wriothesley and Rich tortured her on the rack (page 127). Such desperate measures taken against a gentlewoman were against the law and unusual in practice. On 2 July, Otwell Johnson wrote to his brother to give him news of the current heresy trials, sentences, and recantations. Askew remained steadfast, he wrote, "and yet she hath ben rakked since her condempnacion, as men say, which is a straunge thing, in my understanding."[39] Askew herself remarks that the Privy Council was not pleased "that it shulde be reported abroade, that I was racked in the towre" (page 134), partly, she thinks, because they

---

38. See Janel Mueller's detailed account of Katherine Parr's Protestant circle and writings in "A Tudor Queen Finds Voice: Katherine Parr's *Lamentation of a Sinner,*" in *The Historical Renaissance: New Essays on Tudor and Stuart Literature and Culture,* ed. Heather Dubrow and Richard Strier (Chicago and London: Univ. of Chicago Press, 1988), 15–47.

39. Nichols, Appendix, 306.

fear that the king might find out. Like many Reformers, Askew appears
to exonerate Henry VIII of wrongdoing, preserving the myth of the just
English ruler and preferring to blame his councillors and church officers
for her persecution. Sir William Paget, for instance, is swiftly character-
ized as a man of "many gloryouse wordes" who tells her she can speak
her mind and then deny it later. Askew recounts her lecture to him on
the meaning of the crucial text, Christ's words in Matthew 26:26,
"Take, eate. Thys is my bodye..." (page 99), concluding with her scorn-
ful dismissal of his comparison of the mass to the king's honor. Bale's
accompanying commentary lambastes both Paget and his support for
the Roman Catholic doctrine of the Eucharist. Apparently, when the
Askew-Bale text began to circulate in the new reign of Edward VI (who
had succeeded to the throne in January 1547), these pages were particularly embarrassing to the Protestant regime in which Paget was prominent, especially since Askew's beliefs had by then become official
religious doctrine. On the whole, Askew's *Examinations* were very much
in the spirit of the renewed Reformation under Edward VI, so that only
these references to Paget were politically troubling. Probably to protect
Paget, in an unknown number of copies, the top four lines of page 23
were cut out and the facing page (22v) was glued to the cut page, thus
concealing the lower contents of pages 22v and 23r. Page continuity
seemed to be uninterrupted because the top of page 22v now appeared
through the cut at the top of page 23v. The censored passage begins
with Askew's "Then he compared it unto the kinge..." and concludes
with Bale's "amonge them that perysh for not lovynge the veryte, 2.
Thes. 2" (pages 101–2). Paget's complicity was literally covered over in
part, although the edition published in 1548(?) (STC 852), the first
without Bale's commentary, more sweepingly omitted the entire interview with Paget.

We know that both censored and uncensored texts were distributed,
for one of Askew's chief adversaries, Stephen Gardiner, bishop of Winchester saw them. Writing to Protector Somerset on 6 June 1547, he
complained about the open dissemination of "evil" Reformed books by
those who flouted his authority even in his own seat of Winchester:
"And as for Bales booke called the Elucidacion of Anne Askewes Mar-
terdome, they were in these partes comon, some with leaves unglewed,
where Maister Paget was spoken of, and some with leaves glued. And I

call them common because I saw at the least foure of them."[40] Gardiner's irritation over "evill doers" who distributed these books was perhaps compounded by passages where Askew compares him to Judas (page 97) and Bale calls him "the popes great dansynge beare" (page 69).

Gardiner clearly understood the political implications of Askew's text. In an earlier letter, dated 21 May 1547, he wrote to Protector Somerset objecting bitterly to two of Bale's books, *The true hystorie of the Christen departynge of the reverende man, D. Martyne Luther* and Askew's *Examinations*. Countering both Bale's and Foxe's conferral of martyrdom on Askew, Gardiner complained that the Askew text was "very pernicious, sedicious, and slaunderous," published by "vile inferior subjects" who impeached the honor of the late king by claiming Askew as a martyr. Moreover, Gardiner asserted that Askew's examinations were "utterly misreported." From his point of view, the danger of the Askew-Bale text was that the appropriation of religion and religious discourse by the people would lead to political empowerment: "For if it be perswaded the understanding of Gods law to be at larg in women and children, wherby they may have the rule of that, and then Gods law must be the rule of all, is not hereby the rule of al brought into there hands?"[41] Askew's *Examinations* may thus be seen in the context of the "crisis of authority" initiated by the Reformation.[42]

Anne Askew and John Bale shared religious faith and political ideology, although their style and their understanding of Askew's role as a woman were entirely different. In general, while Bale uses Askew's text to attack the Roman Catholic church and to disseminate Protestant propaganda, often in vivid, slashing language, Askew's resistance consists of the act of bearing witness to her faith and the creation of her own text to record her conflicts with the authorities. She dramatizes her

---

40. *The Letters of Stephen Gardiner,* ed. James Arthur Muller (Cambridge: Cambridge Univ. Press, 1933), 293.

41. *Letters,* 276–80.

42. For a discussion of the "crisis of authority" and the Somerset-Gardiner letters, see Robert Weimann, "'Bifold Authority' in Reformation Discourse: Authorization, Representation, and Early Modern 'Meaning'," in *Historical Criticism and the Challenge of Theory,* ed. Janet Levarie Smarr (Urbana and Chicago: Univ. of Illinois Press, 1993), 167–82.

interrogations, beginning with Christopher Dare and the quest, the lord mayor, the bishop of London's chancellor, and Bishop Bonner himself in *The first examinacyon,* and continuing with the Privy Council at Greenwich and Richard Rich and lord chancellor Wriothesley in the Tower of London in *The lattre examinacyon.* Fully aware of the "expectacion" of her audience of "good people" or her "dere frynde in the lorde," Askew joins generations of dissenters in the fifteenth and sixteenth centuries who recorded their examinations as part of their spiritual struggles.[43] One key difference between Askew's *Examinations* and others collected by Bale and Foxe is that she frequently makes her gender the topic of the dialogue. Continually, she shapes the interviews with these powerful male officials of church and state so that each concludes with the discomfiture of her interrogators by a "weak" woman. Their assumption, articulated by the bishop's chancellor, is that St. Paul "forbode women to speake or to talke of the worde of God." Askew, however, continually defends her right to discuss Scripture as long as she obeys Paul's injunction not to "speake in the congregacyon by the waye of teachynge" (page 30). Her weapons are silence, her own questions, and irony; for example, she answers her interrogators' request to explain the passage from St. Paul with an ironic barb: "I answered, that it was agaynst saynt Paules lernynge, that I beynge a woman, shuld interprete the scriptures, specyallye where so manye wyse lerned men were" (page 54).[44]

While Askew had her enemies, she also names friends who helped her during her first examination, beginning with her cousin Christopher Brittayne who attempts to bail her from the Counter, the City of London prison to which she is sent by the lord mayor. Brittayne, along with the chronicler Edward Hall and Dr. Hugh Weston, intercedes with Bishop Bonner and eventually Askew is freed. Whether she would have been liberated without signing a recantation is a difficult question.

43. See Ritchie D. Kendall, *The Drama of Dissent: The Radical Poetics of Nonconformity, 1380—1590* (Chapel Hill: Univ. of North Carolina, 1986). Kendall defines the importance of the examination in Lollard writing and places Askew within a continuing tradition (123–26).
44. See Elaine V. Beilin, "A Challenge to Authority: Anne Askew," in *Redeeming Eve: Women Writers of the English Renaissance* (Princeton: Princeton Univ. Press, 1987), 29–47.

Askew clearly wished to establish her version of the issue: during her questioning by Bishop Bonner, she records that the bishop went away to write a document, which she saw but does not fully remember. In essence, it was a confession of faith in the Roman Catholic doctrine of the mass (pages 58–59), so that when the bishop read it to her and asked for her agreement, she answered only, "I beleve so moche therof, as the holye scripture doth agre to" (page 60). When the bishop asked for her signature, she claims not to have signed, but to have written, "I Anne Askewe do beleve all maner thynges contayned in the faythe of the Catholyck churche" (page 62).[45] Askew depicts the bishop's fury at the phrase, "Catholyck churche," for she had thus implied her dissent from Roman Catholic doctrine and her belief that the Reformed church was the true "catholic" or universal church.

Directly contradicting Askew's account is the entry in the official diocesan record, the Bishops' Register, of a "trewe copye of the confession and belief of Anne Askewe," dated 20 March 1544/5, a recantation that she allegedly signed and that was witnessed by bishops, clerics, and her own allies, Edward Hall and Frances Spilman. However, the copy was apparently not entered in the record until June 1546; the preamble in the Register indicates that it was entered at that time so that "the woorlde may see what credence ys now to be gyven unto the same wooman who in short a tyme hathe moost dampnably altered and chaunged her opynyon and beleaf and therefore rightfullie in opyn court arrayned and condempned." Such language suggests an attempt to justify Askew's subsequent harsh treatment.[46]

The lattre examinacyon differs from *The first examinacyon* in that it contains less narrative and is often less dramatic. More precisely, it is a collection of documents, each of which marks a stage in Askew's journey to Smithfield. Beginning with an exposition of Askew's belief about the Lord's Supper, the text continues with "The summe of my examynacyon afore the kynges counsell at Grenewyche" on 18 and 19 June

---

45. Askew repeats her version of the recantation episode in *The lattre examinacyon* (page 136).

46. Guildhall MS 9531/12, fol. 109r. Foxe printed the preamble and the confession; see pages 175–77.

1546, when she is questioned about her husband and about her beliefs
concerning the sacrament. She refuses to sign a document recanting
these beliefs and on 20 June is sent, sick, to Newgate prison. There follow a "confessyon" of faith; prayers and meditations; a summary of her
condemnation for heresy at the Guildhall on 28 June when she was
not given the lawful benefit of a "quest"; a letter to Lord Chancellor
Wriothesley; a letter to the king about her beliefs; and a chilling account
of her transfer from Newgate to the Tower where on 29 June Wriothesley and Rich tortured her on the rack.[47] While she recovers at a house,
Wriothesley offers her the choice between recanting or returning to
Newgate before being burned at the stake.[48] Again, Askew insists that
she never recanted during her first examination, and will not now. The
last items are the "confession of her fayth" and her "Balade," which she
purportedly wrote and sang in Newgate. Three stanzas of the ballad
strongly resemble verses from a paraphrase of Ecclesiastes by Henry
Howard, earl of Surrey. Using similar images, Surrey wrote:

> I saw a rioall throne wheras that justice should have sitt.
> In sted of whom I saw, with fyerce and crwell mode,
> Wher wrong was set, that blody beast, that drounke the giltles blode.
> Then thought I thus: "One day the Lord shall sit in dome,
> To vewe his flock, and chose the pure; the spotted have no rome."[49]

Askew and Surrey were in similarly perilous positions in 1546 and their
shared court connections suggest that the poetic influence might go
either way.[50] Askew was burned on 16 July 1546.

---

47. Askew also mentions that Rich came to the Tower with "one of the counsell" (page 121).
In a letter to me of 5 February 1995, Thomas Freeman suggests this councillor is Sir John
Baker, whom Foxe, following his oral sources, names as one of the torturers in the 1570 and
1576 editions of *Actes and Monuments*.

48. In his letter to Anne Hartipole, John Philpot refers to an undated time when "that blessed
woman Ann Askew, (now a glorious martyr in the sight of Jesus Christ,) was harboured in your
house." *The Examinations and Writings of John Philpot...Archdeacon of Winchester*, edited for
the Parker Society by Robert Eden (Cambridge: Cambridge Univ. Press, 1842; Johnson
Reprint Co., 1968), 249.

49. *The Poems of Henry Howard Earl of Surrey*, ed. Frederick Morgan Padelford (Seattle: Univ.
of Washington Press, 1920), 87. Cf. page 150 in the present edition.

50. See H. A. Mason, *Humanism and Poetry in the Early Tudor Period* (London: Routledge and
Kegan Paul, 1959), 243–44. Susan Brigden gives a detailed account of Surrey's political and
religious positions and argues that Askew imitates his poem; see "Henry Howard and the
'Conjured League.'" *Historical Journal* 37 (1994): 507–37.

This volume contains the *Examinations* as they were first published in 1546 and 1547 by the ardent Protestant propagandist John Bale, and as they were later published by the martyrologist John Foxe. After Askew's death, her work left England, perhaps with the Dutch merchants who witnessed her burning and whom Bale credits for bringing it to him "in coppye" in the Duchy of Cleves (page 88). By November, *The first examinacyon* had been printed at Wesel in the Duchy of Cleves (about thirty miles north of present-day Düsseldorf, Germany); *The lattre examinacyon* is dated 16 January 1547. [51] To each part, Bale added a preface and an *Elucidation* in which he placed Askew's life and work within the context of Reformation faith, politics, and propaganda: like the martyrs of the early Christian church, he argued, Askew was a true Christian engaged in a battle with Antichrist, the Roman Catholic Church, and the worldly rulers who supported it. The *Examinations* subsequently appeared in editions with and without Bale's commentary. Perhaps most important for the preservation of Askew's name and story, John Foxe, the historian and martyrologist, published them alone as *The two examinations of the worthy servaunt of God, Maistris An Askew* in his history of the English Reformation, *Actes and Monuments of these latter and perillous dayes* (1563). Foxe had earlier included the *Examinations* in his Latin edition, *Rerum in Ecclesia Gestarum Commentarii* (Basel, 1559). Like Bale, his friend and mentor, Foxe gathered documents and eyewitness accounts to support his narrative of the persecution of Protestants and to record the religious and political struggle to establish the English Protestant Church; Askew's writing provided him with what he called a "singular example" of unswerving belief in Reformed doctrine—and courage—the kind of story that made his "Book of Martyrs" the dominant popular account of the English Reformation. [52] Foxe's version of Askew's *Examinations* appears after Bale's in this volume.

---

51. John N. King suggests that the misleading "Marpurg"—a town 130 miles southeast of Wesel—appears in the text (pages 71, 158) to hide Bale's actual location and to designate him "as the apostolic successor to William Tyndale, who had issued a series of Antwerp imprints under 'Marburg' colophons." *English Reformation Literature: The Tudor Origins of the Protestant Religion* (Princeton: Princeton Univ. Press, 1982), 72.

52. See Rosemary O'Day, *The Debate on the English Reformation* (London: Methuen, 1985), 16–20.

Bale, Askew's first editor, worked methodically to shape a text that supported his own agenda in the mid-1540s: to discredit the Catholic church in England; and to prove with all available historical and exegetical resources that the Reformers were liberating the native English church from centuries of false domination by foreign clerics. The remarkable woodcut printed on the title-page of each *Examination* represents a woman clothed as an early Christian martyr, holding the Bible and a martyr's palm, and trampling the "papist Beast" underfoot.[53] At every possible opening, Bale interrupts Askew to provide this historical context, intending to demonstrate by continual comparison that Askew's words, actions, and beliefs are closer to the Scriptures and to the primitive church than anything written or performed by Roman Catholics for at least the previous nine centuries. Placing his edition of Askew in the context of his other projects at the time reveals how much it belongs to Bale's historical vision and to the Reformers' project of publishing vernacular works supporting the Protestant cause.

In 1545 or 1546, Bale also published *The Image of Both Churches*, a commentary on the Book of Revelation, in which he interpreted the history of the Church through the successive breaking of the seven seals, each seal representing an era in the rise and fall of the true Church. Since the seventh century, Christ's beastly opponent, the Antichrist—that is, the Roman Catholic church—had been persecuting the few remaining true Christians; in the present age, Bale thought, the epic struggle continued, though now edging towards the end of the world and the day of judgment.[54] The large number of references to Revelation or "Apocalypse" in Bale's *Elucidation* indicates how thoroughly he viewed Askew's confrontations with Bishop Gardiner and Lord Chancellor Wriothesley in these terms. Also in 1546, at Antwerp, Bale published his *Actes of English Votaryes*, another "historical" work designed to prove that foreign clerics and their domestic agents had for centuries undermined the true faith of the English. At the end of this work, Bale

---

53. The woodcut is reproduced on pages 1 and 73 of the present edition. For analysis of the woodcut, see John N. King, *English Reformation Literature*, 73; and *Tudor Royal Iconography: Literature and Art in an Age of Religious Crisis* (Princeton: Princeton Univ. Press, 1989), 207–9.

54. See John N. King, *English Reformation Literature*, 61–64.

lists a hundred "Authors names both Englyshe and other, out of whom thys present Boke ys collected."[55] The diversity of his sources indicates the breadth of his library resources, his willingness to copy any useful material from any quarter, and his unswerving determination to legitimate the English Reformation in the long view of providential and human history. He includes Julius Caesar, many medieval authors— Bede, Geoffrey of Monmouth, and Lydgate, for instance—and his own contemporaries, Tyndale and Barnes. The nature of his research, much of which also appears in his edition of Askew, stands in stark contrast to Askew's text: whereas Bale explores the shelves of great libraries, Askew concentrates almost entirely on the Bible, citing, reciting, and interpreting it in the light of Reformist exegesis. Bale also included Askew in his Latin *Summarium,* a biographical and bibliographical catalogue of British writers. Briefly repeating the thesis of his edition of Askew, he describes her as a remarkable young woman endowed with grace and intelligence who resembled the early martyrs Cecilia and Blandina in her struggle to the death with wicked tyrants and idolaters. Of the *Examinations* he says, "She wrote this with her own hand and I illustrated it with prefaces and commentaries."[56] Askew's importance for the Reformers' cause was reiterated when John Foxe printed Askew's *Examinations* in his *Actes and Monuments* of 1563. To his text, Foxe added the "true copy" of Askew's confession from the Bishop's Register in order to argue that her enemies had altered the document and entered it a year later to justify her condemnation. And, memorably, Foxe concluded Askew's text with a woodcut of the scene at Smithfield, one that resembles Bale's description of the four martyrs, the thunderclap from the clouds, and the presence of many witnesses (page 154).[57]

---

55. John Bale, *The Actes of Englysh Votaryes* (Antwerp, 1546), 78v–79r.

56. "Scripsit haec propria manu, quos & ego praefationibus ac scholiis illustravi." *Illustrium maioris Britanniae scriptorum summarium* (Wesel, 1548), 229. Bale uses the phrase "praeclari generis iuvencula," which could mean she was physically "beautiful," "admirable," or "famous." Since Bale never saw Askew, he would probably praise her moral qualities; however, many later writers decide she was beautiful.

57. The woodcut is reproduced on page 164 of the present edition. In *English Reformation Literature,* King shows that Foxe's printer John Day used the woodcut he had previously used in Robert Crowley's 1548 pamphlet, *Confutation of XIII Articles, Whereunto Nicholas Shaxton…Subscribed* (439–40). Shaxton, former bishop of Salisbury, had recanted his Protestant beliefs and preached at Askew's burning.

Bale's analogy between the centurion converted at Christ's death (Matt. 27) and those supposedly converted that day at Smithfield may also parallel the anachronistic details of the woodcut: the soldiers appear to wear Roman dress and the dominant group of dignitaries watching in the background might be more at home in the ancient Coliseum.

An eyewitness of Askew's execution was John Louth, archdeacon of Nottingham, who some years later offered Foxe his "Reminiscences," including further details about Askew's examinations and her appearances before the mayor and the Privy Council; it is unclear, however, whether he worked from notes taken in the 1540s or from later recollections. Louth is the source of an extraordinary story that some time during her stay in London, Askew was under surveillance. He describes how "one great papiste of Wykam Colledge, then called Wadloe, a coursytore of the Chawncery, hott in his religione, and thynkyng not well of hir lyffe, gott hymselfe lodged harde by hur at the nexte howse…" But according to Louth, Askew unknowingly won over her enemy who reported to his master, Lionel Throckmorton, that she was the "devouteste and godliest woman that ever he knew." Beginning to pray at midnight, she "ceaseth not in many howers after, when I and others applye our sleape or do worse."[58] Foxe did not incorporate this material, although later historians have adopted it freely.

Louth's version of Askew's examination by the Lord Mayor of London casts some doubt on his historicity. He situates the interview in the Tower "with the cownsell," even though Askew would have been questioned at the Guildhall, as she herself says. Louth creates a version of the examination expressly designed to ridicule the mayor, whom he names as Martin Bowes; in the process, he also trivializes Askew's dialogue. Unfortunately, his version appealed to almost every subsequent teller of Askew's story, essentially supplanting Askew's own account (page 27). When the mayor examined Askew about her sacramentarian beliefs,

58. *Reminiscences of John Louth*, 40.

Louth writes, he asked whether the communion wafer were not Christ's body:

> *A. Askowghe.* No, it ys bot consecrated bredd, or sacramentall bredd. *L. Maior.* What, yf a mowse eate yt after the consecratione, what shalbecome of the mowse? What sayeste thow, thow folyshe woman? *A. Askowghe.* What shall become of hur, say yow, my lorde? *L. Maior.* I say that that mowse is damned. *A. Askew.* Alacke poore mowse! By this tyme—the lordes had ynowghe of my lorde maiores divinitie, and perceavyng that some cowld not keap in theyr lawghyng, proceeded to the Botchery and slawter that they entended afore thei came thither.(41)

Louth appears to have conflated part of the first examination at the Guildhall with the events of June 1546 when Askew was examined by the Privy Council and sent to the Tower to be questioned and tortured.[59]

Louth claims to have been present at Askew's death in Smithfield, a scene he describes with a mixture of verisimilitude, religious conviction, and self-justification. He helps us to visualize how "they putt fyar to the reedes; the cownsell lookyng on, and leanyng in a wyndow by the spyttle" (the hospital of St Bartholomew). Like Bale and Foxe, he remarks on the divine sign of thunder, but he goes further, claiming also to have felt "a lytle dewe, or a few pleasante droppes apon us that stode by…"[60] However, Louth seems uncomfortable about being a mere witness to so horrific a moment, for he adds that "I could not, for feare of damnatione, stand by and say nothyng agaynste theyre cruelte; therfor I with a lowde voyce, lookyng to the cownsell, sayd, 'I axe advenganse of yow all that thus dothe burne Chrystes member.'"

A brief excerpt from the *Examinations* appears in Thomas Bentley's *Monument of Matrones: conteining seven severall Lamps of Virginitie, or distinct treatises…compiled for the necessarie use of both sexes out of the sacred Scriptures, and other approved authors* (1582). In "The second Lampe," in a section of "Certaine praiers made by godlie women Mar-

---

59. In particular, John Strype preserved and legitimized Louth's additions for later readers. *Ecclesiastical Memorials* (London: John Wyat, 1721), 1: 387–88.

60. *Reminiscences of John Louth*, 44.

tyrs," Bentley includes "The praier of Anne Askue the Martyr, before hir death" (pages 146–48).[61] In the same section are the prayers of the martyrs, Agnes and Eulalia, of John Bradford's mother, and prayers "taken out of the Psalmes" by anonymous gentlewomen.

The two major histories of the sixteenth century, Stow's *Annales* (1592) and Holinshed's *Chronicles* (1587), mention Askew briefly. Stow, who did not often record such executions, notes the date and names of those burned with Askew "for the sacrament," as well as Shaxton's recantation: "...doctor Shaxton somtime bishop of Salisbury preached at the same fire, and there recanted, persuading them to do the like, but they would not."[62] In Holinshed, the entry is attributed to Richard Grafton, and records only Askew's arraignment with "Robert Luken" and "Jone Sautereie" at the Guildhall on 13 June 1545, when "twelve honest substantiall men of the citie (sworne to passe upon their indictments) cleerelie acquited and discharged" them.[63]

Askew's story is again retold in 1605 by the Jesuit Robert Parsons, who included it in his extended attack on Foxe's martyrology. Like Gardiner earlier, he sees the political implications of a narrative "so pittifully related...as he would moove compassion on her side, and hatred against the king and his Councell."[64] Also recognizing Askew's court connections, Parsons claimed that "she did in secrett seeke to corrupt divers people, but especially weomen," particularly Queen Katherine Parr and other highly placed courtiers whom Askew supplied with "hereticall books" (2:494). Askew's gender is, indeed, at the center of Parsons' attack, for while Askew herself and her supporters had insisted on her female modesty, Parsons vilifies her as "a coy dame, and of very evill fame for wantonnesse: in that she left the company of her husband Maister Kyme, to gad up and downe the countrey a ghospelling and gossipinge where she might, and ought not" (2:495). Worse, "she

61. Thomas Bentley, *The Monument of Matrones* (London, 1582), 214.

62. John Stow, *The Annales of England...untill this present yeere 1592* (London, 1592), 999.

63. *The third volume of Chronicles...First compiled by Raphaell Holinshed...Now newlie recognised, augmented, and continued...to the yeare 1586* (London, 1587), 968. Some phraseology echoes that of Wriothesley's *Chronicle*. See above, page xx.

64. Robert Parsons, *The Third Part of a Treatise, Intituled: of three Conversions of England.* By N. D. (London, 1604), 2: 492.

seemed in a sort to disdayne the bearing of his name, calling herselfe
Anne Askue, alias Kime," although Parsons considers the name only a
prelude to the liberties she took in speaking her "proud and presumptu-
ous answers, quips, and nips" (2:496) to the King's Council and the
bishops.

By 1596, when Thomas Nashe mentions it, a "Ballad of Anne
Askew" was circulating; it was first printed as "A Ballad of Anne Askew,
Intituled I am a Woman poore and Blinde," some time after 14 December 1624, and several more editions appeared before the end of the seventeenth century.[65] It is possible that Askew herself might have written
the ballad, the other candidates being writers who recognized the popular appeal of Askew's conflict with powerful authorities.[66] In his *Summarium,* Bale does say that Askew "cantiones quoque plures edidit,"
which could mean that she published "several" or "many" songs, two of
which he includes in his edition of the *Examinations:* Askew's version of
Psalme 54 (page 72) and "The Balade whych Anne Askewe made and
sange whan she was in Newgate" (pages 149–50).

Over the last four centuries, Askew's *Examinations* have been widely
read, edited, and interpreted, reappearing in various forms, and gradu-
ally gathering embellishments and alterations to suit the views and purposes of each reader.

Later references to Askew are common enough to suggest she was in
fact one of the better known English martyrs. In 1673, Bathsua Makin
described Askew as "a person famous for learning and piety," who influenced the Queen and court ladies "and after sealed her profession with
her blood, that the seed of reformation seemed to be sowed by her
hand."[67] In his monumental and influential *Ecclesiastical Memorials* of

---

65. Thomas Nashe refers to "the ballet of Anne Askew" and quotes the first line in *Have With
You to Saffron Walden.* 1596. In *Works,* ed. Ronald B. McKerrow (Oxford: Basil Blackwell,
1958), 3: 113. It was entered in the Stationers' Register on 14 December 1624. The Ballad
appears in Appendix 2 of the present edition.

66. In *English Reformation Literature,* John N. King does not attribute the ballad to Askew, but
sees it as part of the later popularization of the Reformation (444).

67. Bathsua Makin, "An Essay to Revive the Ancient Education of Gentlewomen" (1673), in
The Female Spectator: English Women Writers before 1800, ed. Mary R. Mahl and Helene Koon
(Bloomington and Old Westbury, New York: Indiana Univ. Press and The Feminist Press,
1977), 134.

1721, John Strype appropriated Louth's entire account of Askew's examinations and death.[68]

In the nineteenth century, Askew's story customarily appeared in collections of women's biographies, especially those emphasizing women's piety.[69] While the story could be found in many sources, it is clear that Askew's own writings were also known, for they appeared in anthologies and were consulted by historians, biographers, religious writers, and novelists.[70]

Maria Webb used the *Examinations*, Fuller's *Worthies*, and Strype to write a chapter on Anne Askew in her biography of the Quaker family, *The Fells of Swarthmore Hall*.[71] According to Webb, Askew's son, William Askew, connected the South Kelsey Askews to the Margaret Askew who married Thomas Fell; when Askew's husband, Thomas Kyme, turned her out, she renounced his name for herself and her children. Webb does not reveal her sources for this new information about Askew's children. Above all, she gives the persecuted Quaker Fells a suitable ancestor in an early Protestant martyr. In Webb's version, however, Askew assumes the virtues of Victorian domesticity, for "this lady did not leave her husband till he ordered her to go" and "her coming to London was with the desire to live with her children in peace and retirement" (9). She cites Fuller's remark that Askew was "distinguished for wit, beauty, learning, and religion." But Webb also makes extensive use of the *Examinations* so that the intensity and integrity of Askew's story survive, even with this genteel veneer.

On 11 November 1868, the Reverend Benjamin Oswald Sharp preached a sermon at St. James's, Clerkenwell, in honor of a proposed Smithfield Martyrs Memorial Church. A statue of Anne Askew was planned among others on the exterior, and Sharp calls her "the heroine"

68. John Strype, *Ecclesiastical Memorials* (London: John Wyat, 1721), 1: 387–88.

69. See, for example, James Anderson, *Ladies of the Reformation* (1855), 136–79.

70. Askew's Ballad, "Like as the armed knight," appears, for example, in Frederic Rowton, *The Female Poets of Great Britain* (1853). Facsimile edition, ed. Marilyn L. Williamson (Detroit: Wayne State Univ. Press, 1981), 30–33.

71. Webb's book was published in London in 1865 by Alfred W. Bennett and in Dublin by J. Robertson. A second London edition appeared in 1867 and a Philadelphia edition in 1896.

of his story.[72] Sharp addressed his sermon particularly to women, and in language strikingly close to that of John Bale (whom he later cites), he reminds "Protestant daughters, sisters, wives, and mothers" how much they owe the Reformation that released them from Roman Catholicism (5). In his scheme, Askew represents those martyrs who "have been pure, noble, wise, gentle, and lovely women, pre-eminent for every gift and grace that could adorn humanity" (9). Askew's narrative still retains considerable power in the sermon, even with Strype's alterations and Sharp's impassioned additions. His final plea is to the ladies not to "do all dear Anne Askew died to undo" (14) and to espouse an evangelical Christianity through which "you can do here in Clerkenwell even as Anne Askew did at Smithfield…" (16).

Askew's story was again retold in an anonymous eight-page pamphlet, "Anne Askewe, The Lincolnshire Martyr."[73] Using Strype and Foxe, the author presents what was becoming the standard version of Askew's examinations, featuring her beauty and wit, the priests of Lincoln, the dialogue about the mouse, her racking in the Tower, her execution, and her Ballad, "Like as the armed knight." Perhaps responsive to a turning tide in England, the author does urge readers not to respond by hating Roman Catholics.

Mary E. T. Stirling's biography of Askew appeared in three editions dedicated to the memory of Stirling's grandmother "who was an Askew of the same family as Anne."[74] Stirling consulted the *Examinations,* possibly in an early edition, since she includes Paget's examination at Greenwich. She also cites Strype, Burnet, and Foxe, although there are many unidentified quotations in the text. Askew, who is "very young and remarkably beautiful" (4), reassumes her maiden name after being

---

72. "Anne Askew—Martyr, A. D. 1545" (London: S. W. Partridge and Co., 1869), 3. Sharp preached the sermon again on 6 January 1869 at the Mission Church on the site of the proposed Memorial. The sermon is bound with other sermons preached 1851–69, British Library shelfmark 4905/B45.

73. The copy in the British Library is dated [1870?] and bound with other religious biographies.

74. *A Short Life of Anne Askew* (London: Chas. J. Thynne, [1913]), 24 pp.; *Anne Askew: Her Life and Martyrdom,* 3rd ed. (London: Thynne and Co., [1930]), 31 pp.

disowned by her relatives for becoming a Protestant (5). She comes to London "with her faithful maid" with whom she attends sermons at Paul's Cross (6).[75] Once past these unsupported biographical details, however, Stirling cites the *Examinations* extensively, although she does include the Louth-Strype version of the dialogue about the mouse. The book concludes with "The Ballad of Anne Askew."

Two novels about Askew, written a century apart, also use a considerable amount of material from the *Examinations* as well as the embellished "historical" narratives in circulation. Anne Manning's *The Lincolnshire Tragedy: Passages in the Life of the Faire Gospeller, Mistress Anne Askew* appeared in 1866 and Alison Macleod's *The Heretics* in 1965. Macleod tells the story through Askew's maid, effectively using the dramatic confrontations in the source material.[76]

In a mid-nineteenth-century review of an edition of ballads that included "I am a Woman poore and blinde," the reviewer refers to Anne Askew's story as one that "must be well known to all our readers."[77] The purpose of this present edition of Askew's *Examinations* is to ensure that her reputation as a writer will remain equally strong.

---

75. In the *Examinations*, Askew refers once to her maid who "as she went abroade in the stretes" receives money for Askew from the apprentices (page 124).

76. *The Lincolnshire Tragedy* (London: Bentley, 1866); also published as *Passages in the Life of the Faire Gospeller, Mistress Anne Askew* (New York: Dodd, 1866). *The Heretics* (London: Hodder & Stoughton, 1965); also published as *The Heretic* (Boston: Houghton Mifflin, 1966).

77. "The Roxburghe Ballads," *The North British Review* 6 (1847) [American ed., vol. 1], 21.

Selected Bibliography

Beilin, Elaine V. "A Challenge to Authority: Anne Askew." In *Redeeming Eve: Women Writers of the English Renaissance*. Princeton: Princeton Univ. Press, 1987.

———. "Anne Askew's Dialogue with Authority." In *Contending Kingdoms: Historical, Psychological, and Feminist Approaches to the Literature of Sixteenth-Century England and France*, edited by Marie-Rose Logan and Peter Rudnytsky, 313–22. Detroit: Wayne State Univ. Press, 1991.

Brigden, Susan. *London and the Reformation*. Oxford: Clarendon Press, 1991.

Crawford, Patricia M. *Women and Religion in England, 1500–1720*. New York: Routledge, 1993.

Fairfield, Leslie P. *John Bale: Mythmaker for the English Reformation*. West Lafayette: Purdue Univ. Press, 1976.

Guy, John. *Tudor England*. Oxford: Oxford Univ. Press, 1988.

Kendall, Ritchie D. *The Drama of Dissent: The Radical Poetics of Nonconformity, 1380-1590*. Chapel Hill and London: Univ. of North Carolina Press, 1986.

King, John N. *English Reformation Literature: The Tudor Origins of the Protestant Tradition*. Princeton: Princeton Univ. Press, 1982.

McQuade, Paula. "'Except that they had offended the Lawe': Gender and Jurisprudence in *The Examinations of Anne Askew.*" *Literature & History*, 3d ser. 3 (1994): 1–14.

Mueller, Janel. "A Tudor Queen Finds Voice: Katherine Parr's *Lamentation of a Sinner.*" In *The Historical Renaissance: New Essays on Tudor and Stuart Literature and Culture*, edited by Heather Dubrow and Richard Strier, 15-47. Chicago and London: Univ. of Chicago Press, 1988.

Willen, Diane. "Women and Religion in Early Modern England." In *Women in Reformation and Counter-Reformation Europe: Private and Public Worlds*, edited by Sherrin Marshall, 140-65. Bloomington: Indiana Univ. Press, 1989.

TEXTUAL INTRODUCTION

I. THE FIRST EDITIONS

The first editions of Anne Askew's *Examinations* (STC 848 and 850) were published after her death by John Bale in Wesel in the Protestant Duchy of Cleves.[1] Since Askew had been burned for heresy and Bale was named in the king's proclamation of 8 July 1546 listing forbidden authors, the work could not be printed in England.[2] According to the date at the end of *The first examinacyon*, it was printed in November 1546, and the place is erroneously given as "Marpurg in the lande of Hessen," probably to insure Bale's safety (see Introduction, page xxxiii). *The lattre examinacyon* is dated 16 January 1547, also from "Marpurg." The *STC* lists copies of *The first examinacyon* (STC 848) at eight locations: the British Library; the Bodleian Library; Worcester College, Oxford; Cambridge University Library; Lincoln Cathedral Library; the Folger Shakespeare Library; the Huntington Library; and Houghton Library, Harvard University. There are two copies at the British Library and two copies at the Cambridge University Library. The *STC* lists copies of *The lattre examinacyon* (STC 850) at the same locations except for the Huntington Library. There are three copies at the British Library and two copies at the Cambridge University Library. The first editions of both *Examinations* are octavo volumes remarkable for the identical woodcut on the title pages: the figure of a woman displaying a Bible, bearing a martyr's palm, and trampling a beast wearing the tiara of the Roman papacy. The woodcut is discussed in the Introduction on page xxxiv and is reproduced on pages 1 and 73 of the present edition.

On the last page of *The first examinacyon*, there is another woodcut comprising a tree, the motto "Amor Vincit Omnia," and the initials

---

1. Although the title of the present volume, *The Examinations*, is in modern spelling, the spelling of the first edition has been retained when *The first examinacyon* and *The lattre examinacyon* appear in a sixteenth-century context.

2. The proclamation is STC 7809. See Paul L. Hughes and James F. Larkin, eds. *Tudor Royal Proclamations* (New Haven: Yale Univ. Press, 1964), 1: 373–76.

"IVK"; this is the printer's emblem of Johann van Kempen of Cologne. Nevertheless, the printer of the *Examinations* was Dirik van der Straten, also known as Theodoricus Plateanus. Van der Straten printed a series of works for Bale, all of which may be linked by their type and woodcut initials. Robert Steele describes the type as "that of the 'Marburg Press' of Tyndale on a new body (82mm. = 20 lines), used in conjunction with a larger German fount of the same character."[3] This type was used in the *Examinations;* in a translation by Bale, *The true hystorie of the Christen departynge of the reverende man, D. Martyne Luther* [1546]; in Elizabeth Tudor's *Godly Medytacyon of the christen sowle* (1548); and in several other works.[4] All of these works include woodcut initials matching those in Bale's *Illustrium Maioris Britanniae Scriptorum...Summarium,* a variant of which contains Plateanus' imprint.[5] The initials A, O, H, and F in *The first examinacyon* and the initials I and C in *The lattre examinacyon* match initials in the *Summarium,* although the types differ.[6]

In the first edition, Askew's text is set in type larger than the type for Bale's commentary. Marginal references, some of which are interpretative, may derive from Bale's collaboration with van der Straten.

Pages in some copies of the first edition of *The lattre examinacyon* were cut and glued to conceal some of the text without appearing to lose continuity. The censorship, apparently to protect Sir William Paget, is discussed in the Introduction, page xxviii. Four lines from the top of page 23r–23v (sigs. C7r–C7v) were cut; the facing page, 22v, was glued to page 23r. The result is that the new "22v" is composed of the first three lines of the original 22v, which show through the cut, fol-

3. Robert Steele, "Notes on English Books Printed Abroad, 1525–48," *Transactions of the Bibliographical Society* 11 (1909–1911): 230–36. I am grateful to Hugh Amory, Senior Rare Book Cataloguer, Houghton Library, Harvard University, for this reference.

4. The Houghton Library copies of STC 848 and 850 are bound with *The true hystorie of the Christen departynge of the reverende man, D. Martyne Luther.* See below.

5. The variant of Bale's *Summarium* is STC 1296.

6. For an account of van der Straten's acquisition of the initials and the type of the *Summarium,* see Honor McCusker, "Some Ornamental Initials Used by Plateanus of Wesel," *The Library,* 4th ser., 16 (1936): 452–54.

lowed by the original page 23v minus its top three lines. Askew's text on page 22v and Bale's text on page 23r and the top of page 23v disappear. One copy of *The lattre examinacyon* at the British Library is still cut and glued in this way (shelfmark C.135. a. 23 [2], bound with STC 849). The pages in two other copies at the British Library (shelfmarks C.21.a.4 and G11657) have been separated and repaired with blank paper at the top of the page. There is some damage to the separated pages in G11657, which was also cut less neatly by the original censor. In the copy at the Folger Shakespeare Library, page 23r was cut, but the pages are not glued together and there is no evidence of earlier gluing and separation; however, evidence may have been lost when pages were washed when the book was rebound in the nineteenth century.[7] One copy at Cambridge University Library (shelfmark SSS.47.303) was cut and pasted, then later separated; the other is intact.[8] Copies at the Bodleian Library; Worcester College, Oxford; Lincoln Cathedral Library; and Houghton Library, Harvard University, were not censored.

The Bodleian Library copies of STC 848 and 850, the basetexts for the present edition, are complete and are bound together in a volume which also includes Miles Coverdale's *Confutacion of...John Standish* (shelfmark 8° C.46 Th. Seld.). The volume is in excellent condition.

The British Library possesses two copies of *The first examinacyon*. One copy is bound with *The lattre examinacyon* (shelfmark C.21.a.4) and both *Examinations* are complete except for the excised lines in STC 850 noted above. This British Library copy may be found on University Microfilms Reel 21. The second British Library copy of *The first examinacyon* (shelfmark G11656) lacks the title page, Bale's preface, and the table of contents. The arms of the Right Honourable Thomas Grenville are stamped inside the cover, as they are in the companion volume of *The lattre examinacyon* (shelfmark G11657). The British Library acquired the Grenville library in 1847. On the flyleaf of the second volume "very rare" is handwritten.

---

7. For information about copies of the *Examinations* held by the Folger Shakespeare Library, I am grateful to Georgianna Ziegler, Reference Librarian.

8. I am grateful to Nicholas Smith, Under-Librarian, Rare Books Department, at the Cambridge University Library for his assistance.

The copy of *The first examinacyon* at Lincoln Cathedral Library lacks a title page. It is bound with *The lattre examinacyon;* on a blank page between the two texts is written "Elizabeth Knowles oweth thy" and "god makes him a good women." The second part ends on page 62v (sig. H6v), and is thus lacking Askew's "Balade," Bale's conclusion, and the table of contents. The volume was bequeathed to the Library in 1681 by Michael Honywood, Dean of Lincoln 1660–1681.[9]

The Folger Shakespeare Library copies of STC 848 and 850 were bound together by the London bookbinder Francis Bedford in the nineteenth century. Pages 34r–39v (sigs. E2r–E7v) of *The first examinacyon* and *The lattre examinacyon* have been interchanged, perhaps by Bedford. The title page of *The first examinacyon* has been mended with a facsimile. The copy contains the bookplates of Henry Huth, E. M. Coxe, and Sir R. Lester Harmsworth, and a pencilled note saying that it was sold in the Huth sale of November 1911. *The lattre examinacyon* was censored, as noted above.

The copies of STC 848 and 850 at the Houghton Library, Harvard University, are bound with Bale's translations of *The true hystorie of the Christen departynge of the reverende man, D. Martyne Luther* and *An oracyon or processe rehearced off Philipp Melanchton at the buryall of the Reverende man, Doctour Martyne Luther* (shelfmark Br 1771/3). On a flyleaf appears a handwritten list of the contents of the volume, noting missing leaves, with the signature, "1770 Wm: Herbert." This is William Herbert, the bibliographer (1718–1795) who enlarged Joseph Ames's *Typographical Antiquities* and published his work 1785–90. STC 848, the second item in the volume, lacks a title page. A handwritten title—in a different hand—is apparently based on the title of STC 849: "The Examination of the worthy servant of God, Mystresse Anne Askew younger Daughter of Sir William Askew, lately martyr'd in Smithfield by the Romish Broode." There follows the note, "Bibliotheca Askeviana, N. 10," indicating that this copy appeared as "Number 10" in the 1774 catalogue of the sale of Dr. Anthony Askew's

---

9. I am grateful to Dr. Nicholas Bennett, Lincoln Cathedral Librarian, for this information and for his assistance at the Library.

library. An auctioneer's note from the 1775 sale indicates that the *Examinations* were sold to "Mason" for two shillings.[10] This copy also lacks Bale's preface and the table of contents. At the bottom of page 1 (sig. Ar), partly cut off, is written "Ames p. 507" and "WH. p. 1561," references to Joseph Ames's *Typographical Antiquities* (London, 1749), where the *Examinations* are described on page 507 and to William Herbert's enlarged edition, where the entry appears on page 1561.[11] The same reference to William Herbert's edition of the *Antiquities* appears in the Bodleian Library copy of STC 852 (see page li below).

II. LATER EDITIONS

The first examination was reprinted in London by Robert Waldegrave, apparently in 1585 (STC 849). There are two known copies, one at the British Library and one at the Folger Shakespeare Library. The title page repeats the heading from page 1 (sig. Ar) of STC 848, except that "the Romish Antichristian Broode" is substituted for "the Romysh popes upholders" and the orthography is different. Waldegrave's printer's device, a swan standing on a wreath with a border of intertwined snakes and the motto "God is my Helper" appears above the imprint "At London / Printed by Robert Walde-grave, dwelling / without Temple-bar in the Strond, neere / unto Sommerset house."[12]

The texts of Askew and Bale appear on sigs. Ar to E2v. "The confession of the faith which Anne Askewe made in Newgate afore shee suffered" appears on sigs. [E3r] to [E4v], and is copied from Askew's text in *The lattre examinacyon* (pages 54–62 in STC 850, but without Bale's commentary). The flyleaf of the British Library copy (shelfmark C.

---

10. *Bibliotheca Askeviana, sive Catalogus Librorum Rarissimorum Antonii Askew, M.D.* (London, 1774), 1. Hugh Amory kindly supplied this reference. See below for Anthony Askew's daughter, Deborah Askew Pepys, owner of a copy of another edition of the *Examinations*.

11. Joseph Ames, *Typographical Antiquities*, augmented by William Herbert (London, 1790), 3:1561.

12. See *A Dictionary of Printers and Booksellers in England...1557–1640*, gen. ed. R. B. McKerrow (London: Bibliographical Society, 1910; reprint 1968), s.v. "Waldegrave (Robert)."

135.a.23 [1]) contains the handwritten lines, "Deborah Askew / given her by her Aunt / Anne Askew" and "To Robert Pulleine / from his Affect^e. Aunt / Deborah Pepys." Deborah Askew Pepys was the daughter of Anthony Askew, the physician, classical scholar, and book collector; she married the physician Sir Lucas Pepys on 29 June 1813. Her aunt, Anne Askew, was her father's unmarried sister who died in 1814, aged 76; her nephew was the son of her sister Elizabeth and Henry Pelham Pulleine of Carleton Hall, Yorkshire. The name of Askew was common in the north country and these Askews are not related to the sixteenth-century South Kelsey Askews, whose last male heir died in 1707. This copy is bound with a copy of STC 850, which lacks the title page, Bale's preface, and six pages of text. The Folger Library copy of STC 849 may be found on University Microfilms Reel 635.

In the reign of Edward VI when Protestant publishers had new freedom, the two *Examinations* with Bale's *Elucydacyon* were printed together on continuous signatures, apparently by Nicholas Hill in 1547 (STC 851).[13] *The first examinacion* appears on sigs. Ar to G3v. "Marpurg...1546" appears on sig. G3r, but the orthography and layout differ from the first edition. *The latter examynacyon* appears on sigs. G4r to P2r, with "Marpurg...1547" on P2r. Floral woodcuts mark initial letters on sigs. A2r, Bv, G5r, and H3v, but there are no woodcuts on the title pages. In the passages mentioning William Paget, this edition retains Askew's text beginning "Then came mastre Pagette to me" (STC 850, 20v), but deletes the next phrase, "with many gloryouse wordes." Bale's commentary (STC 850, 21r–22v) is retained, but Askew's text (STC 850, 22v) and Bale's commentary (STC 850, 23r–23v) are missing, suggesting that the printer worked from a copy of STC 850 in which these pages had been cut and glued together, as noted above. The copy at Christ Church, Oxford (shelfmark Wb 8, 11) is now bound in a volume of *Popish Tracts Henry VIII;* it may be found on University Microfilms, Reel 1470.

Another edition of the two *Examinations* was printed, apparently by

---

13. See E. Gordon Duff, *A Century of the English Book Trade* (London: Bibliographical Society, 1905), s.v. "Hill, Montanus or van de Berghe (Nicholas)."

William Hill in 1548, omitting Bale's commentary (STC 852).[14] There
are two known copies, one at the Bodleian Library (shelfmark Douce
A376) and one at the Folger Shakespeare Library. The title page of *The
firste Examinacion* contains the heading from page 1 (sig. Ar) of STC
848, but with different orthography and layout. There is no woodcut,
but the biblical quotations are the same as those on the title page of
STC 848. On the verso of the title page appears a new introductory
paragraph:

> Here, hast thou (gentle reader) the two examinacions of Anne Askewe
> which she wrote with her owne hand, at the instaunte desyre of certain
> faithfull menne and women, by the which (if thou marke dylygently the
> communicacions both of her and of her examiners) thou mayeste, easily
> prove the sprites, as Saint Jhon the Apostle geveth you councel. i. Jhon
> iiiii. and than shalt thou know the tree by the frute and the man by his
> worke. [ornament] Anne Askewe.

This passage resembles Bale's original commentary, combining an
abridgement of Bale's introductory paragraph (STC 848, page 19), and
the address to the reader at the beginning of Bale's conclusions to *The
first examinacyon* (STC 848, page 66) and *The lattre examinacyon* (STC
850, page 151). Even though Bale's commentary is not printed in this
edition, it is possible that Bale—who had probably returned to England
in 1548—wrote this paragraph for the printer. Alternately, the printer
may have cobbled together the paragraph from Bale's original commentary. The phrase, "at the instaunte desyre of certain faithfull menne and
women," which also appears in STC 848 (page 19), is echoed by a
phrase in the title of Katherine Parr's *Lamentation of a Sinner,* printed 5
November 1547 "at the instaunt desire of the right gracious ladie
Caterin Duchesse of Suffolke."[15] This paragraph also appears with different orthography and layout in STC 852, 852.5, 853 and (with variants) in Foxe's Latin and English headnotes. In STC 852, *The firste
Examinacion* extends from sig. A2r to sig. B4r. Sig. B4v is blank and
The latter Examination extends from sig. B5r to sig. D3r. The title page

---

14. See Duff, s.v. "Hill (William)."
15. I am grateful to Janel Mueller for pointing out this parallel.

of *The latter Examination* contains the heading from page 10 (sig. B2r) of STC 850, but with different orthography and layout. The biblical quotations on the title page are the same as those on the title page of STC 850. The orthography of this edition differs from that of STC 848 and STC 850. Floral woodcuts—different from those in STC 851— mark initial letters on sigs. A2r and [B5v]. This is the first edition to omit "The voyce of Anne Askewe oute of the 54. Psalme" (STC 848, page 72), also omitted in subsequent editions. In this edition, all passages referring to William Paget have been omitted, so that Askew's sentence "Then was I commaunded to stande a syde" (STC 850, 20r) is immediately followed by "Then came to me doctor Coxe, and doctor Robynson" (STC 850, 23v). There are some emendations; for instance, where STC 850 prints "racke me their owne handes" (page 127), STC 852 prints "racke me wt [with] ther owne handes" (C5v).

The continued popularity of Askew's *Examinations* is suggested by the printing of two more early editions, neither containing Bale's commentary. One was printed around 1550, apparently by William Copland (STC 852.5); the single known copy is at the Pierpont Morgan Library (PML 984). This edition of *The fyrst Exawinacion* [sic] and *The latter Examinacion* is close to STC 852. On the bottom of sig. D3r is a woodcut ornamental floral band identified in a handwritten note as "used by Copland and his successor, Middleton." The copy was bought by J. P. Morgan in 1906 from Pearson, London.[16]

The last early edition of both *Examinations* was printed around 1560(?) (STC 853); the single known copy is in the British Library (shelfmark Huth 55). On the flyleaf is written, "An excessively rare volume, if not unique. P. H." The title page of *The first examination* contains the heading from page 1 (sig. Ar) in STC 848, except that "Romish upholders" appears instead of "Romish popes upholders." There is no woodcut, but the biblical quotations are the same as those on the title page of STC 848. On the verso of the title page the address to the reader appears as in STC 852, but with different orthography.

---

16. I am grateful to Inge Dupont, Head of Reader Services at the Pierpont Morgan Library, for information about this copy.

The first examination extends from sig. Ar to sig. B4v; *The lattre examinacion* extends from sig. B5r to sig. D3v. As in STC 852, all passages referring to William Paget have been omitted. The orthography of this edition is substantially different from STC 848 and 850. As in STC 852, "racke me their owne handes" (page 127), is corrected to "racke me wyth their owne hands" (sig. C6r) in STC 853.

III. JOHN FOXE, ACTES AND MONUMENTS

John Foxe first printed Askew's *Examinations* in the Latin *Rerum in Ecclesia Gestarum Commentarii* (Basel, 1559). Foxe wrote a brief introduction, and his initials are attached to a concluding thirty-two line Latin eulogy, "In Annæ Askevæ Constantissimæ fœminæ & martyris bustum, Epitaphium Sapphicum. I. F." ("Epitaph in Sapphic Verse upon the tomb of the most steadfast woman and martyr Anne Askew. J[ohn] F[oxe]").[17] Foxe's Latin introduction notes Askew's birth in Lincoln, her father's name, and her education "fitting her birth." He praises her intelligence, "apt for further learning," although what was lacking in her education "divine grace supplied." He admires her sagacity and the readiness of her wit during her interrogations.[18]

In the first English edition, *Actes and Monuments of these latter and perillous dayes, touching matters of the Church* (London, 1563), Foxe includes *The two examinations of the worthy servant of God, Maistris An Askew* without Bale's commentary (pp. 669–678; pp. 673, 674, 677, and 678 are misnumbered). The English edition omits the introduction found in the Latin edition, but it includes an entry from Bishop Bonner's Register, "The true copy of the confession and beliefe of Anne Askew." Foxe points out that the confession was not entered until 1546

---

17. *Rerum in Ecclesia Gestarum Commentarii,* 200. The "Epitaph" and an English translation appear in Appendix 1 of the present edition.

18. "Educationem itaque dignam suis natalibus sortita...Ingenium foelix, ac maioribus etiam aptum disciplinis...Sed quod institutioni diminutum est, divina supplevit gratia...De prudentia eius & ingenii promptitudine ex duplici eius inquisitione constare poterit" (185–86).

and that Askew says she did not sign it (Introduction, page xxxi). Foxe
would have had access to earlier printed editions of Askew.[19]

The *Examinations* appear in subsequent editions of Foxe. In the
1570 edition of *Actes and Monuments,* there are some changes and additions. For instance, in the account of Askew's torture, Foxe changes the
name of one of the torturers from "master Rich" to "Sir John Baker"; in
the 1583 edition, Richard Rich's name is restored.[20] In the 1570 edition, Foxe adds an account of the refusal of the lieutenant of the Tower,
Sir Anthony Knevet, to keep Askew on the rack and of his race to court
to ask the king's pardon for disobeying the lord chancellor.[21] Thomas S.
Freeman reports that a shorter version of this account appears in a scrib-
bled note still extant among Foxe's papers (British Library Harley MS
419, fol. 2r). Since Foxe's account reflects the concerns of Knevet and
the Tower guard, Freeman surmises that Foxe made the notes while
interviewing a soldier who had been present at the Tower in 1546, and
he thus concludes that Foxe drew on both oral and written sources.[22] In
the 1570 edition, Foxe also adds details about Askew's execution,
including the concern of the official witnesses that they were endan-
gered by gunpowder placed around the stakes (p.1420).[23] The 1583
edition retains these additions.[24]

---

19. In a letter to the editor of this volume (5 April 1995), Thomas S. Freeman argues that Foxe
used STC 852.5, the edition that most resembles Foxe's text and one that was published
around 1550, soon after Foxe met Bale in London. A complete collation of editions before
1563 with the Foxe edition might resolve the issue.

20. Baker's name appears in Foxe's holograph note describing Askew's racking, BL Harley MS
419, fol. 2r, discussed below. See John N. King, *English Reformation Literature,* 439.

21. John Foxe, *The second Volume of the Ecclesiasticall history contaynyng the Actes and
Monuments...Newly recognized and inlarged* (London, 1570), 1418–19.

22. Thomas Freeman generously shared these findings in his letter to me of 30 November
1994.

23. Freeman argues that Foxe's source for this addition was also oral, and that it could have
been Francis Russell, second earl of Bedford, whose father, John Lord Russell, the future first
earl of Bedford, was present at the execution. Freeman has found evidence in Foxe's papers that
Francis Russell gave Foxe information about his father after 1563 and before 1570, although
the Askew execution is not specifically mentioned; it is also possible that Francis Russell was
himself present at the execution (letters of 30 November 1994 and 5 February 1995).

24. John Foxe, *The seconde Volume of the Ecclesiasticall Historie, conteining the Acts and
Monuments* (London, 1583), 1234–40.

IV. MODERN EDITIONS

The Religious Tract Society published the *Examinations* in a modernized text in *Writings of Edward the Sixth, William Hugh, Queen Catherine Parr, Anne Askew, Lady Jane Grey, Hamilton and Balnaves.*[25] Two modernized texts were published in 1849. The first, *The Account of the Sufferings of Anne Askew,* may have used STC 852 or 853, or perhaps Foxe, as a basetext and bears an unusual subtitle: *for opposing the / Gross Fiction of Transubstantiation / which is / So Repugnant to Truth and Common Sense, / And Has No Warranty Whatever from / Scripture /* Written by Herself / and Re-Printed by a Catholic / London: / Francis & John Rivington / St Paul's Church Yard, & Waterloo Place / 1849. Whether the "Catholic" is an earlier printer or the present one is unknown.

The second publication of 1849 was the inclusion of the *Examinations* in the *Select Works of John Bale… Containing the Examinations of Lord Cobham, William Thorpe, and Anne Askewe and the Image of both Churches,* edited by the Reverend Henry Christmas for the Parker Society.[26] For the *First Examination,* Christmas appears to have compared and collated two editions. His description suggests that he used a copy of STC 853; perhaps, since STC 853 is undated, Christmas assumed that an edition without Bale's commentary was the first, and he designated it as such in his variants. From his description of the title-page woodcut, the other edition was a copy of STC 848. For the *Latter Examination,* the two copies he "compared and collated" were both cut and pasted at pages 22v–23v, suggesting that they were both copies of STC 850. The one in the British Museum remained pasted (possibly the one still pasted today, C 135 a. 23 [2]), but Christmas separated the leaves of the one owned by George Offor of Grove House, Hackney, although he could not supply the missing lines (205). However, Christmas appears to have worked with a basetext with numerous variants from Offor's copy, which itself seems to conform fully to STC 850. He

---

25. London, n.d., 1831, 1836, 1840, 186?; republished in *British Reformers* (Philadelphia: Presbyterian Board of Publication, 1842), vol. 3.

26. (Cambridge: Cambridge Univ. Press, 1849; reprint, New York: Johnson Reprint Corp., 1968), 135–248.

made many modernizing changes in the text, some substantial, and provided some textual and contextual annotations. Since Christmas does
not identify his basetext, or explain which emendations are his own, it is
difficult to solve this puzzle. Although the evidence above suggests that
he used STC 850, the discrepancies leave open the possibility that he
used a presently unknown variant of STC 850.

V. A BALLAD OF ANNE ASKEW

Askew's name also appears on "A Ballad of *Anne Askew,* Intituled: *I
am a Woman poore and Blind*" (STC 853.5).[27] Although Nashe men-
tions "the ballet of Anne Askew" and quotes the first line in *Have With
You to Saffron-Walden* (1596), the ballad does not appear in the Stationers' Register until 14 December 1624 when "I am a poore woman and
blinde" was entered with 127 other ballads to Master Pavier, John
Wright, Cutbert Wright, Edward Wright, John Grismond, and Henry
Gosson.[28] The single known copy of the 1624 printing is held by the
Central Library in Manchester, England, in a collection bought from T.
Sutton and Son in 1883. According to Christine Lingard, Language
and Literature Librarian at the Central Library, the ballads are
"mounted into volumes and presumably have been since purchase
though as the [Askew] sheet has been doubly mounted they may have
been rebound at a later date." The Askew ballad "is completely separate
from the ballad on the same page and it is impossible to tell whether
they were one sheet."[29] The other ballad is "The shamefull downefall of
the Popes Kingdome Contayning the life and death of Steeven Garnet,
the Popes chiefe Priest in England being executed in Paules Church-
yard in London the 3. of May last. 1606. To the tune of, Triumph and
Joy." Each ballad is headed by two woodcuts. The Askew ballad features
on the left a roughly drawn half-length of a woman wearing a headdress

---

27. The "Ballad" appears in Appendix 2 of the present volume.

28. See Thomas Nashe, *Works,* ed. Ronald B. McKerrow (Oxford: Basil Blackwell, 1958), 3:
113; *A Transcript of the Registers of the Company of Stationers of London 1554–1640,* ed. Edward
Arber (London, 1877; reprint, New York: Peter Smith, 1950), 4: 93.

29. Ms. Lingard kindly provided a photocopy and a description of this copy of the ballad.

and a cross on a chain around her neck, and on the right a woodcut of a "priest" with a tonsure, rosary, and prayerbook, who also wears doublet and hose under a long coat. The other ballad repeats, on the left, the woodcut of the priest and on the right, an elaborately dressed gallant with the heading over both woodcuts, "Garnet, the Popes chiefe wandring Priest, his habite and attire." Ms. Lingard notes that the sheet is "in poor condition but is well preserved and any further deterioration halted. It is extremely discolored...and the print is somewhat smudged, especially in the bottom left hand corner." At the bottom right, "Imprinted at London for TP" is just legible, although the bottom of the initials is missing. Five more editions of the ballad are listed in the Wing catalogue: A3210B, in which the name is spelled "Ann Askew," [1684–86]; A3211 [1693?] and A3212 [1695?] which change the spelling to "An Askew"; A3213, which has "Anne Askew" [1695?]; and A3214, "Ann Askew" [1695?].[30] The woodcuts heading A3212 and A3213 differ from each other and from the woodcut of STC 853.5. A3212 shows a well-dressed woman kneeling in prayer. A3213 shows a draped figure, perhaps blind, bearing a cup, in front of a turreted building. A3212 was republished by the Roxburgh Club.[31] There are numerous variants between the first and later editions of the ballad.

---

30. *Short-Title Catalogue of Books Printed in England, Scotland, Ireland, Wales, and British America And of English Books Printed in Other Countries 1641–1700*, vol. 1, compiled by Donald Wing, 2nd ed., newly revised and enlarged by John J. Morrison and Carolyn W. Nelson, editors, and Matthew Seccombe, assistant editor (New York: Modern Language Association, 1994).

31. *Ancient Songs and Ballads Written on Various Subjects and Printed between the years MDLX and MDCC Chiefly Collected by Robert Earl of Oxford, And purchased at the Sale of the late Mr. West's Library in the Year 1773*, vol. 1 (London, 1774).

Note on the Text

The present edition of Askew's *Examinations* is based on copies of *The first examinacyon* (STC 848) and *The lattre examinacyon* (STC 850) in the Bodleian Library, Oxford (shelfmark 8⁰ C.46. Th. Seld.), used by permission.

The two examinations of...Maistris An Askew is based on the copy of John Foxe's *Actes and Monuments* (STC 11222) in the Huntington Library (shelfmark RB 59840), pages 669–78, used by permission of the Huntington Library, San Marino, California. There are numerous differences (variants, omissions, and additions) between Bale's and Foxe's editions of Askew's text. The notes indicate some omissions in Foxe and differences between the two texts in the transcription of numbers.

"In Annæ Askevæ Constantissimæ fœminæ et martyris bustum, Epitaphium Sapphicum" is based on the copy of John Foxe's *Rerum in Ecclesia Gestarum Commentarii* (Basel, 1559) in the Houghton Library (shelfmark fEC/F8364/559r, vol. 1), page 200, used by permission of the Houghton Library, Harvard University. The English translation, "Epitaph in Sapphic Verse upon the tomb of the most steadfast woman and martyr Anne Askew," is by G. P. Goold, Lampson Professor Emeritus of Latin, Yale University (Appendix 1, page 194).

"A Ballad of Anne Askew" (STC 853.5) is based on the copy at the Language and Literature Library, Central Library, Manchester, England, used by permission (Appendix 2, page 195).

The English texts retain sixteenth-century spelling except that *i, j, u, v, w,* and long *s* have been regularized according to modern usage and contractions and abbreviations such as & (and) have been expanded. In the Latin "Epitaph," however, *i, u,* and *v* appear as in the basetext, and the ampersand (&) has been retained there and in Latin quotations in the text. The abbreviation for "etcetera" (&c.) has been retained. A tilde over a vowel has been expanded to *m* or *n* as needed; a tilde over *n* has been expanded to *un*. Large initials are not carried over. Turned letters have been silently emended. The following sixteenth-century spellings

lviii

occur frequently in the text: "whan" for when; "than" for then; "to" for too; "the" for thee; "-cyons" for -tions.

This edition retains the punctuation of the basetexts with the following silent emendations: virgules have been emended to commas; periods missing at the ends of sentences have been supplied; where there is only one parenthetical mark, the missing mark has been supplied.

Emendations are indicated in the notes to the page on which they occur. Marginalia in the basetext, many of which are editorial comments, have been placed in the notes to the page on which they occur and are indicated by "margin." Page numbers in Bale's Tables of Contents have been altered to refer to pages in this edition.

Contextual notes identifying obscure historical, pseudo-historical, and religious figures are based on a variety of early modern and modern sources. Early sources include Bede, *Ecclesiastical History of the English Nation; The Kalendre of the New Legende of Englande* (1516); John Bale, *The Actes of English Votaryes* (1546) and *Illustrium Maioris Britanniae Scriptorum...Summarium* (1548); and John Foxe, *Actes and Monuments* (1563). Modern reference works include *The New Catholic Encyclopedia; The Oxford Dictionary of the Christian Church;* and *The Book of Saints,* 6th ed. (London: A. & C. Black, 1989).

List of Abbreviations for Biblical References

In the sixteenth century, biblical scholars referred to the Greek Septuagint, the Latin Vulgate, Hebrew scripture, and various English translations, including those of John Wycliffe, William Tyndale, and Miles Coverdale. With the exception of Askew's paraphrase of Psalm 54, references to the Psalms in Askew's and Bale's texts follow the numbering of the Septuagint and Vulgate, a numbering that differs from that of the Hebrew Bible—and also, therefore, from that of the 1611 Authorized Version.[32] Coverdale's English Bible (1535) also follows the Vulgate numbering of the Psalms. For convenience to readers, equivalent numbers of the Psalms in the Authorized (King James) Version are given in contextual notes in the present volume. Biblical quotations in the contextual notes are taken from a modern-spelling edition of the 1611 Authorized Version. Abbreviations in the contextual notes are those in *The Chicago Manual of Style*, 14th edition.

The following list identifies the abbreviations and biblical references used in the basetext of *The Examinations* and in the basetext of *The two examinations* in John Foxe's *Actes and Monuments*.

Abacuch	Habakkuk
Acto.	Acts
Apo., Apoca.	Apocalypse; Revelation.
Apostle Judas	Jude
Baruch	Apocryphal Book of Baruch including Chapter 6, The Letter of Jeremiah.
Corin., Corinthiorum	Corinthians
Dan., Dani.	Daniel
Eccles.	Apocryphal Book of Ecclesiasticus
Esaye, Es., Esa.	Isaiah
Exodi.	Exodus
Ezechielis	Ezekiel
Gala.	Galatians.

---

32. See "Psalms" in the *Encyclopedia Britannica*, 15th ed. for a chart of the differences in numbering between the Hebrew Bible and the Vulgate.

Gene.	Genesis
Hester	Esther
Hiere.	Jeremiah
Jaco.	James.
Joan., Jo., Johannis, Johan.	John
Johel	Joel
Judi.	Judges
Luce	Luke
Macha., Machabeorum	Apocryphal Book of the Maccabees
Mala.	Malachi
Marci., Mar.	Mark
Math., Mathei, Matthei	Matthew
Michee, Miche	Micah
Osee	Hosea
Parali.	Paralipomenon; Chronicles
Petri	Peter
Philippen	Philippians
Pro., Prover., Proverbiorum	Proverbs
Psalmo., Psal.	Psalms
Regum, Reg.	Kings [the division of Samuel and Kings into four books derives from ancient practice in the Septuagint and the Latin Vulgate; the two Books of Samuel were called the First and Second Book of Kings; First and Second Kings were known as the Third and Fourth Book of Kings or 3 and 4 Regum]
Rom., Roma.	Romans
Sapien., Sapi	Apocryphal Book of the Wisdom of Solomon
Thes.	Thessalonians
Treno., Threnorum	Lamentations.
Zach., Zacha.	Zechariah

The first examinacy=
on of Anne Askewe, latelye mar
tyred in Smythfelde, by the wyc=
ked Synagoge of Antichrist,
with the Elucydacyon of
Johan Bale.

The veryte of the lorde endureth for euer.

Psalme 116.

BIB
LIA

Anne Askewe stode fast by thys veryte of
God to the ende.

Fauoure is disceytfull/and bewtye is a vay
ne thynge. But a woman that feareth the
lorde/is worthye to be praysed. She ope=
neth her mouthe to wysdome/and in her lan
guage is the lawe of grace. Prouerb. xxxj.

The title page from John Bale's edition of *The first examinacyon of Anne Askewe* (1546) is reproduced by permission of the Folger Shakespeare Library.

Johan Bale to the Christen readers.

Amonge other most syngular offyces (dylygent reader) whych the lorde hath appoynted to be done in the ernest sprete of Helyas, by the foreronners of hys lattre aperaunce, thys is one verye specyall to be noted. They shall turne the hartes of their auncyent elders into the chyldren, Mala, 4. And the unbelevers of their tyme, to the wysdome of those ryghtouse fathers, as ded Johan Baptyst afore hys first commynge, Luce 1. That is (sayth Bedas ca. 68. de temporum ratione) the faythe and fervent zele of the prophetes and Apostles shall they plant in their hartes, whych shall in those dayes lyve and be amonge men conver- 10 saunt, and than wyll breake fourth (sayth he as a verye true prophete) soche horryble persecucyon, as wyll first of all take from the worlde, those myghtye heliases by tryumphaunt martyrdome, to the terryfyenge of other in the same fayth, of whom some shall becom through that occasyon, most gloryouse martyrs unto Christ also, and some verye wycked Apostataes forsakynge hys lyvelye doctryne. For by the seyd Bedas testymonye in the begynnynge of the same chaptre, two most certayne sygnes shall we than have that the lattre judgement daye is at hande. The returne of Israels remnaunt unto their lorde God, and the horryble persecucyon of Antichrist. 20

Conferre with thys treated scripture and former prophecye of that vertuouse man Bedas, the worldes alteracyon now, with the terryble turmoylynges of our tyme. And as in a most clere myrrour, ye shall wele

---

Line 3. **Helyas:** Elias; the prophet Elijah.

Line 8. **Bedas...ratione:** Bede (673–735), theologian and historian of the English church; Bale refers to chapter 68 in Bede's Latin treatise, *On the Reckoning of Times.* **Bedes prophecye:** margin.

Line 15. **2. sortes.:** margin.

Line 16. **Apostataes:** apostates (Latin); those who forsake their religious faith.

Lines 18–19. **lattre...hande:** God's Last Judgement is near. **2. sygnes.:** margin.

Line 19. **returne of Israel...God:** the conversion of the Jews to Christianity, an event Christians believed would happen just before the Last Judgement.

Line 20. **Antichrist:** the great opponent of Christ who would appear before the end of the world (1 John 2:18); Reformers' derogatory term for the Roman Catholic papacy.

Line 21. **Conferre:** compare.

3

perceyve them at thys present, to be in most quyck workynge. And as concernynge the Israelytes or Jewes, I have both seane and knowne of them in Germanye, most faythfull Christen belevers. Neyther is it in the prophecye (Osee 3.) that they shuld at that daye be all converted, no more than they were at Johan Baptystes preachynge, Luce 1. For as Esaye reporteth, though the posteryte of Jacob be as the see sande
30 (innumerable) yet shall but a remnaunt of them convert than unto their lorde God. Esaie 10. And though the lorde hath syfted that howse of Israel (as broused corne in a syffe) amonge all other nacyons, Amos 9. Yet shall not that remnaunt of theirs perysh, but at that daye be saved, through the onlye eleccyon of grace, Romano. 11. Now concernynge the afore seyd foreronners, in thys most wonderfull change of the worlde before the lattre ende therof. I thynke within thys realme of Englande, besydes other nacyons abroade, the sprete of Helyas was not all a slepe in good Wyllyam Tyndale, Robert Barnes, and soche other more, whome Antichristes vyolence hath sent hens in fyre to heaven, as
40 Helyas went afore in the fyerye charett, 4. Regum 2.

These turned the hartes of the fathers into the chyldren, soche tyme as they toke from a great nombre of our nacyon, by their godlye preachynges and writynges, the corrupted beleve of the pope and hys mastrye workers (whych were no fathers, but cruell robbers and destroyers, Joan. 10.) reducynge them agayn to the true faythe of Abraham and Peter, Gene. 15. and Math. 16. The pure beleve in Christes

---

Line 25. **Israelytes.**: margin.

Line 32. **broused**: bruised. **syffe**: sieve.

Line 34. **eleccyon of grace**: central Reformist doctrine of salvation by grace not works; see Rom. 11:5–6. **preachers**: margin.

Lines 35–36. **change of the worlde**: the change after the last trumpet at the end of time; see 1 Cor. 15:51–52.

Line 38. **Wyllyam Tyndale**: Reformer (ca. 1494–1536) who translated the Bible into English (New Testament, 1526; Old Testament, 1530) and was burned for heresy at Vilvorde in Belgium. **Robert Barnes**: Reformist author and evangelical preacher (1495–1540) who was burned for heresy at Smithfield. **Tyndale. Barnes.**: margin.

Line 40. **fyerye**: emended from "frerye".

Line 45. **reducynge**: leading back.

birthe and passyon, whych Adam and Noe sucked out of the first promes of God, Jacob and Moses out of the seconde, David and the prophetes out of the thirde, and so fourth the Apostles and fathers out of the other scriptures, so firmelye planted they in the consciences of 50 manye, that no cruell kynde of deathe coulde averte them from it. As we have for example their constaunt dyscyples, and now stronge witnesses of Jesus Christ, Johan Lassels and Anne Askewe, with their other. ii. companyons, verye gloryouse martyrs afore God, what though they be not so afore the wronge judgynge eyes of the worlde whom the bloudye remnaunt of Antichrist put unto most cruell deathe in Smythfelde at London, in the yeare of our lorde, M. D. XLVI. in Julye.

If they be onlye (as was Johan Baptyst) great afore the lorde by the holye scriptures allowaunce, whych are strongelye adourned with the graces of hys sprete, as faythe, force, understandynge, wysdome, pa- 60 cyence, love, longe sufferaunce and soche lyke. I dare boldelye afferme these 4. myghtye witnesses also to be the same, so well as the martyrs of the prymatyve or Apostles churche. For so strongelye had these those vertues as they, and so boldelye objected their bodyes to the deathe for the undefyled Christen beleve, agaynst the malygnaunt Synagoge of Sathan, as ever ded they, for no tyrannye admyttynge anye create or corruptyble substaunce for their eternall lyvynge god. If their blynde

---

Line 47. **Noe:** Noah. **The fathers.**: margin.

Line 53. **Johan Lassels:** Reformer from Nottinghamshire and an attendant of the King's Chamber (d. 1546). See pages 133, 154. **other...companyons:** see Introduction, pages xxii–xxiii. **Martyrs.**: margin.

Line 56. **Smythfelde:** Smithfield, open area outside London wall and just inside London city limits; after 1400 the place of execution for heretics.

Line 58. **as was Johan Baptyst...lorde:** see Luke 7:28.

Line 63. **primatyve...churche:** the church during the first centuries after Christ. **Christen martyrs.**: margin.

Line 64. **objected:** exposed to danger or evil.

Lines 65–66. **Synagoge...Sathan:** see Rev. 2:9; in hostile controversy, the Reformers' term for the Roman Catholic clergy.

Lines 66–67. **anye...god:** the Roman Catholic doctrine of transubstantiation, that during the mass the consecrated bread and wine are changed into Christ's body and blood. **Breade.**: margin.

babyes to prove them unlyke, do object agaynst me, the myracles
shewed at their deathes more than at these, as that unfaythfull genera-
70   cyon is ever desyerouse of wonders Math. 12. I wolde but knowe of
them, what myracles were shewed whan Johan Baptystes head was cut
of in the preson? Marci 6. and whan James the Apostle was byheaded at
Hierusalem? Acto. 12. These 2. were excellent afore God, what though
they were but myserable wretches, lyght fellawes, sedycyouse heretykes,
busye knaves, and lowsye beggers in the syght of noble kyng Herode
and hys honorable counsell of prelates. For had not rochettes and syde
gownes bene at hande, haplye they had not so lyghtlye dyed.

    If they allege Steven, to maynteyne their purpose, that he at hys
deathe be helde heaven open. I aske of them agayne what they were
80   whych se it more than hys owne persone? Sure I am that their wycked
predecessours there present, se it not. For they stopped their eares,
whan he tolde them therof, Actorum 7. If they yet brynge fourth the
other hystoryes of Apostles and martyrs. I answere them, that all they
are of no soche autoryte, as these here afore. The popes martyrs in
dede, were moche fuller of myracles than ever were Christes, as hysselfe
tolde us they shulde be so, Mathei 24. Yet wrought fryre Forest, Johan
Fisher and Thomas More no myracles, what though manye be now
regestred in their lyves and legendes by the fryres of Fraunce, Italye,
and Spayne. Besydes that Johan Cochleus hath written of them, ad
90   Paulum Pontificem, ad regem Henricum, and also in their defence agaynst

---

Line 72. **myracles**: margin.

Line 76. **rochettes**: ecclesiastical vestments worn by bishops and abbots. **syde gownes**: long garments, hanging far down. **rochettes**: margin.

Line 79. **Steven.**: margin.

Line 82. **Legendes.**: margin.

Lines 86–87. **fryre Forest**: John Forest (1474–1538), Franciscan friar who opposed the king's supremacy and was burned at Smithfield. **Johan Fisher**: John Fisher (1469–1535), bishop of Rochester; he opposed the king's supremacy and the royal divorce, and was beheaded on Tower Hill. **Thomas More**: lord chancellor, Catholic, and author (1478–1535); he opposed the king's supremacy and was beheaded on Tower Hill. **Forest. Fysher. More.**: margin.

Line 89. **Johan Cochleus**: Johannes Cochlaeus (1479–1552), German Catholic theologian who supported Henry VIII's attack on Luther.

Lines 89–90. **ad...Pontificem**: to Pope Paul (Latin). **ad...Henricum**: to king Henry (Latin).

doctor Sampson. With that Erasmus ded also ad Huttenum. P. M. ad
Gasparem Agrippam, Albertus Pighius, Rivius, Fichardus, and a great
sort more. And as for the holye mayde of kent with Doctor Bockynge,
though they wrought great wonders by their lyfe, yet apered non at
their deathes. Of hys owne chosen martyrs, Christ loketh for non other
myracle, but that onlye they persever faythfull to the ende, Math. 10.
And never denye hys veryte afore men. Luce 12. For that worthye vyctorye of the synnefull worlde, standeth in the invyncyblenesse of faythe,
and not in myracles and wonders, as those waverynge wittes suppose, 1.
Joan. 5.

Ryght wonderfullye wyll thys apere in the ii. myghtye conflyctes here
after folowynge, whych the faythfull servaunt of Jesu Anne Askewe, a
gentylwoman verye yonge, dayntye, and tender, had with that outra-
gynge Synagoge, in her ii. examynacyons, about the xxv. yeare of her
age, whom she sent abroade by her owne hande writynge. The handelynges of her other iii. companyons, shall be shewed in other severall
treatyses at layser. For the glorye and great power of the lorde, so manyfestlye aperynge in hys elect vessels, maye not now perysh at all handes,
and be unthankefullye neglected but be spred the worlde over, as wele

---

Line 91. **doctor Sampson:** Richard Sampson (d. 1554), bishop of Coventry and Lichfield, who argued for the king's supremacy. **Erasmus:** Desiderius Erasmus (1469–1536), Dutch humanist and biblical scholar.

Lines 91–92. **ad Huttenum:** Erasmus's Latin discourse to Ulrich von Hutten (1488–1523), German humanist and Reformer. **P. M.:** possibly Philip Melanchthon (1497–1560), friend and co-worker of Luther. **ad Gasparem Agrippam:** unidentified. **Albertus Pighius:** Dutch Catholic theologian (1490–1542). **Rivius:** Johannes Rivius, author of *A treatise against the folishness of men in differringe the reformation of their living* [English trans. 1550?].

Line 92. **Fichardus:** possibly Thomas Fich (d. 1517), ecclesiastic and compiler. **Writers.:** margin.

Line 93. **holye mayde of kent:** Elizabeth Barton (ca. 1506–1534), the serving woman whose prophecies warned against the royal divorce; she was executed for treason. **Doctor Bockynge:** Dr. Edward Bocking, a monk and Barton's spiritual director.

Line 95. **Christen martyrs.:** margin.

Line 102. **servaunt;** emended from "setvaunt". **Anne Askewe.:** margin.

Line 107. **Goddes power.:** margin.

Line 108. **elect vessels:** chosen people.

110 in Latyne as Englysh, to the perpetuall infamye of so wyllfullye cruell
and spyghtfull tyrauntes. Nothynge˙ at all shall it terryfye us, nor yet in
anye poynt lett us of our purpose, that our bokes are now in Englande
condempned and brent, by the Byshoppes and prestes with their frantyck affynyte, the great Antichristes upholders, whych seke by all practyses possyble to turne over the kynges most noble and godlye
enterpryse. But it wyll from hens forth occasyon us, to set fourth in the
Latyne also, that afore we wrote onlye in the Englysh, and so make their
spirytuall wyckednesse and treason knowne moche farther of. What
avayled it Joakim to burne Hieremyes prophecye by the ungracyouse
120 counsell of hys prelates? Hiere. 36. Eyther yet Antiochus to set fyre on
the other scriptures? 1. Macha. 1.

       After the Apostles were brought afore the counsell and strayghtlye
commaunded to cease from preachynge, they preached moche more
than afore. Acto. 4. In most terryble persecucyons of the prymatyve
churche, were the examynacyons and answers, tormentes and deathes of
the constaunt martyrs written, and sent abroade all the whole worlde
over, as testyfyeth Eusebius Cesariensis in hys ecclesyastyck hystorye.
Their coppyes habounde yet everye where. Great slaughter and
burnynge hath bene here in Englande for Johan wycleves bokes, ever
130 sens the yeare of our lorde. M. CCC. LXXXII. Yet have not one of them
throughlye peryshed. I have at thys houre the tytles of a C. and XLIIII.
of them, whych are manye more in nombre. For some of them undre
one tytle comprehendeth ii. bokes, some iii. some iiii. Yea, one of them

---

Line 112. **lett:** hinder.

Lines 112–13. **our bokes...brent:** a proclamation of 8 July 1546 ordered the collecting and
burning of heretical books written by Frith, Tyndale, Wycliffe, Bale, Barnes, Coverdale, and
others; on 26 September confiscated books were burned at St. Paul's Cross. **Bokes
condempned.:** margin.

Line 117. **Latyne:** Latin, the international language of diplomacy, religion, and law. **Latyne.:**
margin.

Line 119. **prophecye:** emended from "proyhecye".

Line 122. **God wyll be knowne.:** margin.

Line 127. **Eusebius Cesariensis:** Eusebius of Caesarea (fl. fourth century), first major historian
of the Christian church. **ecclesyastyck hystorye:** Eusebius's *Ecclesiastical History.*

Line 129. **Johan wycleve:** John Wycliffe (ca. 1330–1384), preeminent religious reformer and
translator of the Bible into English. **Johan wycleves bokes.:** margin.

contayneth xii. I thynke not the contrarye, but ere the worlde be at a full ende, God wyll so gloryfye that twentye tymes condempned here-tyke, execrated, cursed, spytted, and spatled at, that all your popysh writers before hys tyme and after, wyll be reckened but vyle swyne-heardes to hym, for the good faver he bare to Christes holye Gospell. A verye madnesse is it to stryve agaynst God, whan he wyll have the longe hydden inyquytees knowne. As the godlye wyse man Gamaliel sayd, Acto. 5. If thys enterpryse that is now taken agaynst yow, be of God, ye shall never be able with all your tyrannouse practyses to dyssolve it.

Now concernynge that blessed woman Anne Askewe, whych latelye suffered the tyrannye of thys worlde for ryghtwisnesse sake. In Lyncolne shyre was she borne of a verye auncyent and noble stocke, Sir Wyllyam Askewe a worthye knyght beynge her father. But no worthynesse in the flesh, neyther yet anye worldlye noblenesse avayleth to godwarde, afore whome is no acceptacyon of persone, Actorum 10. Onlye is it faythe with hys true love and feare, whych maketh us the accept, noble and worthye chyldren unto God, Joan. 1. Wherof by hys gyft, she had won-derfull habundaunce. Soch a won was she, as was Lydia the purple sellar, whose harte the lorde opened by the godlye preachynge of Paule at Thyatira, Acto. 16. For dylygent hede gave she to hys worde whan it was ones taught without superstycyon, and wolde no longar be a false worshypper or ydolatour after the wycked scole of Antichrist. But became from thensfourth a true worshypper, worshyppyng her lorde God (whych is a sprete and not breade) in sprete and in veryte, accor-dynge to that worde of hys, Joan. 4. The Gospell of Christ bare she in her harte, as ded the holye mayde Cecilia, and never after ceased from

Line 135. **Canonyse**: margin.
Line 136. **spatled**: spat.
Line 140. **Gamaliel**: see Acts 5:34. **gamaliel**: margin.
Line 143. **Anne Askewe.**: margin.
Line 144. **ryghtwisnesse**: righteousness.
Line 147. **to godwarde**: in relation to God.
Line 148. **no...persone**: God is no respecter of worldly eminence; see Acts 10:34. **True nobylyte.**: margin.
Line 151. **Lydia**: see Acts 16:14. **Lydia.**: margin.
Line 159. **Cecilia**: third-century Roman martyr and saint. **Cecilia.**: margin.

160   the stodye therof, nor from godlye communycacyon and prayer, tyll she
was clerlye by most cruell tormentes, taken from thys wretched worlde.

    By her do I here (dere fryndes in the lorde) as ded the faythfull Breth-
erne in Fraunce, at the cyties of Lyons and Vienna by a lyke faythfull
yonge woman called Blandina. Whych was there put to deathe with. iii.
myghtye companyons more amonge other (as thys was) for her Christen beleve, about the yeare of our lorde, C. and LXX. in the prymatyve
sprynge of their Christyanyte. They wrote unto their Bretherne in the
landes of Asia and Phrygia verye farre of, her myghtye stronge sufferynges for Christes fayth, whych they knewe nothynge of afore. I write
170   here unto yow in Englande the double processe of thys noble woman,
wherof ye are not ignoraunt, for so moche as it was there so manyfestlye
done amonge yow. Coupled I have these ii. examples togyther, bycause I
fynde them in so manye poyntes agree. Blandina was yonge and tender.
So was Anne Askewe also. But that whych was frayle of nature in them
both, Christ made most stronge by hys grace. Blandina had iii. ernest
companyons in Christ, Maturus, Sanctes, and Attalus, so ferventlye
faythfull as her selfe. So had Anne Askewe iii. fyre fellawes, a gentylman
called Johan Lassels her instructour, a preste, and a tayler called Johan
Adlam, men in Christes veryte unto the ende most constaunt. With
180   Blandina were in preson, to the nombre of x. whych renyed the truthe
and were clerelye forsaken of God for it. How manye fell from Christ
besydes Crome and Shaxton, whan Anne Askewe stode fast by hym, I
am uncerteyne. But I counsell them, as saynt Johan counselled the
Laodycyanes, in the myserable estate they are now in, to bye them

---

Line 163. **Vienna:** Vienne, in southeast France.

Line 164. **Blandina:** slave martyred at Lyons A.D. 177; see Eusebius, *Ecclesiastical History,*
Book 5, chapters 1–3. **Blandina.:** margin.

Line 170. **processe:** proceedings; narrative.

Line 172. **Anne Askewe.:** margin.

Line 176. **Companyons.:** margin.

Line 180. **renyed:** renayed; renounced or denied. **Recanters.:** margin.

Line 182. **Crome:** Dr. Edward Crome, London Reformer and popular preacher who publicly
recanted 27 June 1546. **Shaxton:** Nicholas Shaxton (1485?–1556), former bishop of
Salisbury; condemned for heresy at the Guildhall, 28 June 1546, he recanted and preached at
Askew's burning.

Lines 183–84. **saynt...Laodycyanes:** see Rev. 3:14–22.

through tryed golde of Christ, least they perysh all togyther, Apoca. 3. If they had not styll remayned in that chauncell, whome Christ commaunded Johan in no wyse to measure, Apoca. 11. They had never so shamefullye blasphemed, lyke as Bedas also toucheth in hys former prophecye.

Prompt was Blandina, and of most lustye corage, in renderynge her 190 lyfe for the lyberte of her faythe. No lesse lyvelye and quyck was Anne Askewe in all her enprysonynges and tormentes. Great was the love, Blandina had to Christ. No lesse was the love of Anne Askewe. Blandina never faynted in torment. No more ded Anne Askewe in sprete, whan she was so terrybly racked of Wrysleye the chaunceller and Ryche, that the strynges of her armes and eyes were peryshed. Blandina deryded the cruelte of the tyrauntes. So ded Anne Askewe the madnesse of the Byshoppes and their speche men. Reade burnynge plates of yron and of brasse had Blandina put to her sydes.

So had Anne Askewe the flamynge brandes of fyre. Full of God and 200 hys veryte was Blandina. So was Anne Askewe to the verye ende. Christ wonderfullye tryumphed in Blandina. So ded he in Anne Askewe, whan she made no noyse on the racke, and so ernestlye afterwarde rejoyced in hym. Blandina was geven fourth to wylde beastes to be devoured. So was Anne Askewe to cruell Byshoppes and prestes, whom Christ calleth ravenynge wolves, devourers, and theves. Math. 7. and Joan. 10. Blandina upon the scaffolde boldelye reprehended the pagane prestes of their errour. So ded Anne Askewe whan she was fast tyed to the stake,

---

Line 185. **Tryed Golde.**: margin.

Line 186. **that chauncell**: the space outside the temple, off-limits to the believer; see Rev. 11:2. **The chauncell.**: margin.

Line 191. **Corage.**: margin.

Line 194. **Racked.**: margin.

Line 195. **Wrysleye**: Sir Thomas Wriothesley (1505–1550), lord chancellor who became first earl of Southampton in 1547; he was a prominent conservative determined to stop the Reformers.

Line 195. **Ryche**: Richard Rich (1496?–1567), member of the conservative court faction.

Line 198. **Reade**: red.

Line 199. **Burned.**: margin.

Line 204. **Beastes.**: margin.

with stomack rebuke that blasphemouse apostata Shaxton with the
210 Byshoppes and prestes generacyon, for their manyfest mayntenaunce of
ydolatrye.

Blandina at the stake shewed a vysage unterryfyed. So ded Anne
Askewe a countenaunce stowte, myghtye and ernest. Infatygable was
the sprete of Blandina. So was the sprete of Anne Askewe. The love of
Jesus Christ, the gyft of the holye Ghost, and hope of the crowne of
martyrdome, greatlye mytygated the payne in Blandina. So ded these
iii. worthye graces, the terrour of all tormentes in Anne Askewe. The
stronge sprete of Christ gave stomack to Blandina, both to laugh and
daunce. The same myghtye sprete (and not the popes desperate sprete)
220 made Anne Askewe both to rejoyce and synge in the preson. So bolde
was Blandina (sayth Eusebius) that with a presumpcyon of stomack she
commoved with Christ unseane. I suppose Anne Askewes lattre examynacyon, wyll shewe her, not to do moche lesse. Gentyll was Blandina to
the christen belevers, and terryble to their adversaryes. So was Anne
Askewe verye lowlye to true teachers, but scornefull and hygh stomaked
to the enemyes of truthe. Manye were converted by the sufferaunce of
Blandina. A farre greatter nombre by the burnynge of Anne Askewe.
Though Blandina were yonge, yet was she called the mother of martyrs.
Manye men have supposed Anne Askewe. for her Christen constancye
230 to be no lesse. Blandina prayed for her persecuters. So ded Anne Askewe
most ferventlye. The ashes of Blandina and of other martyrs, were
throwne into the flood of Rhodanus. What was done with the Ashes of
Anne Askewe and her companyons, I can not yet tell.

Line 209. **Shaxton.**: margin.
Line 213. **Infatygable:** indefatigable.
Line 215. **Graces.**: margin.
Line 218. **stomack:** spirit or courage. **Sprete.**: margin.
Line 222. **commoved:** moved in mind or feeling.
Line 223. **Hygh stomacke.**: margin.
Line 225. **hygh stomaked:** proud or haughty.
Line 228. **Mother.**: margin.
Line 231. **Ashes.**: margin.
Line 232. **flood of Rhodanus:** Rhone river.

All these former reportes of Blandina and manye more besydes, hath
Eusebius in Ecclesiastica historia, libro 5. cap. 1. 2. and 3. Hugo Floriacensis, Hermannus Contractus, Vincentius, Antoninus, Petrus Equilinus, and other hystoryanes more. And as touchynge Anne Askewe,
these ii. examynacyons, with her other knowne handelynges in
Englande, are wytnesses for her suffycyent. Thus hath not the fyre taken
Anne Askewe all whole from the worlde, but left her here unto it more   24
pure, perfyght, and precyouse than afore, as it wyll also Johan Lassels
within short space. So that concernynge her, it maye wele be sayd, that
Paule verefyeth, 2. Cor. 12. The strength of God is here made perfyght
by weakenesse. Whan she semed most feble, than was she most stronge.
And gladlye she rejoyced in that weakenesse, that Christes power myght
strongelye dwell in her. Thus choseth the lorde, the folysh of thys
worlde to confounde the wyse, and the weake to deface the myghtye.
Yea, thynges despysed and thought verye vyle, to brynge thynges unto
nought whych the worlde hath in most hygh reputacyon. I thynke yf
thys martyr were ryghtlye conferred, with those canonysed martyrs,   25
whych have had, and yet hath styll, sensynges and syngynges, massynges
and ryngynges in the popes Englysh churche, cause with cause and reason with reason (as haplye here after they shall) she shuld be a great
blemysh unto them. An example of stronge sufferaunce myght thys
holye martyr be, unto all them that the lorde shall after lyke maner put
forewarde in thys horryble furye of Antichrist, to the glorye of hys persecuted churche. Amen.

Lines 235–37. **Hugo Floriacensis**: Hugh of Fleury (d. after 1118), author of *Historia
Ecclesiastica* (*Ecclesiastical History*). **Hermannus Contractus**: Herimannus Contractus (1013–
1054), ecclesiastical chronicler. **Vincentius**: Vincent of Beauvais (ca. 1190–1264), church
father and historian. **Antoninus**: Saint Antoninus (1389–1459), Antonino Pierozzi, author of
Chronicles. **Petrus Equilinus**: also one of Bale's sources for *Actes of Englysh Votaryes*. **Autors.**:
margin.

Line 239. **Not all dead.**: margin.

Line 244. **Weakenesse.**: margin.

Line 249. **hygh**: emended from "hyght".

Line 251. **Martyrs**: margin.

Lines 251–52. **sensynges...ryngynges**: censing (burning incense), singing, saying masses, and
ringing bells for canonized martyrs are all Roman Catholic rituals.

Line 255. **Example**: margin.

A table compendyouse of thys first boke.

God save the kynge.

THE FIRST EXAMINACION

of the worthye servaunt of God mastres Anne Askewe
the yonger doughter of Sir Wyllyam Askewe knyght
of lyncolne shyre, latelye martyred in Smithfelde
by the Romysh popes upholders.

The censure or judgement of Johan Bale therupon,
after the sacred Scriptures and Chronycles.

Of no lesse Christen constancie was thys faythfull wytnesse and holye
martyr of God, Anne Askewe, nor no lesse a fast membre of Christ by
her myghtye persystence in hys veryte at thys tyme of myschefe, than   10
was the afore named Blandina in the prymatyve churche. Thys shall
wele apere in her ii. examynacyons or tyrannouse handelynges here
folowynge, whome she wrote with her owne hande, at the instant desyre
of serten faythfull men and women, yea rather at the secrete mocyon of
God, that the truth theroff myght be knowne the worlde over. As
within short space yt wyll be, yf the latyne speche can carye yt.
Markc wele the communycacyons here both of her and of her exam-
yners, so provynge their spretes as S. Johan the Apostle geveth yow counsell.
1. Jo. 4. And than shall ye knowe the tree by his frute, and the man by
hys worke.   20

Anne Askewe.

To satisfie your expectation, good people (sayth she) this was my first
examynacyon in the yeare of oure Lorde M. D. xlv and in the moneth
of Marche, first Christofer dare examyned me at Sadlers hall, beynge

---

Line 9. **membre of Christ:** a member (or limb) of Christ's "body."

Line 13. **whome:** which.

Line 16. **carye:** emended from "cayrye".

Line 18. **Spretes:** margin.

Line 24. **Christofer dare:** Christopher Dare; otherwise unidentified, one of twelve men
appointed to the quest. **Sadlers hall:** hall belonging to the Company of Saddlers in Wood
Street near the Guildhall (destroyed in World War II). **Christofer dare.:** margin.

one of the quest, and ásked yf I ded not beleve that the sacrament hang-
ynge over the aultre was the verye bodye of Christ reallye. Then I
demaunded thys questyon of hym, wherfore S. Steven was stoned to
deathe? And he sayd, he coulde not tell. Then I answered, that no more
wolde I assoyle hys vayne questyon.

₃₀   *Johan Bale.*

A sacrament (sayth Saynt Augustyne) ys a sygne, shappe, or symylytude
of that yt representyth, and no God nor yet thynge represented. Thys
worde reall or reallye, ys not of beleve, for yt ys not in all the sacred
scriptures. Onlye ys yt sophystycallye borowed of the paganes lernynge
by wynchestre and hys fellawes, to corrupt our Christen faythe. Beware
of that fylthye poyson. The perfyght beleve of Steven, Actorum vii. of
Paule Act. 17. and of Salomon, 3. Regum 8. et 2. Parali. 6. was, that
God dwelleth not in temples made with handes. Agreable unto thys was
the faythe of thys godlye woman, whych neyther coulde beleve that he
₄₀   dwelleth in the boxe. God sayth, Esaie lxvi. Heaven is my seate, not the
boxe. David sayth, Psalm. 113. oure God is in heaven, not in the pixt.
Christ taught us to saye, whan we praye, Matth. 6. Luce 11, our father
which art in heaven, and not our father which art in the boxe. Now dis-
cerne and judge.

                                          Anne Askewe.

Secondly he sayd, that there was a woman, whych ded testyfye, that I
shuld reade, how God was not in temples made with handes. Then I
shewed hym the vii. and the xvii. chaptre of the Apostles actes, what

---

Line 25. **quest**: body of persons appointed to hold an inquiry; see Introduction, page xxvi.

Line 29. **assoyle**: resolve.

Line 33. **of beleve**: part of belief. **Reallye.**: margin.

Line 34. **sophystycallye**: fallaciously; with deceptive subtlety.

Line 35. **wynchestre**: Stephen Gardiner (ca. 1497–1555), bishop of Winchester, prominent
conservative and royal advisor; see Introduction, pages xxvii–xxix.

Line 41. **pixt**: pyx; box in which is kept the consecrated bread of the sacrament. **The boxe**:
margin.

Line 47. **Temples.**: margin.

Steven and Paule had sayd therin. Wherupon he asked me, how I toke those sentences? I answered, that I wolde not throwe pearles amonge swyne, for acornes were good ynough.

Johan Bale.

An ignoraunt woman, yea a beast with out faythe, ys herin allowed to judge the holye scriptures heresye, and agaynst all good lawes admitted to accuse thys godlye woman the servaunt of Christ, for an haynouse heretyke, for the onlye readinge of them. As perverse and blasphemouse was thys qwestmonger as she, and as beastlye ignoraunt in the doctryne of helthe, yet is neyther of them judged yll of the worlde, but the one permitted to accuse thys true membre of Christ, and the other to condempne her. Wherfor her answere out of the vii. chaptre of Matthew, was most fytt for them. For they are no better than swyne, that so contempne the precyouse treasure of the Gospell, for the myre of mennys tradycyons.

Anne Askewe.

Thirdly he asked me, wherfor I sayd, that I had rather to reade fyve lynes in the Bible, than to heare fyve masses in the temple. I confessed, that I sayd no lesse. Not for the dysprayse of eyther the Epistle or Gospell. But bycause the one ded greatlye edyfye me, and the other nothinge at all. As saynt Paule doth witnesse in the xiiii chaptre of hys first Epistle to the Corinthes, whereas he doth saye. If the trumpe geveth an uncertayne sounde, who wyll prepare hymselfe to the battayle?

Johan Bale.

A commaundement hath Christ geven us, to serche the holye scriptures, Johan. 5. for in them onlye is the lyfe eternall. Blessed is he (sayth Christ unto Johan) whych readeth and heareth the wordes of thys prophecye, Apo. 1. But of the latyne popysh masse, is not one worde in all the Byble, and therfor it perteyneth not to faythe. A strayght com-

---

Line 56. **Accusers.**: margin.
Line 58. **helthe**: salvation. **yll**: ill; evil.
Line 66. **Masses**: margin.

maundement have almyghtye God geven, Deutro. 12. that nothynge be
added to hys worde, nor yet taken from it. Put thu nothynge unto his
80   wordes (saith Salomon, Prov. 30.) least thu be founde in so doynge, a
reprobate persone and a lyar. S. Paule wylled nothynge to be uttered in a
dead speche. 1. Corin. 14. (as are your masse and mattens) but sylence
alwayes to be in the congregacyons, where as is no interpretour, for fyve
wordes (sayth he) avayleth more to understandynge, than x. thousande
wordes with the tonge. Thys proveth temple servyce of the papystes all
the yeare, to be worth nothynge.

Anne Askewe.

Fortlye he layed unto my charge, that I shuld saye, If an yll prest
mynystred, it was the devyll and not God. My answere was, that I never
90   spake soche thynge. But thys was my sayenge, That what so ever he
were, whych mynystred unto me, hys yll condycyons coulde not hurte
my faythe. But in sprete I receyved never the lesse, the bodye and
bloude off Christ.

Johan Bale.

Christ sayth, Joan. 6. Have not I chosen yow xii. and yet one of yow is a
devyll, meanynge Judas that false and unfaythfull prest. No lesse sayth
Peter. 2. Pet. 2 of those lyenge curates, by whome the truthe is blasphemed, and the people made merchaundyce of in their covetousnesse.
If the yll frute than, be all one with the yll tree in noughtynesse, the
100 worke of a devyll must be devylysh. God sayd unto the wycked prestes,
Esa. i. Hier. 6. Amos 5. and Mala. 2. that he abhorred their sacryfyces,
and also hated them, even at the verye hart, wyllynge both heaven and
earthe to marke it. Into Judas entered Sathan, after the soppe was geven
hym, Joan. 13. where as the other Apostles receyved the bodye and
bloude of Christ. The table was all one to them both, so was the breade

---

Line 79. **Gods worde.**: margin.
Line 88. **The prest**: margin.
Line 96. **Judas.**: margin.
Line 101. **Sacryfyces.**: margin.

which their mouthes receyved. The inwarde receyvynges than in Peter
and in Judas, made all the dyversyte, whych was beleve and unbeleve, or
faythe and unfaythfulnesse, as Christ largelye declareth in the vi. of
Johan, where as he shewed afore hande, the full doctryne of that mystycall supper. Onlye he that beleveth, hath there the promes of the lyfe   110
everlastinge, and not he that eateth the materyall breade. Of God are
they taught, and not of men, whych trulye understande thys doctryne.

Anne Askewe.

Fiftly he asked me, what I sayd concernynge confession? I answered
hym my meanynge, whych was as Saynt James sayth, that everye man
ought to acknowlege hys fautes to other, and the one to praye for the
other.

Johan Bale.

Thys confessyon onlye do, the scripture appoynt us, Jac. 5. as we have
offended our neyber: But yf we have offended God, we must sorowful-   120
lye acknowlege it before hym. And he (sayth Saynt Johan, 1. Johan. 1.
hath faythfullye promysed to forgeve us our synnes, yf we so do, and to
clense us from all unryghtousnesse. If the lawe of truthe be in the
prestes mouthe, he ys to be sought unto for godlye counsell, Mala. 2.
But yf he be a blasphemouse hypocryte or superstycyouse fole, he ys to
be shourned as a most pestilent poyson.

Anne Askewe.

Sixtly he asked me, what I sayd to the kynges boke? And I answered
hym, that I coulde saye nothynge to it, bycause I never sawe it.

Line 108. **The vi. of Johan.**: margin.

Line 114. **Confession**: margin.

Lines 115–16. **everye man...other:** James 5:16.

Line 121. **hym. And:** emended from "hym=And".

Line 124. **Prestes.**: margin.

Line 126. **shourned:** shunned.

Line 128. **the kynges boke:** *A Necessary Doctrine and Erudition for Any Christen Man* (STC
5168), issued by the king's authority 29 May 1543; it restored essential Roman Catholic
doctrine as the official national standard. **The kynges boke.**: margin.

₁₃₀
Johan Bale.

All craftye wayes possyble, sought thys quarellynge qwestmonger, or els the devyll in hym, to brynge thys poore innocent lambe to the slaughter place of Antichrist. Moche after thys sort sought the wycked Pharysees by serten of their owne faccyon or hyered satellytes with the Herodyanes, to brynge Christ in daunger of Cesar, and so to have hym slayne, Mat. 22. Mar. 12. Luce 21.

Anne Askewe.

Seventhly he asked me, if I had the sprete of God in me? I answered if I had not, I was but a reprobate or cast awaye.

₁₄₀
Johan Bale.

Electe are we of God (sayth Peter) through the sanctyfyenge of the sprete. i. Petri i. In everye true Christen belever dwelleth the sprete of God. Jo. 14. Their sowles are the sanctyfyed temples of the holye Ghost. 1. Corin. 3. He that hath not the sprete of Christ (sayth Paule) is non of Christes, Roma. 8. To them is the holye Ghost geven, whych heareth the Gospell and beleveth it, and not unto them whych wyll be justyfyed by their workes. Gala. 2. All these worthye scryptures confirme her saynge.

Anne Askewe.

₁₅₀
Then he sayd, he had sent for a prest to examyne me, whych was there at hande. The prest asked me, what I sayd to the Sacrament of the aultre? and requyred moche to knowe therin my meaninge. But I desyred hym agayne, to holde me excused concernynge that matter. Non other answere wolde I make hym, because I perceyved hym a papyst.

Line 133. **after...sort**: in the preceding sense. **Pharysees.**: margin.

Line 142. **The sprete.**: margin.

Line 151. **Ap:** : margin.

Line 155. **papyst**: papist; Roman Catholic.

Johan Bale.

Mockynge prestes (sayth Esaye) hath rule of the lordes people. Whose voyces are in their drunckennesse. Byd that maye be bydden, forbyd that maye be forbydden. kepe backe that maye be kept backe, here a lyttle and there a lyttle. Esaie xxviii. A plage shal come upon these, for why, they have chaunged the ordynaunces, and made the everlastinge testament of non effect, Esa. 24. They witholde (sayth S. Paule) the veryte of God in unryghtousnesse, Roma. 1. They brede cockatryce egges (sayth Esaye) and weve the spyders webbe. Who so eateth of their egges, dyeth. But if one treadeth upon them, there cometh up a serpent, Esaie 59.

Anne Askewe.

Eyghtly he asked me, if I ded not thynke, that pryvate masses ded helpe sowles departed. And I sayd, it was great Idololatrye to beleve more in them, than in the deathe whych Christ dyed for us.

Johan Bale.

Here, ryseth the serpent of the cockatryce egges, worckemanlye to fulfyll the afore alleged prophecye. If their Masses had bene of Gods creacyon, ordynaunce or commaundement, or if they had bene in anye poynt necessarye for mannys behove, they had bene regestred in the boke of lyfe, whych is the sacred Byble. But therin is, neither mencyon of Masse pryvate nor publyque, severall nor commen, syngle nor double, hygh nor lowe, by fote not on horsebacke, or by note as they call it. If they be thynges added by mannys invencyon (as they can be non other, not beynge there named) than am I sure that the scriptures call them fylthynesse, rust, chaffe, draffe, swylle, dronckennesse, fornyca-

160

170

180

Line 157. **Mockers.**: margin.

Line 163. **cockatryce**: fabulous monster; serpent with a fatal gaze. **A serpent ryseth.**: margin.

Line 173. **Masses pryvate.**: margin.

Line 177. **severall nor commen**: individual nor communal.

Line 178. **hygh:** mass celebrated with the assistance of deacon and subdeacon, with incense and music. **lowe:** mass without music and with minimal ceremony.

Line 178. **by note:** with music.

cyon, menstrue, mannys dyrt, adders egges, poyson, snares, the breade
of wycked lyes, and the cuppe of Gods curse. Their orygynall grounde
shulde seme to be taken of the Druydes or pagane Prestes, whych inhab-
yted thys realme longe afore Christes incarnacyon, and had than practysed sacryfyces publyque and pryvate. Loke Cornelius Tacitus, Caius
Julius, Plinius, Strabo, and soch other authours. That name of pryvacyon added unto their Masse, clerelye depryveth it of Christen communyon, where one man eateth up all, and dystrybuteth nothynge.

190   How soche ware shulde helpe the sowles departed, I can not tell. But
wele I wote, that the wounded man betwixt Hierusalem and Hierico,
had no helpe of them, Luce 10. The Samarytane whych was rekened
but a pagane amonge them, was hys onlye comfort. In the most popysh
tyme was never more horryble blasphemye, than thys is. Thys wyckednesse impugneth all the promyses of God concernynge faythe and
remyssyon of synnes. It repugneth also to the whole doctryne of the
Gospell. The applycacyon of Christes supper, avayleth them onlye that
be alyve, takynge, eatynge, and drynkynge that is therin mynystered.
Nomore can the prestes receyvynge of that sacrament profyght another
200   man, than can hys receyvynge of Baptysme or of penaunce, as they call
it. If it profyteth not the qwyck, how can it profyght the dead? No sac-
ryfyce is the Masse, nor yet good worke, but a blasphemouse prophana-
cyon of the Lordes holye supper, a manyfest wyckednesse, an horryble
Idololatrye, and a fowle abhomynacyon, beynge thus a ryte of worshyp-
pynge without the worde, yea agaynst the expresse worde of God.

Line 182. **menstrue:** menstrual discharge.

Line 184. **Druydes.:** margin.

Line 186. **Cornelius Tacitus:** Roman historian (ca. 55–ca. 117), author of *Annales* (*Annals*).

Lines 186–88. **Caius Julius:** Julius Caesar (100 B.C.–44 B.C.) described Britain in his
Commentarii Belli Gallici (*Commentaries on the Gallic War*). **Plinius:** Pliny the Younger (ca.
61–113), author of *Epistolae* (*Letters*), a record of contemporary Roman society. **Strabo:**
historian (b. ca. 63 B.C.) of the Roman Empire. **pryvacyon:** private mass at which the
congregation is present, but does not receive communion.

Line 190. **For sowles.:** margin.

Line 192. **Samarytane:** the good Samaritan; see Luke 10:29–37.

Line 196. **repugneth:** is contrary or opposed to.

Line 199. **The prestes receyvynge.:** margin.

Anne Askewe.

Then they had me from thens, unto my lorde Mayre. And he examyned me, as they had before, and I answered hym dyrectlye in all thynges, as I answered the qweste afore.

Johan Bale.

After thys sort was Christ ledde from the examinacyon of the clergye to Pylate, Matth. 27. In that the examynacyon of the qweste and of the Mayre was all one, ye maye wele knowe that they had both one scole mastre, even the brutysh byshopp of London. The ignoraunt magystrates of Englande wyll neyther be godlye wyse with David and Salomon, nor yet enbrace the ernest instruccyons of God, to be lerned in the scriptures, Psa. 2. Sapien. 6. but styll be wycked mynysters, and cruell servaunt slaves to Antichrist and the devyll, Apoc. 17. More fyt are soche wytlesse mayres and gracelesse offycers, as knoweth not whyght from blacke, and lyght from darkenesse. Esa. 5. to fede swyne or to kepe kaddowes, than to rule a christen commynalte. A terryble daye abydeth them, whych thus ordereth the innocent. Jaco. 2.

Anne Askewe.

Besydes thys my lorde mayre layed one thynge unto my charge, which was never spoken of me, but of them. And that was, whether a mouse eatynge the hoste, receyved God or no? Thys questyon ded I never aske, but in dede they asked it of me, wherunto I made them no answere, but smyled.

Johan Bale.

Is not here (thynke yow) wele faverd and wele fashyoned dyvynyte, to establysh an artycle of the Christen faythe? Wylye wynchestre answereth

210

220

230

Line 207. **lorde Mayre:** William Laxton, October 1544–October 1545; Martin Bowes, October 1545–October 1546. See Introduction, pages xxi–xxii. **Mayre.:** margin.

Line 214. **byshopp of London:** Edmund Bonner, bishop 1540–1549, 1553–1559; he was an active persecutor of Reformers. **Bonner.:** margin.

Line 219. **Ignoraunce.:** margin.

Line 221. **kaddowes:** caddows; crows.

Line 231. **Wynchestre.:** margin.

thys questyon as folysh as it is, in hys wyse detectyon of the devyls
sophystrye, fo. 16. Beleve (sayth he) that a mouse can not devoure God.
Yet reporteth he after, in fo. 21. that Christes bodye maye as wele dwell
in a mouse as it ded in Judas. Than foloweth fryre fynke, fryre Peryn I
shuld saye, a bachelar of the same scole. And he answereth in the ende
of hys thirde sermon, that the Sacrament eaten of a mouse, is the verye
and reall bodye of Christ. And whan he hath affermed it to be no dero-
gacyon to Christes presens, to lye in the mawe of that mouse. He devy-
240 deth me the one from the other, the sacrament from Christes bodye,
concludinge. That though the sacrament be digested in the mouses
mawe, yet ys not Christes bodye there consumed. O blasphemouse
beastes, and blynde bloderynge Balaamytes.

Bycause these ii. workemen be scant wyttye in their owne occupacyon, I shal brynge them forth here ii. olde artyfycers of theirs to helpe
them, Guimundus Aversanus a byshopp, to helpe byshopp Steven, and
Thomas walden a fryre, to helpe fryre Peryn. The sacramentes (saye
they both) are not eaten of myce, though they seme so to be in the
exteryour symylytudes. For the vertues (sayth Guimundus) of holye
250 men, are not eaten of beastes, whan they are eaten of them, li. 2. de corpore & sanguine domini. No marrye (quoth walden) nomore is the
paynters occupacyon destroyed, whan a picture is destroyed. Marke
thys gere for your lernynge. But now cometh Algerus a monke, more

---

Lines 232–33. **wyse...fo. 16.**: Gardiner's *Detection of the Devils Sophistrie, Wherwith He Robbeth the Unlearned People, of the True Byleef, in the Sacrament of the Aulter* (1546), fol. 16.

Line 235. **fryre...Peryn**: William Peryn (d. 1558), Dominican friar and author of *Three Notable and Godly Sermons* (1546). **Peryn.**: margin.

Line 236. **bachelar**: graduate.

Line 239. **Divisio**: margin.

Line 243. **bloderynge**: blundering. **Balaamytes**: Balaam's ass sees God's angel before Balaam does in Num. 22–24.

Line 246. **Guimundus Aversanus**: Guitmund of Aversa (d. ca. 1090), author of a treatise on the Eucharist. **byshopp Steven**: Bishop Stephen Gardiner. **Guimundus.**: margin.

Line 247. **Thomas walden**: Thomas Walden, also known as Thomas Netter (d. 1430), a Carmelite author who opposed Wycliffe and Hus. **Waldenus.**: margin.

Lines 250–51. **de...domini**: *Concerning the body and blood of the lord* (Latin).

Line 253. **Algerus.**: margin.

craftye than they both, and he sayth li. 2 cap. 1. de Eucharistia, that as wele is thys meate spirytuall, as materyall, because David calleth it the breade of Angels, and a breade from heaven, Psa. 77. That whych is materyall in thys breade (sayth he) is consumed by dygestyon, but that whych is spirytuall remayneth uncorrupted.

If we wolde attende wele unto Christes dyvynyte, and lete these oyled dyvynes dyspute amonge olde Gossypes, we shuld sone dyscharge myce 260
and rattes, weake stomakes and parbreakynge dronkardes, of a farre other sort than thus, he that eateth my fleshe (sayth Christ) Jo. 6. and dryncketh my bloude, dwelleth in me and I in hym. Thys eatynge is all one with the dwellynge, and is neyther for myce nor rattes, brent chauncels not dronken prestes. For as we eate we dwell, and as we dwell we eate, by a graunded and perfyght faythe in hym. The substaunce of that most godlye refeccyon lyeth not in the mouth eatynge nor yet in the bellye feadynge, though they be necessarye, but in the onlye spirytu-all or sowle eatynge. No wyse man wyll thynke, that Christ wyll dwell in a mouse, nor yet that a mouse can dwell in Christ, though it be the 270
doctryne of these doughtye dowsepers, for they shall fynde no scriptures for it. If these men were not enemyes to faythe and fryndes to Idolatrye, they wolde never teache soche fylthye lernynge. More of thys shall I wryte (God wyllynge) in the answere of their bokes.

Anne Askewe.

Then the Byshoppes chaunceller rebuked me, and sayd, that I was moche to blame for utterynge the scriptures. For S. Paule (he sayd) for-

---

Line 254. **li. 2...Eucharistia:** book 2, chapter 1 of *De Sacramento* (*Concerning the Sacrament*), a Latin work written by Algerus, a monk of Cluny, against Berengar of Tours who had argued that the Eucharist was a symbol.

Line 261. **parbreakynge:** spewing; vomiting. **Christus.:** margin.

Line 264. **brent:** burnt.

Line 265. **chauncels:** chancels; part of church where the service is conducted; controversy surrounded the possible destruction of the host by fire.

Line 266. **graunded:** grounded.

Line 269. **Faythe.:** margin.

Line 271. **doughtye:** valiant or worthy. **dowsepers:** douzepers; illustrious grandees.

Line 273. **Nota.:** margin.

bode women to speake or to talke of the worde of God. I answered
hym, that I knewe Paules meanynge so well as he, whych is, i. Corin-
280   thiorum xiiii. that a woman ought not to speake in the congregacyon by
the waye of teachynge. And then I asked hym, how manye women he
had seane, go into the pulpett and preache. He sayde, he never sawe
non. Then I sayd, he ought to fynde no faute in poore women, except
they had offended the lawe.

Johan Bale.

Plenteouse ynough is her answere here, unto thys quarellynge, and (as
apereth) unlerned chancellour. Manye godlye women both in the olde
lawe and the newe, were lerned in the scriptures, and made utteraunce
of them to the glorye of God. As we reade of Helisabeth, Marye, and
290   Anna the wydowe, Lu. 1. and 2. yet were they not rebuked for it. yea,
Marye Christes mother retayned all, that was afterwarde written of
hym, Luc. 2. yet was it not imputed unto her an offence. Christ blamed
not the woman that cryed whyls he was in preachynge, happye is the
wombe that bare the, Luce 11. The women whych gave knowlege to hys
dyscyples, that he was rysen from deathe to lyfe, dyscomfyted not he,
but solaced them with hys most gloryouse aperaunce. Mat. 28. Jo. 20.
In the prymatyve churche, specyallye in Saynt Hieromes tyme, was it a
great prayse unto women to be lerned in the scriptures. Great commen-
dacyons geveth our Englysh Cronycles to Helena, Ursula, and Hilda,

---

Line 278. **Women.**: margin.

Line 283. **faute:** fault.

Line 287. **Scripture women.**: margin.

Line 294. **the:** thee.

Line 294. **Women:** margin.

Line 297. **Hierome:** Saint Jerome (342–420), Church Father.

Line 299. **our Englysh Cronycles:** Bale consulted Matthew Paris (d. 1259), John Capgrave (d. 1464), Robert Fabian (d. 1513), and others. **Helena:** learned mother of Emperor Constantine (ca. 255–ca. 330), whom medieval historians confused with a later Helen born in Britain. **Ursula:** in medieval chronicles, daughter of Dionotus, king of Cornwall (fourth century); according to legends, she was one of 11,000 virgins killed at Cologne. **Hilda:** learned abbess of Whitby (614–680) who defended Celtic church rituals against Roman clerics at the Synod of Whitby in 664. **Englysh women.**: margin.

women of our nacyon, for beynge lerned also in the scriptures. Soche a   300
woman was the seyd Hilda, as openlye dysputed in them agaynst the
superstycyons of certen byshoppes. But thys chancellour by lyke,
chaunced upon that blynde popysh worke whych Walter Hunte a whyte
fryre, wrote iiii. score yeares ago, Contra doctrices mulieres, agaynst
scole women, or els some otherlyke blynde Romysh beggeryes.

Anne Askewe.

Then my Lorde mayre commaunded me to warde. I asked hym, if suretees wolde not serve me, And he made me short answere, that he wolde
take non. Then was I had to the Countre, and there remayned xii.
dayes, no frynde admytted to speake with me.   310

Johan Bale.

Here is Christ yet troden on the hele, by that wycked serpent whych
tempted Eva. Gene. 3. Hys faythfull membre for belevynge in hym, is
here throwne in preson. And no marvele, for it was hys owne promes, ye
shall be brought before rulers and debytees (sayth he) for my truthes
sake Mat. x ye shall be betrayed of your owne nacyon and kyndred, and
so throwne in preson, Luc. 21. If they have persecuted me, thynke not
but they wyll also persecute yow, Jo. 15. Thys serpent is agayne
becomen the prynce of thys worlde, and holdeth the governers therof
captyve, Jo. 14. Suertees wolde have bene taken for a thefe or a mour-   320
therer, but not for Christes membre, the byshoppes chauncellour beynge at hande, nor yet her fryndes permytted to confort her.

Line 303. **Walter Hunte:** Carmelite friar and theologian (d. 1478). **Walter hunte.:** margin.

Lines 304–5. **Contra...women:** Bale translates the title of a Latin work written ca. 1460.
scole: learned.

Line 307. **warde:** prison. **Preson.:** margin.

Lines 307–8. **suretees:** sureties; personal guarantors.

Line 309. **Countre:** the Counter; prison attached to the London city court, under the
jurisdiction of the lord mayor.

Line 312. **Christ troden on the hele.:** margin.

Line 315. **debytees:** deputies.

Anne Askewe.

But in the meane tyme there was a prest sent to me, whych sayd that he was commaunded of the byshopp to examyne me, and to geve me good counsell, whych he ded not. But first he asked me for what cause I was put in the Counter? And I tolde hym I coulde not tell. Then he sayd, it was great pytie that I shulde be there without cause, and concluded that he was verye sorye for me.

Johan Bale.

O temptacyon of Sathan. Christ beynge in the solitarye wyldernesse alone, was after thys flatterynge sort assaulted first of hys enemye, Matt. 4. Thys Judas was sent afore to geve a fryndelye kysse, the more depelye to trappe the innocent in snare. But Gods wysdome made her to perceyve what he was. A false prophete is sone knowne by hys frutes, amonge them that are godlye wyse. Mat. 7. She consydered with Salomon, that more to profyght are the strypes of a frynde, than the fraudolent kysses of a deceytfull enemye, Proverb. 27.

Anne Askewe.

Secondly he sayd, it was tolde hym, that I shuld denye the sacrament of the aultre. And I answered hym agayne, that that I had sayd, I had sayd.

Johan Bale.

In thys brefe answere, she remembred Salomons counsell, Answere not a fole, all after hys folyshnesse. Be ware of them (sayth Christ) whych come in shepes clothynge, for inwardlye they are most ravenynge wolves, Mat. 7. God destroyeth the craftes of the wycked (sayth Job) so that they are not hable to perfourme that they take in hande. Job 5

Anne Askewe.

Thirdly he asked me, if I were shryven, I tolde hym no. Then he sayd,

Line 324. **A prest.**: margin.
Line 333. **Judas.**: margin.
Line 340. **The Sacrament.**: margin.
Line 349. **shryven**: after confession, absolved of sin by a priest.

he wolde brynge one to me, for to shryve me. And I tolde hym, so that 350
I myght have one of these iii. that is to saye, doctor Crome, syr Gyllam,
or Huntyngton, I was contented, bycause I knewe them to be men of
wysdome. As for yow or anye other, I wyll not dysprayse, bycause I
knowe ye not. Then he sayd, I wolde not have yow thynke, but that I or
an other that shall be brought yow, shall be as honest as they. For if we
were not, ye maye be sure, the Kynge wolde not suffer us to preache.
Then I answered by the saynge of Salomon. By commonynge with the
wyse, I maye lerne wysdome, but by talkynge with a fole, I shall take
skathe, Prover. i.

Johan Bale. 360

Se how thys adversarye compaseth lyke a ravenynge lyon, to devoure
thys lambe 1. Pet. 5. Now tempteth he her with Confessyon, whych
hath bene soche a bayte of theirs, as hath brought into their nettes and
snares the myghtyest prynces of the worlde, both kynges and emprours.
Se here if they leave anye subtylte unsought, to obtayne their praye. He
reckened by thys to wynne hys purpose, which waye so ever she had
taken. If she had bene confessed to hym, he had knowne whych waye
she had bene bent. If she had utterlye refused confessyon, he had more
matter to accuse her of. O subtyle sede of the serpent. Thys part played
your olde generacyon the Pharysees and prestes with Christ, to brynge 370
hym in daunger of the lawe, Mat. 22. and Jo. 8. No Christen erudycyon
bryngeth thys prest, nor yet good counsels of the scripture. But as Esaye

---

Line 350. **Shriffte.**: margin.
Line 351. **syr Gyllam:** Sir William, otherwise unidentified.
Line 352. **Huntyngton:** John Huntingdon, former priest, and an ardent Reformist preacher.
Line 356. **Prechers.**: margin.
Line 357. **commonynge:** conversing.
Line 359. **skathe:** harm.
Line 361. **compaseth:** contrives.
Line 362. **Confessyon:** margin.
Line 365. **praye:** prey.
Line 366. **Practyse:** margin.

sayth. The hypocryte ymagyneth abhomynacyon agaynst God, to
famysh the hungrye, and witholde drynke from the thirstye. Yet shall
not the eyes of the seynge be dymme, nor the eares of the hearynge be
deffe, Esa. 32. If the kynge admyt soche preachers (as I can not thynke
it) a sore plage remayneth both to hym and to hys people.

Anne Askewe.

Fortly he asked me, if the host shuld fall, and a beast ded eate it,
380 whether the beast ded receyve God or no? I answered, Seynge ye have
taken the paynes to aske thys questyon, I desyre yow also to take so
moche payne more, as to assoyle it your selfe. For I wyll not do it,
bycause I perceyve ye come to tempte me. And he sayd, it was agaynst
the ordre of scoles, that he whych asked the questyon, shuld answere it.
I tolde hym, I was but a woman, and knewe not the course of scoles.

Johan Bale.

Beastlye was that questyon, and of a more beastlye brayne propouned to
thys woman. Lyttle nede shall other men have to manyfest their blasphemouse folyes, whan they do it so playnelye their selves. Who ever
390 hearde afore, that their host was a God, and myght fall, and be eaten of
a beast, tyll they now so beastlye tolde the tale? Though Saynt Paule,
where as it is ryghtlye mynystred, doth call it the bodye of the Lorde. i.
Corin. 11. Yet doth he not call it a God. Though Christ sayth, Thys is
my bodye, Matth. 26. Marci 14. Luce 22. yet sayth he not thys is a
God. For God is a sprete, and no body, Joannis 4. Where God is eaten,
it is of the sprete, and neyther of mouse nor ratte, as Wynchestre and
Peryn, with other lyke popysh heretykes have taught now of late by

---

Line 373. **hypocryte**: margin.
Line 376. **Prechers**: margin.
Line 379. **The host.**: margin.
Line 384. **ordre of scoles**: rules of scholastic debate associated with Catholic scholarship.
Line 387. **propouned**: propounded.
Line 390. **A fallynge God.**: margin.
Line 396. **Wynchestre.**: margin.

their owne hande wrytynges. Oure God is in heaven, and cannot fall nor yet be eaten of beastes. If they have soche a God, as maye both fall, and so be eaten, as thys prest here confesseth, it is some false or counter- 400 fett God of their owne makynge. If he maye putryfye or be consumed of wormes, moule, rust, beast, or fyre, Baruch sayth, it is an Idoll, and no God. Baruch 6.

These witlesse ydolatours have no grace in thys age, to hyde their olde legerdemaynes. They fare lyke those dronken Gossypes, whych tell more than all, whan their headers be full of wele gyngerdeale. The proude crowne of the dronken Ephraemytes (sayth Esaye) shall be tro-den under fote. The prestes and the prophetes do stacker, they are so overseane with wyne, Esa. 28. They stomble in the stretes, and have stayned themselves with bloude. Treno. 4. All the dwellers of Juda 410 (sayth the lorde) shall I fyll with dronckennesse, both the kynges and the prestes. I wyll neyther perdon them, spare them, nor yet have pytie on them, Hiere. 13. And where as that dronckennesse is (sayth Salomon) there is no counsell kept, Pro. 31. In the ende, thys hypocryte full lyke hymselfe, allegeth to thys woman, a maner used of hys olde predecessours in the scholes of falsehede. But from the scole of truthe he bryngeth nothynge to the confort of her conscyence. He declareth full workemanlye in thys, what he and hys generacyon seketh, by soche their spyrituall and justyfyenge workes, ex opere operato.

Line 398. **Peryn.**: margin.

Line 401. **An Idoll.**: margin.

Line 402. **moule**: mold.

Line 405. **Lyke olde Gossyppes.**: margin.

Line 407. **Ephraemytes**: in Isa. 28:1, inhabitants of the northern kingdom of Israel.

Line 408. **stacker**: stagger.

Line 411. **Dronckennesse.**: margin.

Line 414. **hypocryte**: margin.

Line 419. **ex opere operato**: by the work done (Latin); a technical term for the Catholic dogma that grace of the sacrament comes from the sacramental rite validly performed and not from the merits of the recipient or minister.

Anne Askewe.

Fyftly he asked me, if I intended to receyve the sacrament at easter, or no? I answered, that els I were no Christen woman, and that I ded rejoyce, that the tyme was so nere at hande. And than he departed thens, with manye fayre wordes.

Johan Bale.

Thys hongrye wolfe practyseth by all craftye wayes possyble, to sucke the bloude of thys innocent lambe. Is not that (thynke yow) an holye congregacyon, whych is thus spyrytuallye occupyed? Some godlye wyse men wyll wondre, that they be not ashamed. But marvele not of it. For 430 the holye Ghost sayth, in hys fore judgementes, that the same holye mother whych hath hatched them up in oyles and in shavynges, is an unshamefast whore, Apo. 17. et Dan. 8. Than of verye nature must her whelpes be shamelesse chyldren. Soche shamelesse dogges are they (sayth Esaye) as be never satisfyed. Es. 56. whan they kylle yow (sayth Christ) they shall thynke they do God good servyce, Jo. 16. so greatlye have their malyce blynded them, Sapien 2. whych is partlye the droken- nesse afore spoken of.

Anne Askewe.

And the xxiii. daye of Marche, my cosyne Brittayne came into the 440 Counter to me, and asked there, whether I myght be put to bayle or no? Then went he immedyatlye unto my lorde Mayre, desyerynge of hym to be so good lorde unto me, that I myght be bayled. My lorde answered hym, and sayd, that he wolde be glad to do the best that in

---

Line 421. **Howsell.**: margin.

Line 427. **Spirituallye.**: margin.

Line 431. **mother:** emended from "mothet".

Line 431. **oyles...shavynges:** the holy oil to anoint priests and the shaving of priests' heads.

Line 432. **unshamefast whore:** Reformers associated the scarlet woman on the scarlet beast in Revelation 17 with the Roman Catholic church and the Papacy. **A whore.**: margin.

Line 433. **Dogges.**: margin.

Line 439. **cosyne Brittayne:** Christopher Brittayn, a lawyer of the Middle Temple, one of the Inns of Court.

Line 440. **Baylynge.**: margin.

hym laye. Howbeyt he coulde not bayle me without the consent of a
spirytuall offycer. So requyrynge hym to go and speake with the chauncellour of London. For he sayd, lyke as he coulde not commytt me to
pryson without the consent of a spirytuall offycer, nomore coulde he
bayle me without consent of the same.

Johan Bale.

True is it here, that is written of S. Johan in the Apocalyppes, that Anti-   450
christ is worshypped of the potentates and kynges of the earthe, Apo.
13. The mayre of London, whych is the kynges liefetenaunt, and repre-
senteth there hys owne persone, standeth here lyke a dead Idoll, or lyke
soche a servaunt slave as can do nothynge within hys owne cytie concernynge their matters. Who is lyke the Beast (sayth Saynt Johan) who
is able to warre with hym? He hath brought all landes and their kyngedomes in feare (sayth Esaye) the strength of their cyties hath he taken
awaye, and restrayned the delyveraunce of their presoners, Esa. 14. The
parentes of hym that was borne blynde, feared thys spyrituall tyrannye
or captyvyte of theirs, soch tyme as they were examyned of the   460
byshoppes for the syght of their sonne. Joan. 9. Soche as beleved in
Christ amonge the chefe rulers of the Jewes, wolde not be acknowne
therof, for feare of lyke vyolence, Joan. 12. No newe thynge is it than in
that spyrituall generacyon, but a custome of olde antyquyte. Both
Christ and hys Apostles have suffered lyke tyrannye under them. But
never ded they yet mynystre it to anye creature after their exemple.

Anne Askewe.

So upon that he went to the chancellour, requyrynge of hym as he ded

---

Line 445. **spirytuall offycer:** church official.

Lines 445–46. **chauncellour of London:** the church official to whom the bishop delegated his
authority.

Line 450. **antichrist:** margin.

Line 455. **The beast:** margin.

Line 459. **Examples:** margin.

Line 462. **acknowne:** acknowledged.

Line 463. **A custome.:** margin.

Line 468. **The chaunceller.:** margin.

afore of my lorde mayre. He answered hym, that the matter was so hay-
470 nouse, that he durst not of hymself do it, without my Lorde of London
were made prevye therunto. But he sayd, he wolde speake unto my
lorde in it. And bad hym repare unto hym the next morowe and he
shuld wele know my lordes pleasure.

Johan Bale.

Ryghtwysnesse judge they synne, and synne ryghtwysnesse, Es. 5. so
unperfyght is their syght, Jo. 12. in that God hath geven them up to
their owne lustes, Rom. i. What an haynouse matter is it holden here, to
beleve in Christ after the scriptures, and not after their superstycyouse
maner? For non other cause coulde they laye to thys woman, as ye have
480 hearde here afore, and as ye shall here after perceyve more largelye.
What so ever it be to offende God or man, their offence maye be no
lesse than pryson and deathe. The Turke is not more vengeable, than is
thys spyghtfull spirytuall generacyon. Yet boast they Christes religion,
and the holye mother churche.

Anne Askewe.

And upon the morowe after, he came thydre, and spake both with the
chauncellour, and with my lorde byshopp of London. My lorde
declared unto hym, that he was verye wele contended that I shuld come
forth to a communycacyon. And appoynted me to apere afore hym the
490 next daye after, at iii. of the clocke, at after none. More over he sayd
unto hym, that he wolde there shulde be at that examynacyon, soche
lerned men as I was affeccyoned to. That they myght se, and also make

---

Line 470. **my Lorde of London:** Edmund Bonner, bishop of London.

Line 471. **prevye:** privy; aware.

Line 473. **know:** emended from "knowne".

Line 478. **Fayth in Christ.:** margin.

Line 482. **Tyrannye.:** margin.

Line 483. **generacyon:** class or kind of persons.

Line 486. **thydre:** thither; there.

Line 489. **communycacyon:** conference.

Line 491. **Wylye. Wylye.:** margin.

Line 492. **affeccyoned:** well disposed.

report, that I was handeled with no rygour. He answered hym, that he
knewe no man that I had more affeccyon to than other. Than sayd the
byshopp. Yes, as I understande, she is affeccyoned to Doctor Crome, Sir
Gyllam, Whyteheade, and Huntyngton, that they myght heare the matter. For she ded knowe them to be lerned, and of a godlye judgement.

Johan Bale.

A foxysh faver was thys, both of the chauncellour and byshopp, and
soche a benyvolent gentylnesse, as not onlye sought her bloude, but also 500
the bloude of all them whych are here named, yf they had than come to
thys examynacyon. For the evenynge afore (as I am credyblye
infourmed) the Byshopp made boast amonge hys owne sort, that if they
came thydre, he wolde tye them a great dele shorter. A voyce was thys
full lyke to hym that uttered it. For therby he apereth, not one that wyll
save and fede, but rather soche a one as seketh to kyll and destroye.
Johannis 10. The foxes runne over the hyll of Syon (sayth Hieremye)
because she is fallen from God, Threnorum 5. O Israel (sayth the
Lorde) thy prophetes are lyke the wylye foxes upon the drye feldes,
Ezechielis 13. The Poete hath a byworde, that happye is he whych can 510
take hede by an other mannys hurte. I adde thys here, that ye shuld be
ware, if ye come in lyke daunger of anye soche foxish byshopp. By one
of hys daye devyls, whom thys Cayphas sent to commen with the
woman in preson, he knewe part of her meanynge, and what they were
also whych favered her opynyons. Yea, he craftelye undermyned thys
gentylman whych intreated for her, if ye marke it wele. Trust not to
moche in the flatterouse faunynge of soche wylye foxes.

Line 495. **Subtyle.**: margin.

Line 496. **Whyteheade**: David Whitehead (1492?–1571), Reformist disputant and tutor to
Charles Brandon, duke of Suffolk.

Line 502. **A wolfe.**: margin.

Line 507. **Foxes**: margin.

Line 513. **Cayphas**: Caiaphas, the high priest who questioned Jesus; see John 18:13–28.
commen: commune; talk. **A prest.**: margin.

Line 517. **flatterouse**: flattering.

Anne Askewe.

Also he requyred my cosyne Bryttayne, that he shulde ernestlye persuade me to utter, even the verye bottom of my harte. And he sware by
hys fydelyte, that no man shuld take anye advauntage of my wordes.
Neyther yet wolde he laye ought to my charge, for anye thynge that I
shuld there speake. But if I sayd anye maner of thynge amys, He with
other more wolde be glad to reforme me therin, with most godlye counsell.

Johan Bale.

O vengeable tyraunt and devyll. How subtyllye sekyst thu the bloude of
thys innocent woman, undre a coloure of fryndelye handelynge. God
ones commaunded the ernestlye, in no case to compasse thy neyber
with deceyt, to the effusion of hys bloude, Lev. 19. But hys commaundement, thu reckenest but a Caunterburye tale. By swearynge by thy
fydelyte, thu art not all unlyke unto Herode, whom Christ for lyke
practyses, first to put Johan, and than hym to deathe, called also a most
craftye cruell foxe, Luce 13. Thu laborest here, to have thys woman in
snare, with serten of her fryndes. But God put in her mynde at thys
tyme, to recken the a dogge and a swyne. Matth. 7. and therupon to
have fewe wordes.

Anne Askewe.

On the morowe after, my lorde of London sent for me, at one of the
clocke, hys houre beynge appoynted at thre. And as I came before hym,
he sayd, he was verye sorye of my trouble, and desyred to knowe my
opynyon in soche matters, as were layed agaynst me. He requyred me
also in anye wyse, boldelye to utter the secretes of my harte, byddynge
me not to feare in anye poynt. For what so ever I ded saye within hys

---

Line 520. **A thefe.**: margin.
Line 527. **vengeable**: vengeful. **Judas.**: margin.
Line 532. **Herode.**: margin.
Line 540. **A false lyar.**: margin.
Line 544. **O trayter.**: margin.

house, no man shuld hurte me for it. I answered. For so moche as your Lordeshypp appoynted iii. of the clocke, and my fryndes shall not come tyll that houre, I desyre yow to pardon me of gevynge answere tyll they come.

Johan Bale.

In thys preventynge of the houre, maye the dylygent reader perceyve the 550
gredynesse of thys Babylon Byshopp, or bloudthurstie wolfe, concernynge thys praye. Swyft are their fete (sayth David) in the effusion of
innocent bloude, whych have fraude in their tunges, venym in their
lyppes, and most cruell vengeaunce in their mouthes. Psal. 13. David in
that Psalme moche marveleth in the sprete that takynge upon them the
spirytuall governaunce of the people, they can fall in soche frenesye or
forgetfulnesse of themselves, as to beleve it laufull thus to oppresse the
faythfull, and to devoure them with as lyttle compassyon, as he that
gredylye devoureth a pece of breade. If soche have redde anye thynge of
God, they have lyttle mynded their true dewtye therin. More swyft 560
(sayth Hieremye) are our cruell persecuters, than the egles of the ayre.
They folowe upon us over the mountaynes, and laye prevye wayte for us
in the wyldernesse. Trenorum 4. He that wyll knowe the craftye
haukynge of Byshoppes to brynge in their praye, lete hym lerne it here.
Judas (I thynke) had never the x. part of their connynge warkeman-
shyppe. Marke it here, and in that whych foloweth.

Anne Askewe.

Then sayd he, that he thought it mete, to sende for those iiii. men
whych were afore named, and appoynted. Then I desyred hym, not to

---

Line 550. **preventynge**: anticipating.

Line 551. **Babylon Bysshop:** Reformers associated the Babylon of Revelation 17–18 with Rome and the Roman Catholic church. **A tyraunt.**: margin.

Line 556. **Murtherers.**: margin.

Line 561. **Egles.**: margin.

Line 562. **prevye**: privy; secret.

Line 568. **thought**: emended from "thougt".

Line 568. **mete**: meet; fitting.

Line 569. **More lambes to devoure.**: margin.

570 put them to the payne. For it shuld not nede, bycause the ii. gentylmen
whych were my fryndes, were able ynough to testyfye that I shuld saye.
Anon after he went into his gallerye with mastre Spylman, and wylled
hym in anye wyse, that he shuld exhort me, to utter all that I thought.

Johan Bale.

Christ sheweth us in the vii. chaptre of Mathew, and in other places
more of the Gospell, how we shall knowe a false prophete or an hypocryte, and wylleth us to be ware of them. Their maner is as the devyls is,
flatteryngly to tempt, and deceytfullye to trappe, that they maye at the
lattre, most cruellye slee. Soche a won (sayth David) hath nothynge in
580 hys tunge, but playne deceyt. He layeth wayte for the innocent, with no
lesse cruelte than the lyon for a shepe. He lurketh to ravysh up the
poore. And whan he hath gotten hym into hys nette, than throweth he
hym downe by hys autoryte. Psalm. 9. Thys is the thirde temptacyon of
thys byshopp, that the woman shuld utter, to her owne confusyon.

Anne Askewe.

In the meane whyle he commaunded hys Archedeacon to commen with
me, who sayd unto me. Mastres wherfor are ye accused? I answered. Axe
my accusers, for I knowe not as yet. Then toke he my boke out of my
hande, and sayd. Soche bokes as thys is, hath brought yow to the trou-
590 ble ye are in. Be ware (sayth he) be ware, for he that made it, was brent
in Smythfelde. Then I asked hym, if he were sure that it was true that he
had spoken. And he sayd, he knewe wele, the boke was of Johan frithes
makynge. Then I asked hym, if he were not ashamed for to judge of the
boke before he sawe it within, or yet knewe the truthe therof. I sayd

---

Line 572. **mastre Spylman**: Francis Spylman, a witness of Askew's "Confession"; see Foxe,
page 177.

Line 577. **Lyke the devyll.**: margin.

Line 579. **slee**: slay.

Line 586. **Archedeacon**: John Wymesley; he witnessed Askew's "Confession." **Archedeacon.**:
margin.

Line 592. **Johan frithe**: John Frith (1503–1533), Reformist theologian, author of *A Boke
Made by J. Frith…Answering unto M. Mores Lettur* (1533); he was burned for heresy. **A Lyar.**:
margin.

also, that soche unadvysed and hastye judgement, is a token apparent of a verye slendre wytt. Then I opened the boke and shewed it hym. He sayd, he thought it had bene an other. for he coulde fynde no faulte therin. Then I desyred hym, nomore to be so swyft in judgement, tyll he throughlye knewe the truthe. And so he departed.

Johan Bale.   600

Here sendeth he fourth an other Judas of hys, to betraye this true servaunt of God. Marke the good workemanshypp hardelye, and tell me if they be not the of sprynge of the serpent. Moche are they offended with bokes, for that they so playnelye do manyfest their myschefes. Johan Frith is a great moate in their eyes, for so turnynge over their purgatorye, and heavynge at their most monstruose Masse, or mammetrouse Mazon, whych sygnyfyeth breade or feadynge. Notwithstandynge Daniel calleth it Maozim, betokenynge strength or defence, Dan. 11. because the false worshyppynges therof shuld be so myghtelye defended by worldlye autoryte and power. No newe thynge is it, that   610 good men and their bokes are destroyed now a dayes, whan they touche the myschefes of that generacyon. For Joakim the kynge of Juda, cutt Hieremyes prophecyes in peces with a penne knyfe, and in hys madnesse threwe them into the fyre, commaundynge both Hieremye whych taught them, and Baruch that wrote them, to be put to deathe. Hieremie 36. Whan kynge Antiochus had sett upon the aultre of God, the abhomynable Idoll of desolacyon (whych is now the popysh masse, Mat. 24) the bokes of Gods lawe commaunded he to be torne in peces

---

Line 601. **Judas.**: margin.
Line 604. **Johan Frith.**: margin.
Line 605. **moate**: mote; speck.
Line 606. **mammetrouse**: maumetrous (from "Mahomet"); idolatrous.
Line 607. **Mazon**: bread (Hebrew).
Line 608. **Maozim**: stronghold (Hebrew).
Line 610. **Bokes condempned**: margin.
Line 613. **penne knyfe**: knife used to sharpen the scribe's quill.
Line 617. **popysh**: emended from "poysh".
Line 618. **Bokes brent.**: margin.

and brent in the fyre, sendynge fourth therupon, thys cruell proclama-
620 cyon. That what so ever he was, whych had a boke of the Lordes Testament founde about hym, or that endevoured themselves to lyve after
the lawes of God, the Kynges commaundement was, they shuld be put
to death. 1. Machabeorum 1.

Anne Askewe.

Immedyatlye after came my cosyne Bryttayne in with dyverse other, as
Mastre Hawe of Grayes inne, and soche other lyke. Then my lorde of
London persuaded my cosyne Bryttayne, as he had done oft before,
which was, that I shuld utter the bottom of my harte in anye wyse.

Johan Bale.

630 Thys is the fort temptacyon, or craftye callynge upon, to utter her
mynde, that he myght saye of her, as Cayphas sayd of Christ. Matt. 26.
what nede we anye more witnesses? Lo, now ye have hearde a blasphemye or an heresye. How saye ye now to it, whych are her fryndes? Is she
not gyltye of deathe? If they shuld have sayd naye, unto thys, they shuld
have bene so, in as depe daunger as she. Thys serpentyne practyse, was
as wele to trappe them as her, lete it not be unmarked.

Anne Askewe.

My lorde sayd after that unto me, that he wolde I shuld credyte the
counsell of my fryndes in hys behalfe, whych was, that I shuld utter all
640 thynges that burdened my conscyence. For he ensured me, that I shuld
not nede to stande in doubt to saye anye thynge. For lyke as he promysed them (he sayd) he promysed me, and wolde perfourme it.
Whych was, that neyther he, nor anye man for hym, shuld take me at

---

Line 626. **Mastre Hawe:** the chronicler Edward Hall (d. 1547). **Grayes inne:** one of the four
Inns of Court where lawyers were trained. **Her fryndes.:** margin.

Line 631. **Cayphas:** margin.

Line 634. **gyltye:** guilty; deserving.

Line 635. **practyse:** treachery. **Practyse.:** margin.

Line 639. **Sathan.:** margin.

Line 640. **ensured:** assured.

advauntage of anye word I shuld speake. And therfor he bad me, saye my mynde without feare. I answered hym, that I had nought to saye. For my conscyence (I thanked God) was burdened with nothynge.

Johan Bale.

Styll foloweth thys ghostlye enemye, hys former temptacyon, and calleth upon mortall utteraunce, or utteraunce full of deathe, that he myght crye with Cayphas, Luc. 22. what nede we further testymonye? Her owne mouthe hath accused her. We are able witnesses therof, for our owne eares have hearde it. Thus laye they wayte for bloude (sayth Salomon) and lurke pryvelye for the innocent, without a cause, Proverbiorum 1. Consent not (sayth he) unto soche tyrauntes, if they entyce the. For though their wordes apere as honye, Proverbiorum 16. Yet shalt thu fynde them in the ende, so bytter as wormewode, Proverbiorum 5. Though that whorysh generacyon pretendeth a coloure of gentylnesse, yet byteth it at the lattre lyke a serpent, and styngeth lyke an adder, throwynge fourth poyson. Prov. 23.

Anne Askewe.

Then brought he fourth thys unsaverye symylytude, That if a man had a wounde, no wyse surgeon wolde mynystre helpe unto it, before he had seane it uncovered. In lyke case (sayth he) can I geve yow no good counsell, unlesse I knowe wher with your conscyence is burdened. I answered, that my conscience was clere in all thynges. And for to laye a playstre unto the whole skynne, it might apere moche folye.

Line 644. **Tempter:** margin.
Line 650. **Cayphas:** margin.
Line 651. **witnesses:** emended from "withnesses".
Line 654. **enemyes.:** margin.
Line 656. **wormewode:** wormwood; plant proverbial for bitter taste.
Line 657. **coloure:** semblance.
Line 662. **surgerye.:** margin.
Line 664. **Counsell.:** margin.
Line 666. **playstre:** plaster.

Johan Bale.

Hath not he (thynke yow) moche nede of helpe, whych seketh to soche
a surgeon. Uncircumspect is that pacyent, and most commonlye unfor-
670 tunate, whych goeth to a commen murtherer to be healed of hys dys-
ease. Christ bad us evermore to be ware of all soche, unlesse we wolde
be woryed, Matthei 7. The nature of these, Lorde (sayth David) is not
to make whole, but to persecute them whom thu hast smytten, and to
adde woundes unto wounde, Psalmo 68. Their owne botches are insanable, Esaie 1. for the multytude of their myschefes, Hiere. 30. The prest
and the Levyte, whych travayled betwin Hierusalem and Hierico,
healed not the wounded man, yet were they no wounders. Lu. 10. Who
can thynke that he wyll unburden the conscyence, whych stodyeth
nothynge els but to over loade it with most grevouse and daungerouse
680 burdens? Math. 23.

Anne Askewe.

Then ye dryve me (sayth he) to laye to your charge, your owne report,
whych is thys. Ye ded saye, he that doth receyve the sacrament by the
handes of an yll prest or a synner, he receyveth the devyll, and not God.
To that I answered, that I never spake soche wordes. But as I sayd afore
both to the qwest and to my Lorde Mayre, so saye I now agayne, that
the wyckednesse of the prest shuld not hurte me, but in sprete and
faythe I receyved no lesse, the bodye and bloude of Christ. Then sayd
the byshopp unto me, what a saynge is thys? In sprete. I wyll not take
690 yow at that advauntage. Then I answered, My lorde without faythe and
sprete, I can not receyve hym worthelye.

Johan Bale.

Now sheweth thys Cayphas where about he Goeth, for all hys false flat-

---

Line 670. **A murtherer.**: margin.

Line 674. **botches:** boils, sores. **insanable:** incurable. **Botches.**: margin.

Line 683. **Gathered store.**: margin.

Line 687. **sprete:** spirit. **Sinon caste.**: margin. **Sinon:** In Virgil's *Aeneid*, the Greek who
convinced the Trojans to bring the wooden horse into Troy; symbol of treachery. **caste:** cast;
overthrown.

terynge colours afore. And seynge he can winne non advauntage to hys
cruel purpose, of her owne communycacyon, he shaketh the bowgettes
of hys provyded Judases and betrayers of innocent bloude. He bryngeth
fourth soche stuffe and store, as that wycked qwest had gathered of her
answere to them, to flatter and to please hys tyrannye therwith. It ys to
be feared, that as farre was the feare of God here from them, as from
hym, Psal. 13. for as wele practysed they thys myschefe agaynst her, as   700
he. Marke here the natural workynge of a verye full Antichrist. He
defendeth synne in hys own generacyon, and condemneth vertue in
Christes dere membre. Malice, pryde, whoredome, sodometrye, with
other most devylysh vyces, reckeneth he not to hurte the mynystracyon
of a prest, yet judgeth it he an heresye, no lesse worthye than deathe, to
beleve that Christes fleshe and bloude is receyved in faythe and sprete.
What though it be Christes most ernest doctryne, Joan. 6. what a
saynge (sayth thys Bishopp) is thys? In sprete. I wyll not take yow at the
worst, sayth he. As though it were a most haynouse heresye. But most
dyscrete and godlye was the womannys answere, declarynge her a ryght   710
membre of Christ, where as those prestes, whom he here defendeth, are
unworthye receyvers and members of the devyll, Joan. 13. and i. Corin.
11. Thus is an Antichrist here knowne by hys frutes. For he uttereth
blasphemyes agaynst God, Daniel 7. Apoc. 13. he calleth evyll Good,
and Good evyll, Esa. 5. and Proverbiorum 3.

Anne Askewe.

Then he layed unto me, that I shuld saye, that the sacrament
remaynynge in the pixte, was but breade. I answered that I never sayd
so: But in dede the qwest asked me soche a qwestion, wherunto I wolde

---

Line 695. **bowgettes:** budgets; wallets. **Bowgettes.**: margin.
Line 701. **Antichrist.**: margin.
Line 703. **sodometrye:** sodomy.
Line 707. **A sore heresie.**: margin.
Line 711. **Prestes.**: margin.
Line 717. **shuld saye:** did say.
Line 718. **Breade.**: margin.

720 not answere (I sayd) tyll soche tyme as they had assoyled me thys question of myne. Wherfor Steven was stoned to deathe. They sayd, they
knewe not. Then sayd I agayne, no more wolde I tell them what it was.

Johan Bale.

O Idolouse shepehearde (sayth Zach.) thu sekest not to heale the
wounded, but to eate the fleshe of the fatte. Zach. 11. The watche men
of Israel (sayth the lorde) are verye blynde beastes, and shamelesse
dogges. They have no understandynge, but folowe their owne beastlye
wayes for covetousnesse, Esaie 56. Who ever redde in the scripture or
autorysed Chronycle, that breade in a boxe shuld be Christes bodye?
730 Where or whan commaunded he hys most holye bodye, so to be
bestowed? What have ye to laye for thys doctryne of yours? Are ye not
yet ashamed of your unreverent and blasphemouse beastlynesse? wyll ye
styll plucke our Christen beleve from the ryght hande of God the eternall father, and sende it to a boxe of your braynysh devysynge?
     The first boxer of it, was pope Honorius the thyrde in the yeare of
our lorde, M. CC. XVI. after the manyfolde revelacyons of dyverse
relygyouse women. Neyther was there anye great honour geven unto it
of the common people, tyll a sorye solytarye syster or Ankorasse in the
lande of Leodium or Luke, called Eva after serten visions, had procured
740 of pope Urbanus the fort, in the yeare of our Lorde. M. CC. LXIIII. the
feast of Corpus Christi to be holden solempne all Christendome over.

Line 721. **Steven.**: margin.

Line 726. **Beastes.**: margin.

Line 730. **The boxe.**: margin.

Line 731. **laye**: put forward.

Line 734. **braynysh**: brainish; headstrong.

Line 735. **first boxer**: the ritual of reserving the consecrated bread for veneration rather than congregational communion. **Honorius**: margin.

Lines 738–39. **Ankorasse...Eva**: Eva of Liege (ca. 1210–ca. 1266), a recluse and confidante of the nun Juliana whose visions inspired the creation of the Feast of Corpus Christi. **Eva reclusa**: margin.

As testyfyeth Arnoldus Bostius, Epist. 6. ad Joannem Paleonydorum. In al the xii. hondred yeares afore that, was it neyther boxed nor pixed, honoured nor sensed unyversallye. And se what an horrible worke here is now, for the boxinge therof, and what a great heresie it is to beleve that Christ dwell not therin, contrarye both to hys owne and to hys Apostles doctryne. Marke also how thys Gods creature is handeled here for it, and how subtyllye she is betrayed of the Byshoppes begles and lymmes of the devyll.

Anne Askewe.

750

Then layd it my Lorde unto me, that I had alleged a serten text of the scripture. I answered that I alleged non other but S. Paules owne saynge to the Athenianes, in the xvii. chaptre of the Apostles actes. That God dwelleth not in temples made with handes. Then asked he me. what my faythe and beleve was in that matter? I answered hym. I beleve as the scripture doth teache me. Then enquired he of me, what if the scripture doth saye, that it is the bodye of Christ? I beleve (sayd I) like as the scripture doth teache me. Then asked he agayne, what if the scripture doth saye, that it is not the bodye of Christ? My answere was styll, I beleve as the scripture infourmeth me. And upon thys argument he tar-
760
ryed a great whyle, to have dryven me to make hym an answere to hys mynde. Howbeit I wolde not, but concluded thus with hym, that I beleved therin and in all other thynges, as Christ and hys holye Apostles ded leave them.

Line 742. **Arnoldus Bostius:** Carmelite theologian (1445–1499) from Ghent. **Epist. 6...**
Paleonydorum: Letter 6 to John Paleonydorus (Latin); "Paleonydorus" or "old water" (Greek) was a pen name of John of Oudewater, a Dutch Carmelite theologian. Bale's transcript of the correspondence between Bostius and John of Oudewater is now in the Bodleian Library, MS Selden, supra, 41. **Bostius:** margin.

Line 743. **neyther:** emended from "neyter".

Line 746. **Judases.:** margin.

Line 751. **alleged:** quoted.

Line 754. **Temples:** margin.

Line 756. **A tempter.:** margin.

Line 762. **Howbeit:** however.

Johan Bale.

Se what an horryble synne here was. She alleged the scripture for her
beleve, whych is a sore and a daungerouse matter. For it is against the
popes canon lawes, and agaynst the olde customes of holye churche.
Sens kynge Henryes dayes the fort, hath it bene a burnynge matter,
770 onlye to reade it in the Englysh tunge, and was called wycleves lernynge,
tyll now of late years. And it wyll not be wele with holye churche, tyll it
be brought to that poynt agayne. For it maketh manye heretykes
agaynst holye churche. O insipient papystes. These are your corrupted
practyses and abhomynable stodyes, to dryve the symple from God, and
yet ye thynke, he seyth yow not, Psalme 13. Saynt Paule sayth (Roma.
15.) what so ever thynges are written in the scriptures, are written for
our lernynge, that we through pacyence and comfort in them, myght
have hope, and ye wyll robbe us therof. Christ commaunded all peo-
ples, both men and women (Johan. 5.) to serche the scryptures, if they
780 thynke to have everlastynge lyfe, for that lyfe is no where but in them.
Yet wyll yow in payne of deathe kepe them styll from them.

For ye take upon ye to sytt in Gods stede, and thynke by that
usurped offyce, that ye maye turne over all, 2. Thes. 2. But Christ bad
us to be ware both of yow and your chaplaynes, whan he sayd. There
shall aryse false Christes and false prophetes, workynge manye great
wonders, and saynge, Lo, here is Christ, and there is Christ. Beleve
them not. Matt. 24. And therfor alleged thys woman unto your qwestmongers (the dogges that Christ warned us of, Mathei 7.) and now unto
yow that saynge of S. Paule, Acto. 17. That God dwelleth not in tem-
790 ples made with handes, whych also were the wordes both of Salomon
longe afore 3. Reg. 8. and of Steven, Acto. 7. in hys tyme. That scripture

---

Line 767. **Scripture.**: margin.

Line 771. **late:** recent.

Line 774. **practyses.**: margin.

Line 778. **Christ.**: margin.

Line 782. **In Gods stede.**: margin.

Lines 787–88 **qwestmongers:** those who make a business of conducting inquests.

Line 789. **Temples.**: margin.

so moche offended yow, that ye wolde nedes knowe therof the under-standynge. For soche textes as agre not with the cloynynges of your con-jurers, and the conveyaunces of your sorcerers must nedes be seasoned with Aristotles Physyckes, and sawced with Johan Donses subtyltees. Here make ye a wonderfull turmoylynge to wrynge out of thys Wo-mannis beleve in that matter, that she myght eyther become a creature of your olde God the pope, or els be burned. yet have she not ones re-moved her fote from the harde foundacyon or savynge rocke Jhesus Christ. 1. Corinth. 11. Blessed be hys holye name for it.   800

Anne Askewe.

Then he asked me, whye I had so fewe wordes? And I answered. God hath geven me the gyfte of knowlege, but not of utteraunce. And Salomon sayth, that a woman of fewe wordes, is a gyfte of God, Prover. 19.

Johan Bale.

Whan Christ stode before Cayphas, he asked hym, moche after thys sort, wherfor he had so fewe wordes? Thu answerest not (sayth he) to those thynges which are layed Here agaynst the of these men. Neverthe-lesse he held hys peace. Mar. 14. But whan he was ones throughlye   810 compelled by the name of the lyvynge God, to speake, and had uttered a verye fewe wordes, he toke hym at soche advauntage, though they were the eternall veryte, as he was able through them, to procure hys deathe, Matth. 26. lyke as thys bloudye Bishopp Bonner, of the same wycked generacyon, ded at the lattre, by thys faythfull woman.

Line 793. **cloynynges:** deceivings.

Line 794. **conveyaunces:** underhand dealings. **sorcerers must:** emended from "sorcerers. must".

Line 795. **Johan Donses:** John Duns (1265?–1308?), scholastic author and editor of Aristotle. **Arystotle Dons.:** margin.

Line 797. **myght:** emended from "myghe".

Line 802. **Fewe wordes.:** margin.

Line 810. **Sylence:** margin.

Line 814. **Bonner.:** margin.

Anne Askewe.

Thirdlye my lorde layed unto my charge, that I shuld saye, that the
Masse was ydolatrye I answered hym. No, I sayd not so. Howbeyt (I
sayd) the qwest ded aske me, whether pryvate Masses ded releve sowles
820 departed, or no? Unto whome than I answered. O Lorde, what ydolatrye is thys? that we shuld rather beleve in pryvate masses, than in the
helthsom deathe of the dere sonne of God. Than sayd my lorde agayne.
What an answere was that? Though it were but meane (sayd I) yet was it
good ynough for the questyon.

Johan Bale.

About the lattre dayes of Johan wycleve, in the yeare of our lorde a
M. CCC. LXXXII. as Henrye Spenser than Byshopp of Norwych, was
with a great nombre of Englysh warryours besiegynge the Towne of
Hypers in Flaunders, in the quarell of pope Urbanus the vi. The vessels
830 of perdycyon or verye organes of Sathan, the iiii. orders of beggynge
fryres, preached all Englande over, that that most holye father of theirs,
had lyberallye opened the welle of mercye, and graunted cleane
remyssyon to all them that wolde eyther fyght, or geve anye thynge
towardes the mayntenaunce of those warres in that quarell of holye
churche agaynst scysmatykes and heretykes. For than was thys matter of
their popysh Masse, in great controversye lyke as it is now. More over
they promysed by vertu of hys great pardons, to sende the sowles
departed, to heaven. And dyverse of them sayd, they had seane them

---

Line 818. **Howbeyt:** however.

Line 819. **Pryvate Masses.:** margin.

Line 822. **helthsom:** healthsome; bestowing spiritual health.

Line 823. **meane:** unadorned.

Line 827. **Henrye Spenser:** Henry Despenser, bishop of Norwich (1370–1406), the "fighting bishop." **Henrye Spenser.:** margin.

Line 829. **Hypers:** Ypres; town in the north of France. **Urbanus:** Urban VI (ca. 1318–1389), Italian pope (1378–1389) supported by England in his war against the French pope Clement VII.

Lines 830–31. **iiii...fryres:** mendicant friars, whom Wycliffe had attacked. **Frires.:** margin.

Line 835. **scysmatykes:** schismatics; those who divided the church.

Line 836. **Masse.:** margin.

flye up, out of the churche yeardes from their graves thydre warde.

Thys most devylysh blasphemye with soche other lyke, provoked 840
the seyd Johan wycleve, the verye organe of God, and vessell of the
holye Ghost not onlye to replye than agaynst them at Oxforde in the
open scooles, but also to write a great nombre of bokes agaynst that
pestylent popysh kyngedome of theirs. lyke as Martyne Luther hath
done also in our tyme, with manye other godlye men. And lyke as those
false prophetes the fryres ded than attribute unto the popes pardons,
the remyssyon of synnes, the deliveraunce from dampnacyon, and the
fre enteraunce of heaven, whych peculyarlye belongeth to the precyouse
payment of Christes bloude. i. Petri 1. and 1. Joan. 1. So do these false
anoynted, or blasphemouse Byssoppes and prestes now, attrybute them 850
agayne unto theyr pryvate and publique Masses, the popes owne wares
as prowlynge and pelferynge as the pardons, with no lesse blasphemye.
The devylyshnesse of thys newe doctryne of theyrs, shall be refelled in
my bokes agaynst fryre Peryn and Wynchestre, and therfor I write the
lesse here.

Anne Askewe.

Then I tolde my lorde, that there was a prest, whych ded hearc what I
sayd there before my lorde mayre and them. with that the chaunceller
answered, whych was the same prest. So she spake it in verye dede
(sayth he) before my lorde the mayre and me. Then were there serten 860
prestes as doctor Standysh and other, whych tempted me moche to

---

Line 839. **thydre warde:** in that direction.

Line 841. **Johan wycleve:** margin.

Line 843. **open scooles:** rooms at the university for organized disputation, often associated
with scholastic (Catholic) theologians.

Line 846. **Pardons.:** margin.

Line 851. **Druydes.:** margin.

Line 852. **prowlynge:** plundering.

Line 853. **refelled:** refuted.

Line 854. **Perin.:** margin.

Line 858. **Chaunceler.:** margin.

Line 861. **doctor Standysh:** John Standish (1507?–1570), Bishop Bonner's appointee as rector
of St. Andrew Undershaft. **Standysh.:** margin.

knowe my mynde. And I answered them alwayes thus. That I have sayd
to my lorde of London, I have sayd.

Johan Bale.

By thys ye maye se, that the Byshoppes have every wher ther wachmen.
least the kynges offycers shuld do anye thynge, contrarye to their
bloudye behove. Thys Chauncellour wolde not have thus answered
hardelye, so agreablye to her tale, had it not bene to their advauntage
agaynst her, as here after wyll apere. Marke here the fashyon of these
870   temptynge serpentes, Standysh and hys fellawes, And tel me if they be
not lyke unto those vypers whelpes whych came to Johans Baptym,
Matthei 3. and to Christ Jesus preachynge, Luce 11. I thynke ye shall
fynde them the same generacyon.

Anne Askewe.

And then doctor Standish desyered my lorde, to byd me saye my
mynde, concernynge that same text of S. Paule. I answered, that it was
agaynst saynt Paules lernynge, that I beynge a woman, shuld interprete
the scriptures, specyallye where so manye wyse lerned men were.

Johan Bale.

880   It is not yet halfe a score of yeares ago, sens thys blasphemouse Idyote
Standish, compared in a lewde sermon of hys, the dere pryce of our
redempcyon, or precyouse bloude of Christ, to the bloude of a fylthye
swyne, lyke hymselfe a swyne. And for hys good doynge, he is now
becomen a dawe, a doctor I shuld saye, of the popes dyvynyte, and a
scolastical interpretour of the scriptures to hys behove. Here wolde the

---

Line 865. **Watchemen.**: margin.
Line 867. **behove**: behoof; advantage.
Line 871. **Vypers.**: margin.
Line 875. **A tempter.**: margin.
Line 881. **lewde**: ignorant. **Standish.**: margin.
Line 884. **dawe**: crow; simpleton. **Doctor.**: margin.

swynysh gentylman have proved, both that S. Steven dyed an heretyke, and S. Paule a scysmatyke, for teachynge that God dwelleth not in temples made with handes Act. 7. and 17. if he myght have reasoned out the matter with thys woman. But she toke a swyne for a swyne, and wolde laye no pearles afore hym, as Christ had charged her afore. Matthei 7. For all their interrogacyons are now about the temple and the temple wares. Matthei 26.

Anne Askewe.

Then my lorde of London sayd he was infourmed, that one shulde aske of me, if I wolde receyve the Sacrament at Easter, and I made a mocke of it, Then I desyered that myne accuser myght come fourth, whych my lorde wolde not. But he sayd agayne unto me. I sent one to geve yow good counsell, and at the first worde ye called hym papyst. That I denyed not. for I perceyved, he was no lesse. yet made I non answere unto it.

Johan Bale.

No confortable scriptures, nor yet anye thynge to the sowles consolacyon, maye come out of the mouthes of these spyrytuall fathers, But dogges rhetoryck and curres curtesye, narrynges, brawlynges, and quarellynges. Whan she was in the myddes of them, she myght wele have sayd wyth David. Delyver me lorde from the quarelouse dealynges of men, that I maye kepe thy commaundementes. I deale with the thynge that is lawfull and ryght, O geve me not over to these oppressers, lete not these proude quarellers do me wronge. Psalm. 118. But amonge all these quarellynges, her accusers myght not be seane, whych were the grounders of them.

890

900

910

Line 887. **Swyne.**: margin.
Line 895. **Accuser.**: margin.
Line 904. **narrynges**: dog-like growlings. **Dogges rhetoryck**: margin.
Line 909. **Quarellers.**: margin.
Line 911. **grounders**: instigators.

Anne Askewe.

Then he rebuked me, and sayd, that I shuld report, that there were bent agaynst me, thre score prestes at Lyncolne. In dede (quoth I) I sayd so. For my fryndes tolde me, if I ded come to Lyncolne, the prestes wolde assault me and put me to great trouble, as therof they had made their boast. And whan I hearde it, I went thydre in dede, not beynge afrayed, because I knewe my matter to be good. More over I remayned there. vi. dayes, to se what wolde be sayd unto me. And as I was in the mynster,
920 readynge upon the Byble, they resorted unto me by ii. and by ii. by v. and by vi. myndynge to have spoken to me, yet went they theyr wayes agayne with out wordes speakynge.

Johan Bale.

Rebukes in that generacyon, are moch more redye at hande, than eyther Christen admonyshmentes, or gentyll exhortacyons, though they be all spyrytuall: And that cometh by reason of their lordeshyppes, whych wanteth due fournyshynge out, unlesse they have tyrannouse bragges and braulynges. Herin folowe they the examples of their naturall predecessours the Jewysh byshoppes, pharysees, and prestes, Joan. 7. and 9.
930 She myght full wele saye, that the prestes were agaynst her. For hypocresye and Idolatrye were never yet with hym, whose blessed quarell she toke. Marke the fort chaptre of Johan, and so fourth almost to the ende of hys Gospell. Beholde also how hys Apostles and disciples were handeled of the prestes, after hys gloryouse ascencyon, Acto. 4. and all that boke folowynge, and ye shall fynde it no new thynge. The servaunt is no better than her mastre whych suffred of that malygnaunt generacyon lyke quarellynges and handelynges, Joan. 15. Se here how they wondered upon her by couples, for readynge the Byble, as their fore fathers wondered upon Christ for preachynge and doynge miracles.

Line 913. **Thre score prestes.**: margin.
Line 918. **Prestes.**: margin.
Line 919. **mynster:** cathedral church.
Line 926. **Lordshyp:** margin.
Line 927. **fournyshynge out:** occupying a position.
Line 930. **Hypocresye.**: margin.
Line 937. **Wonderers.**: margin.

Anne Askewe. 940

Then my lorde asked, if there were not one that ded speake unto me. I tolde hym, yeas, that there was one of them at the last, whych ded speake to me in dede. And my lorde than asked me, what he sayd? And I tolde hym, hys wordes were of so small effecte, that I ded not now remembre them.

Johan Bale.

So farre was not Lyncolne from London, but the Byshopp there had knowlege of thys tragedye. Hereby maye ye se their spirytuall occupyenge agaynst Christ and hys faythfull membirs. Soch is the stody (sayth S. Johan) of that congregacyon, whych is a spirytualte, called Sodome 950 and Egypte. They rejoyce in myschefes amonge themselves, and sende massenges one to another agaynst Gods wytnesses, whan they are vexed by them, Apoca. 11.

Anne Askewe.

Then sayd my lorde, There are manye that reade and knowe the scripture, and yet do not folow it, nor lyve therafter. I sayd agayne. My lorde, I wolde wyshe, that all men knewe my conversacyon and lyvynge in all poyntes, For I am so sure of my selfe thys houre, that there are non able to prove anye dyshonestie by me. If yow knowe anye that can do it, I praye yow brynge them fourth. 960

Johan Bale.

I marvele that Byshoppes can not se thys in themselves, that they are also no folowers of the scriptures. But paraventure they never reade

---

Line 942. **was:** emended from "wat".

Line 942. **A prest.:** margin.

Lines 948–49. **occupyenge:** being busy. **Occupyenge.:** margin.

Line 950. **spirytualte:** group of religious people.

Line 951. **Sodome and Egypte:** traditional representations of wickedness in Christian theology; see Rev. 11:8.

Line 952. **massenges:** messengers or messages.

Line 956. **Scripture.:** margin.

Line 959. **dyshonestie:** unchastity.

Line 963. **paraventure:** perhaps. **Folowers.:** margin.

them, but as they fynde them by chaunce in their popish portyfolyoms
and maskynge bokes. Or els they thynke all the scriptures fulfylled,
whan they have sayd their mattens and their masses. Christ sayd to the
hypocryte. Whye seist thu a moate in thy neybers eye, and consyderest
not the great beame that is in thyne owne eye? Luce 6. Matth. 7. Christ
forbode hys Byshoppes undre payne of dampnacyon to take anye lord-
970 shyppes upon them. Luce 22. How is thys folowed of our prelates? He
commaunded them also to possesse neyther golde nor sylver. Matth. 10.
How is thys commaundement obeyed? If we loked so ernestlye to
Christes instytucyons, as we loke to the popes to be observed, these
wolde also be seane to, by acte of parlement, so wele as prestes marryage
whom Christ never inhibyted. I doubt it not, but thys wyll also be one
daye seane to. Godly ded thys woman in defendynge here her innocencye. For S. Peter sayth, i. Petri 4. Se that non of yow suffre as an evyll
doer. But in your harde sufferynges, committ your sowles unto God
with wele doynge, as unto your faythfull creator.

980   *Anne Askewe.*
Then my lorde went awaye, and sayd, he wolde entytle sumwhat of my
meanynge. And so he writte a great cyrcumstaunce. But what it was, I
have not all in memorye. For he wolde not suffre me to have the coppie
therof. Onlye do I remembre thys smal porcyon of it.

Johan Bale.
Here wrote he serten artycles of the popes Romish faythe, wyllynge her
to subscrybe unto them, and so blaspheme God or els to burne. Hys

---

Line 964. **portyfolyoms:** corruption of medieval Latin *portiforium;* portable breviary, which
contained daily readings to be recited by Catholic clergy.
Line 965. **maskynge:** masking; masquerading.
Line 966. **mattens:** matins; morning prayers in the Catholic breviary.
Line 969. **Lordshyppes possessyons.:** margin.
Line 974. **Marryage.:** margin.
Line 981. **entytle:** to write down under proper titles or headings.
Line 982. **cyrcumstaunce:** detailed and circuitous narrative. **He writeth.:** margin.

sekynge was here, to make her to worshyp the first beast, whose deadlye wounde is healed agayne Apoc. 13. But she wolde not so have her name raced out of the lambes boke of lyfe. Apoca. 20. Rather wolde she con- 990 tende to the ende, hopynge by the myght of hys sprete, at the last to overcome, and so to be clothed wyth the promysed whyte aparell, Apoca. 3.

Anne Askewe.

Be it knowne (sayth he) to all men, that I Anne Askewe, do confesse thys to be my faythe and beleve, notwithstandynge my reportes made afore to the contarye. I beleve that they whych are howseled at the handes of a prest, whether hys conversacyon be good or not, do receyve the bodye and bloude of Christ in substaunce reallye. Also I do beleve it after the consecracyon, whether it be receyved or reserved, to be no lesse 1000 than the verye bodye and bloude of Christ in substaunce. Fynallye I do beleve in thys and in all other sacramentes of holye churche, in all poyntes accordynge to the olde catholyck faythe of the same. In witnesse wherof, I the seyd Anne have subscrybed my name. There was sumwhat more in it, whych because I had not the coppie, I cannot now remembre.

Johan Bale.

All the worlde knoweth, that neyther in Christes tyme, nor yet in the dayes of hys Apostles, was anye soche confession of faythe, Neyther yet in the churche that folowed after, by the space of moche more than a M. 1010 yeares, What have Christen mennes conscience than to do with soche a

---

Line 988. **the first beast**: the beast of Rev. 13:1–3; Bale alludes to the Roman Catholic church. **Worshyp the beast**: margin.

Line 990. **the lambes boke of lyfe**: see Rev. 20:12–15; Christ is the "lamb of God" and saved souls are written in the book of life.

Line 997. **howseled**: received communion. **Holye lecherye**: margin.

Line 998. **conversacyon**: conversation; behaviour.

Line 1000. **whether...reserved**: whether the consecrated elements are handed out or retained for other purposes. **papystyck.**: margin.

Line 1009. **Newe faythe.**: margin. **faythe**: emended from "fatyhe".

prodygyouse confessyon? Are not Christ and hys Apostles, teachers suffycyent ynough for our Christen beleve, and their holye doctrynes lawfull, but we must have these unsaverye brablementes? We must now
beleve in the bawdrye of prestes, or that their Sodometrye and Whoredome for want of marryage, can be no impediment to their God-
makynge. What is it els to be sworne unto the beleve of soche artycles,
but to honour their abhomynable lecherye? O most swynish sacryfyers
of Baal peor, Psalme 105. Yow is it that the Apostle Judas, in hys
1020   canonycall epystle speaketh of. Ye have turned the grace of God, into
your lecherie, denyenge our onlye governour Jhesus Christ. The holye
Ghost sheweth us. Apoca. 21. and 22. that non are of the newe hallowed cytie or congregation of the lorde, whych worketh abhomynacyon or maynteyneth lyes, as ye do them both here.

Anne Askewe.

Then he redde it to me, and asked me, if I ded agre to it. And I sayd
agayne, I beleve so moche therof, as the holye scripture doth agre to.
Wherfor I desyre yow, that ye wyll adde that therunto. Then he
answered, that I shuld not teache hym what he shuld write, With that,
1030   he went forth into hys great chamber, and redde the same byll afore the
audyence, whych envegled and wylled me to sett to my hande, saynge
also that I had faver shewed me.

Line 1012. **prodygyouse:** emended from "progydyouse"; prodigious, portentous.

Line 1014. **brablementes:** noisy quarrelling.

Line 1015. **bawdrye:** unchastity.

Line 1016. **Canonysed lecherie.:** margin.

Lines 1018–19. **swynish...peor:** Psalm 105 (Ps. 106 in the King James version) enumerates the sins of the Hebrews, including worship of the Canaanite god, Baal, whose cult was at Beth-peor.

Lines 1019–20. **Apostle...epystle:** the biblical Letter of Jude which attacks false teachers.

Line 1021. **Priapystes.:** margin.

Lines 1022–23. **newe...cytie:** the heavenly Jerusalem.

Line 1027. **Scripture.:** margin.

Line 1030. **great chamber:** the bishop's formal court at St. Paul's.

Line 1031. **envegled:** inveigled; cajoled.

Johan Bale.

In everye matter concernynge our Christen beleve, is the scripture reckened unsuffycyent of thys wycked generacyon. God was not wyse
ynough in settynge the order therof, but they must adde therunto their
swybber swylle, that he maye abhorre it in us, as he ded the Jewes ceremonyes, Esa. 1. Hiere. 7. Zacha. 7. Amos 5. Michee 6. But thys godlye
woman wolde corrupt her faythe with no soche beggerye, least she in so
doynge shuld admitt them and their pope to sytt in her conscyence   1040
above the eternall God, whych is their daylye stodye, 2. Thes. 2, A vyrgyne was she in that behalf, redemed from the earthe and folowynge the
lambe, and havynge in her forehead the fathers name written. Apoca-
lypsys 14.

Anne Askewe.

Then sayd the Byshopp, I myght thanke other and not myselfe, of the
faver I founde at hys hande. For he consydered (he sayd) that I had
good fryndes, and also that I was come of a worshypfull stocke. Then
answered one Christofer, a servaunt to mastre Dennye. Rather ought ye
(my lorde) to have done it in soche case. for Gods sake than for mannys.   1050

Johan Bale.

Spirytuall wyll these fathers be named, and yet they do all to be seane of
men, Math. 23. Their olde condycyons wyll they change, whan the
blacke moreane change hys skynne, and the catte of the mountayne her
spottes, Hieremye 13. If I sought to please men (sayth S. Paule) I were

---

Line 1035. **Unsuffycyent.**: margin.

Line 1037. **swybber swylle:** a nauseous concoction.

Line 1041. **The pope:** margin.

Line 1047. **Faver.**: margin.

Line 1048. **worshypfull stocke:** a family of distinguished character or rank.

Line 1049. **Christofer:** emended from "Christofet". **mastre Dennye:** Anthony Denny
(1501–1549), Henry VIII's chief gentleman of the privy chamber, close adviser, and a
Reformist sympathizer.

Line 1052. **Falshede:** margin.

Line 1054. **blacke moreane:** blackamorian; Ethiopian or African.

not the servaunt of Christ. Gala. 1. Whan thys tyrannouse Byshopp can
do no more myschefe, than flattereth he the worlde, sekynge to have
thankes where he hath non deserved. And as concernynge the love
or true feare of God (as is here layed unto hym) he hath non at all,
1060 Psal. 13.

Anne Askewe.

Then my lorde sate downe, and toke me the wrytynge to sett therto my
hande, and I writte after thys maner, I Anne Askewe do beleve all maner
thynges contayned in the faythe of the Catholyck churche. Then
because I ded adde unto it, the Catholyck churche, he flonge into hys
chambre in a great furye. With that my cosyne Brittayne folowed hym,
desyerynge hym for Gods sake to be good lorde unto me. He answered
that I was a woman, and that he was nothynge deceyved in me. Then
my cosyne Brittayne desyred hym to take me as a woman, and not to
1070 sett my weake womannys wytt, to hys lordshyppes great wysdome.

Johan Bale.

Was not thys (thynke yow) a sore matter to be so grevoslye taken of thys
prelate? But that they are naturallye geven to soche quarellynges, Matth.
23. Thys worde Catholyck was not wonte to offende them. How
becometh it than now a name so odyouse? Paraventure through thys
onlye occasyon. They knewe not tyll now of late years (for it come of
the Greke) the true sygnyfycacyon therof. As that it is so moche to saye
in the Englysh, as the unyversall or whole. Afore tyme, they toke it to
meane their oyled congregacyon alone. But now they perceyve that it
1080 includeth the layte so wel as them no longar they do esteme it. Other

---

Line 1057. **Flatterye:** margin.

Line 1064. **Catholyck churche:** "catholic" was a hotly contested term between Roman
Catholics and Reformers. See Introduction, page xxxi. **catholick:** margin.

Line 1068. **A woman.:** margin.

Line 1074. **wonte:** accustomed. **Catholick:** margin.

Line 1078. **the Englysh:** emended from "the. Englysh".

Line 1079. **From oyle.:** margin.

Line 1080. **layte:** laity.

cause can I non conjecture, whye they shuld now more contempne it than afore.

Anne Askewe.

Then went in unto hym doctor weston, and sayd, that the cause whye I ded write there the Catholyck church, was, that I understode not the churche written afore. So with moche a do, they persuaded my lorde to come out agayne, and to take my name with the names of my suerties, which were my cosyne Brittayne and mastre Spylman of Grayes inne.

Johan Bale.

For an holye churche wyll they be taken, and seme moche to differ from 1090
the lewde lowsye layte or prophane multytude of the common people, by reason of their holye unccyons and shavynges whych came from their pope. Most specyallye because they have nothynge a do with mar-ryage, reckened a most contagyouse poyson to holye orders, as their foreseyd Romysh father hath taught, whych bryngeth up all hys chyl-dren in Sodome and Gomor. Jude 1. Apoc. 11. And thys poynt have they lerned of their predecessours the olde pharysees and prestes, whych were not, sicut ceteri hominum, as the common sort of men are, but holye, spyrytuall ghostlye fathers, Luce 18. Wherfor they wyll not now be called a catholyck, but an holye spyrytual churche.   1100

Anne Askewe.

Thys beynge done, we thought that, I shuld have bene put to bayle immedyatlye, accordynge to the order of the lawe. Howbeit he wolde not so suffre it, but commytted me from thens to preson agayne untyll

---

Line 1084. **doctor weston:** Hugh Weston, conservative rector of St. Botolph Bishopsgate, London. **Weston.:** margin.

Line 1090. **Layte.:** margin.

Line 1091. **lowsye:** lousy; vile or contemptible.

Line 1092. **unccyons:** unctions; anointing with oil.

Line 1096. **Sodomytes.:** margin.

Line 1098. **sicut...are:** Latin, which Bale translates.

Line 1103. **Manye delayes.:** margin.

the next morowe. And than he wylled me to apere in the guylde halle, and so I ded. Notwithstandynge they wolde not put me to bayle there neyther, but redde the Bishoppes writynge unto me as before, and so commaunded me agayne to preson.

Johan Bale.

1110 A verye servitute of Egipte is it, to be in daunger of these papystyck Byshoppes, as in thys acte doth apere. Se what cavyllacyons thys Pharao ded seke here to holde thys Christen woman styll undre hys captivite, so louth is the gredye wolfe to depart from hys desyred praye Joan. 10. These delayes and these sendynges from Cayphas to Pilate, and from Pylate agayne to Annas in Paules, were not els but to seke more matter agaynst her, and to knowe more depelye who were her fryndes and maynteners. They that shall conferre the fashyons of thys termagaunt Byshopp concernynge thys woman, with the cruell maners of great Pharao in the deliveraunce of the people of Israel at Gods commaunde-
1120 ment, Exo. 5. or with the handelynges of the Jewes spirytualte con-cernynge Christ, Math. 26. and Johan. 18. they shall not fynde them all unlyke.

Anne Askewe.

Then were my suerties appoynted to come before them on the next morowe in Paules churche, whych ded so in dede. Not withstandynge they wolde ones agayne have broken of with them, bycause they wolde

---

Line 1105. **guylde halle:** Guildhall; the administrative headquarters of the City of London.

Line 1107. **writynge:** emended from "witynge".

Line 1110. **servitute of Egipte:** the captivity of the Jews under Pharoah in Egypt; see Exod. 1–3.

Line 1111. **cavyllacyons:** unfair charges in legal proceedings.

Line 1112. **Pharao.:** margin.

Line 1115. **Annas:** see John 18:13,24; Annas sent Jesus bound to his son-in-law, Caiaphas, the high priest. **Paules:** St. Paul's Cathedral, the bishop of London's seat.

Line 1116. **Practyse.:** margin.

Line 1117. **conferre:** compare. **fashyons:** actions.

Line 1126. **Knaverye spirytuall:** margin.

not be bounde also for an other woman at their pleasure. whom they knewe not, nor yet what matter was layed unto her charge. Notwithstandynge at the last, after moche a do and reasonynge to and fro, they toke a bonde of them of recognysaunce for my fourth commynge. And thus I was at the last, delyvered. Written by me Anne Askewe. 1130

Johan Bale.

No veryte (sayth Oseas the Prophete) no mercye, nor yet knowlege of God, is now in the earthe, but abhomynable vyces have everye where gotten the overhande, one bloudgyltynesse folowynge an other, Osee 4. Thynke yow that the Byshoppes and prestes coulde take so cruell wayes, and wolde worke so false feates, if they had the true feare of God, or yet reckened to fele a ryghtwyse judge at the lattre daye? Suppose it not. Not onlye mynded they to shewe no mercye to thys woman, but also to werye all her fryndes and acquayntaunce, whych is most extreme cruelte 1140 and malyce.

The other woman, whom they wolde here most craftelye have delyvered with thys (as I am credyblye infourmed) was a serten popysh queane, whych they had afore provyded both to betraye her, and accuse her. In more depe daunger of the lawe at that tyme, was thys for her false accusement without recorde, than was the other whych was so falselye accused. Fayne wolde the prelates therfor have had her at lyberte, but they feared moche to be noted parcyall. Marke thys craftye

---

Line 1130. **bonde...recognysaunce**: recognizance; obligation.
Line 1130. **fourth commynge**: coming forward (when summoned by the court).
Line 1135. **overhande**: the "upper hand" or victory. **With prestes.**: margin.
Line 1136. **prestes**: emended from "prestea".
Line 1137. **wolde**: would.
Line 1138. **reckened...fele**: considered too much.
Line 1139. **Tyrauntes**: margin.
Line 1140. **werye**: worry; to seize by the throat as would a wolf.
Line 1143. **popysh**: Roman Catholic.
Line 1144. **queane**: disparaging term for "woman."
Line 1145. **Practyse**: margin.
Line 1146. **recorde**: evidence.

poynt for your lernynge, and tell me if they be not a subtyle generacyon.
1150 More of their spirytuall packynges and conveyaunces, for the deathe of thys faythfull woman, and most dere membre of Christ Anne Askewe, shall ye wele perceyve in the lattre part here folowynge, by her owne confession and handewritynge also to the honoure of God and their great dishonour. So be it.

> Vayne is the conversacyon, whych ye receyved by the tradycyons of your fathers, 1. Petri 1.

> The veryte of the lorde endureth forever. Psalm.116.

The Conclusyon.

Here hast thu (gentyll reader) the first examynacyon of the faythfull
1160 martyr of Christ Anne Askewe wyth my symple elucydacyon upon the same. Wherin thu mayst clerely beholde our Byshoppes and prestes so spirytuallye to be occupyed now a dayes, as is the gredye wolfe that ravenouslye ronneth upon hys praye. For the tyrannouse behaver in their cruell predecessours have they no maner of shame. Neyther yet repent they their owne blasphemouse treason agaynst God and hys veryte, what though their most wretched conscyences do daylye accuse them therof. The kyngedome of God, whych is a true faythe in hys worde, or a perfyght knowlege of the gospell, do not they seke to upholde. But vyolentlye they speake yll of it, trouble it, persecute it, chace it, and
1170 bannish it, bycause it is of hym and from within Luce 17. The kyngedome of the pope whych cometh with outwarde observacyon of dayes, persones, places, tymes, meates, garmentes, and ceremonyes, they magnyfye above the mone, bycause it is from without, and to their peculiar advauntage in the loyterynge reigne of ydelnesse.

Line 1149. **Subtylte:** margin.

Line 1150. **packynges:** plottings.

Line 1157. **Psalm 116:** Ps. 117 in the King James version.

Line 1161. **Byshoppes.:** margin.

Line 1167. **Kyngedom of God.:** margin.

Line 1171. **Popes kyngedom.:** margin.

They have thought and yet thynke by their terryble turmoylynges to turne over all, and to change the most noble enterprise of our kynge, yet ones agayn layserlye, to their popes behove. But the godlye wyse man Salomon sayth, There is no polycye, there is no practyse, noo, there is no counsell that can anye thynge prevayle agaynst the lorde, Proverbiorum 21. They recken that with fyre, water, and swerde they are able 1180 to answere all bokes made agaynst their abuses, and so to dyscharge their invyncyble argumentes (for otherwyse they have not assoyled them as yet) but trulye they are sore deceyved therin, as shall wele apere. They suppose by consumynge of a score or ii. in the fyre, they have gotten the felde of the lambe and hys host. Apoca. 17. No, they rather by that meanes, adde strength therunto, and so demynysh their owne. I dare boldelye saye unto them, that by burnynge Anne Askewe and her .iii. companyons, they have one thousande lesse of their popysh beleve than they had afore. They thynke also by condempnynge and burnynge our bokes, to put us to sylence. But that wyll surelye brynge double 1190 upon them, if they be not ware, Apoca.18. For if we shuld be styll, the verye stones wolde speake in these dayes, Luce 19. And detect their horryble treason agaynst God and the kynge.

If they mynde to holde their ydel offices styll, and here after to have profyght of their olde sale wares, as Diriges, Masses, and soche other. My counsel were that they ded by them, as they now do by their pope the great mastre and first founder of them. A subtyle sylence is amonge them concernynge hym, and hath bene ever sens hys first puttynge downe. Ye shall not now heare a worde spoken agaynst hym at Paules

---

Line 1176. **A change**: margin.

Line 1177. **layserlye**: leisurely; deliberately.

Line 1181. **Polycye.**: margin.

Lines 1184–85. **gotten the felde**: won the battlefield; conquered. **No felde**: margin.

Line 1189. **Bokes.**: margin.

Line 1194. **Counsell.**: margin.

Line 1195. **Diriges**: direct (Latin); "dirige" is the first word of the antiphon at Matins in the Roman Catholic Office of the Dead.

Line 1197. **the**: emended from "rhe".

Line 1199. **Sylence.**: margin.

1200 crosse, nor yet agaynst hys olde juglynge feates. And in dede it is a good
wyse waye to sett hym up agayne. Wynchestre and Sampson made a lyttle bragge at the begynnynge, to seme yet to do sumwhat, but sens they
have repented, and made a large amendes for it other wayes. Fryre Peryn
beganne to wryte in defence of their monstruouse Masse, but now of
late dayes, and he can not fynde therin one blasphemouse abuse justlye
to be reprehended. Men saye, there be craftye knaves abroade in the
worlde in all ages. Well, thys polytyck sylence wold do wele also
paraventure in other matters. For the more ruffelynges they make, and
the more murther they do, for that ydell kyngedom of theirs, the more
1210 clere the veryte apereth, and the more vyle their sorcerouse wares. For
the more dyrt be shaken (they saye) the more it stynketh.

So outragyously to rayle in their preachynges, of the noble and lerned
Germanes (whych of all nacyons loveth our kynge most inteyrlye) for
secludynge their pope and changynge their masses, they do not most
wyselye for themselves. They are not so ill beloved of their cuntraye
merchauntes, whych customablye travayle thydre, but they know what
is ther both sayd and done agaynst them. By that meanes came Peryns
boke of hys iii. most ydolatrouse and foxysh sermons, first of all to my
handes. Wherin he rhetorycallye calleth them, in the hote zele of hys
1220 Romysh father, the erronyouse Germanes, subtyle witted heretykes,
obstynate adversaryes, newe fangled expositours, perverse sacramenta-
ryes, blasphemouse apostataes, wycked wretches, devylysh lyars, lewde
lyvers, and abhomynable belevers, with soche other lyke. But certaynelye
I knowe, that they wyll one daye be even with hym and with other lyke

---

Line 1203. **Perryn.**: margin.
Line 1208. **ruffelynges:** dissensions or disturbances.
Line 1208. **take hede:** margin.
Lines 1212–13. **noble...Germanes:** many German principalities had converted to Luther-
anism. **Germanes.**: margin.
Line 1214. **secludynge:** banishing.
Lines 1215–16. **cuntraye merchauntes:** the German merchants.
Line 1216. **customablye:** customarily.
Line 1216. **thydre:** thither; to England.
Lines 1217–18. **Peryns...sermons:** See page 28. **Peryns sermons.**: margin.

apes of Antichrist, for it. Whan the popes great dansynge beare, a proude prankynge prelate of thers, was the last yeare with the emprour Charles at hys fourth goynge agaynst the seyd Germanes, hys braggynge begles were not ashamed to boast it in the open stretes of Utrecht in Hollande, that the pope shuld agayne have hys full swaye in Englande. Of a lykelyhode they knowe there, some secrete mysteryes in workynge. 1230 I saye yet, be ware of that subtyle generacyon, whych seketh not els but to worke all myschefe.

Gentyll and soft wyttes are oft tymes offended, that we are now a dayes so vehement in rebukes. But thys wolde I fayne knowe of them, what modestye they wolde use (as they call it) if they were compelled to fyght with dragons, hyders, and other odyble monsters. How pacyent they wolde be and how gentyll, if a ravenouse wolfe came upon them, they havynge able weapon to put hym a syde. Surelye I knowe no kynde of Christen charytye to be shewed to the devyll. Of non other nature is Moses serpent, but to eate up the serpentes of Pharaoes sorcerers, Exod. 1240 7. If we ded suffre anye longar the oke grove of Baal to stande aboute the aultre of the lorde, we shuld moche offende hys commaundement. Judi. 6. If I shuld holde my peace and not speake in thys age, the veryte so blasphemcd, my conscyence wolde both accuse me and condempne me of the unconsyderaunce of my lorde God. More precyouse is the thynge whych is in daylye controversye and parell (whych is now Gods true honoure) than is all thys worldes treasure here. What Christen hart can abyde it, to se the creature yea not of God but of

---

Line 1225. **Wynchestre.**: margin.

Line 1226. **prankynge**: dressing showily.

Lines 1226–27. **emprour Charles**: Charles V of Germany, Holy Roman Emperor (1500–1558); he was an enemy of the German Protestant princes.

Line 1228. **begles**: beagles; those who scent out and hunt down; spies.

Line 1235. **modestie**: margin.

Line 1236. **hyders**: hydras; many-headed snakes. **odyble**: hateful or odious.

Line 1241. **oke...Baal**: see Judg. 6:25–33; Gideon built an altar to God, then destroyed the altar to Baal and the grove around it. **Oke grove.**: margin.

Line 1245. **unconsyderaunce**: lack of consideration. **Conscyence.**: margin.

Line 1246. **parell**: peril.

man, to be worshypped in the stede of God, and saye nothynge therin?
1250 Salomon sayth, there is as wele a tyme to speake, as a tyme to kepe
sylence, and a tyme as wele to hate, as a tyme to love, Ecclesiastes 3.
With a perfyght hate, lorde (sayth David) have I hated those bloudthurstye enemyes whych were in their presumpcyon agaynst the, Psalme
118. Stronglye and with most myghtye stomack, are hypocrytes to be
invaded, whych wyll not geve place to the veryte. Marke how myghtelye
Moses resysted Pharao, Helyas kynge Achab, Helyseus Joram, Zachary
Joas, Daniel the ydolaters, Johan Baptist the Pharysees and Herode,
Steven the Jewes, the Apostles the Byshoppes and prestes. Christ
rebuked hys dyscyple Peter, and bade hym, come after hym devyll,
1260 Math.16. Yet called he Judas hys frynde, Math. 26. Necessarye is it that
the elect flocke of God, do hate the uncleane fowles, whych yet holde
their habytacyon in Babylon, Apoca. 18. Johan wycleve and Johan Huss
confesse in their writynges, that they were by stronge force inwardlye
constrayned of God to worke agaynst the great Antichryst. Erasmus
boldelye uttered it, that God for the evyls of thys lattre age, hath provyded sharpe phesycyanes. Quenche not the sprete (sayth S. Paule)
despyse not prophecyes, 1. Thessalon. 5. I put my ernest wordes into
thy mouthe (sayd the lorde to Hieremye) that thu shuldest both
destroye and buylde. Hieremye 1. Lete thys suffyse ye concernynge our
1270 rebukes, for they are Gods enemyes whom we invade.

If ye perceyve it and fele it on the other syde, that the waves of the see

---

Line 1251. **hate them.**: margin.

Line 1256. **Helyas...Achab**: see 1 Kings 18; the prophet Elijah resisted King Ahab. **Helyseus Joram**: see 2 Kings 9; the prophet Elisha resisted King Joram. **Examples.**: margin.

Lines 1256–57. **Zachary Joas**: see 2 Chron. 24; Zechariah resisted King Joash. **Daniel the ydolaters**: see Dan. 2; Daniel interpreted King Nebuchadnezzar's dream when magicians, enchanters, and sorcerers could not. **Johan...Herode**: see Matt. 3:7–12 and Matt. 14.

Line 1258. **Steven the Jewes**: see Acts 6:8–15. **Apostles...prestes**: in Acts 23, the Apostle Paul resists the high priest Ananias.

Line 1259. **come...devyll**: paraphrase of Matt. 16:23.

Line 1261. **elect...God**: those God chooses for salvation.

Line 1262. **Johan Huss**: Jan Hus (1369–1415), Czech preacher and scholar influenced by Wycliffe and burned for heresy. **Wycleve and huss.**: margin.

Line 1266. **phesycyanes**: physicians.

Line 1267. **Sprete.**: margin.

are great also, and doth horryblye rage in these dayes, Psalme 92. Consydre agayne (sayth David) that the lorde whych dwelleth on hygh, is a great dele myghtyer than they. As he is of power to cease the storme and to make the wether caulme, Psalme 106. So is he able to change a kynges indignacyon (whych is but deathe) into most peaceable faver and lovynge gentylnesse, Proverbiorum 16. For the hart of a kynge is evermore in the hande of God, and he maye turne it whych waye he wyll, Prover. 21. Hys eternall pleasure it is, that ye shuld honoure your kynge as hys immedyate mynyster concernynge your bodyes and lyves 1. Petri 2. and that ye shuld with all gentylnesse obeye the temporall rulers, Romano. 13. But soche spirytuall hypocrytes, both Byshoppes and prestes, as are continuall haters of hys heavenlye verite, wolde he that we shuld holde for most detestable apostataes and blasphemouse reprobates, as ded Christ and hys Apostles whych never obeyed them, but most sharpelye rebuked them, Mathei 23. Acto. 20. and 2. Petri 2. The grace of that lorde Jhesus Christ, be ever with them, whych ryghtlye hate that synagoge of Sathan, as ded Anne Askewe, Amen.

God standeth by the generacyon of the ryghteouse, Psal. 13.

Thus endeth the first examynacyon of Anne Askewe, latelye done to deathe by the Romysh popes malycyouse remnaunt, and now canonysed in the precyouse bloude of the lorde Jesus Christ. Imprented at Marpurg in the lande of Hessen, in Novembre, Anno 1546.

Line 1272. **Waves.**: margin.
Line 1277. **Praye and obeye.**: margin.
Line 1284. **Abhorre.**: margin.
Line 1289. **Psal. 13**: Ps. 14 in the King James version.

The voyce of Anne Askewe out of the 54. Psalme of David, called. Deus in nomine tuo.

For thy names sake, be my refuge,
  And in thy truthe, my quarell judge.
Before the (lorde) lete me be hearde,
  And with faver my tale regarde
Loo, faythlesse men, agaynst me ryse,   5
  And for thy sake, my deathe practyse.
My lyfe they seke, with mayne and myght
  Whych have not the, afore their syght
Yet helpest thu me, in thys dystresse,
  Savynge my sowle, from cruelnesse.   10
I wote thu wylt revenge my wronge,
  And vysyte them, ere it be longe.
I wyll therfor, my whole hart bende,
  Thy gracyouse name (lorde) to commende.
From evyll thu hast, delyvered me,   15
  Declarynge what, myne enmyes be.
            Prayse to God.

Who so ever lyveth, and beleveth in me, shall never dye. Joan. 11.

He that heareth my wordes, and beleveth on hym that sent me, hath everlastynge lyfe, and shall not come into dampnacyon, but passe from deathe unto lyfe. Joan. 5.

Title. **54. Psalme:** also Ps. 54 in the King James version. **Deus...tuo:** in thy name, Lord (Latin).
Line 11. **wote:** known.

Who...Joan. 11: Below this line in the basetext is the printer's emblem of Johann van Kempen. See Textual Introduction, pages xlv–xlvi.

The lattre examinacy
on of Anne Aſkewe, latelye mar
tyred in Smythfelde, by the wyc=
ked Synagoge of Antichriſt,
with the Elucydacyon of
Johan Bale.

The verite of the lorde endureth for euer.

Pſalme 116.

Anne Aſkewe ſtode faſt by thys verite of God to the ende.

I wyll poure out my ſpýzte vpõ all fleſh (ſayth God) ýcur ſonnes and your dough= ters ſhall prophecye. And who ſo euer call on the name of the lorde/ſhall be ſaued.
Johel. ij.

The title page from John Bale's edition of *The lattre examinacyon of Anne Askewe* (1547) is reproduced by permission of the Houghton Library, Harvard University.

Johan Bale to the Christen Readers.

In the prymatyve churche, as the horryble persecucyons increased, manye dylygent wryters collected the godlye answers and tryumphaunt
sufferynges of the martyrs, as necessarye examples of Christen constancye to be folowed of other. Of thys nombre was Lucas, whych wrote the
Apostles actes. So were after hym Linus, Marcellus, Egesippus, Meliton
Asianus, Abdias Babylonius, Josephus Antiochenus, Clemens Alexandrinus, Antherus, Phileas, Eusebius, Nicephorus, and a great sort more.
Fabianus, not a chayre Byshopp, but a pulpet Byshopp of Rome,
ordayned in hys tyme for that onlye offyce vii. deacons and so manye   10
notayres, aboute the yeare of our lorde. CC. XXXVI. that they shuld
faythfullye regestre ther martyrdomes, to holde them in contynuall
remembraunce, as witnesseth Platina, Polydorus, Masseus, and soch
other chronyclers. No lesse necessarye is that offyce now, though fewe
men attempt it, nor no lesse profytable to the christen commonwelth
than it was in those terryble dayes. For now are persecucyons all Chris-

---

Line 5. **Lucas:** Luke.

Line 6. **Linus:** bishop of Rome (ca. 67–ca. 76). **Marcellus:** bishop of Rome (308–
309). **Egesippus:** Hegesippus (d. ca. 180), church historian. **Writers.:** margin.

Lines 6–7. **Meliton Asianus:** theologian and bishop of Sardis (d. ca. 180). **Abdias
Babylonius:** Abdias, legendary first-century bishop of Babylon; sixteenth-century writers
thought he was the author of legends about the Apostles. **Josephus Antiochenus:** possibly
Saint Joseph (Josippus) of Antioch, a church deacon and martyr.

Lines 7–8. **Clemens Alexandrinus:** Clement of Alexandria (ca. 150–ca. 215), Greek church
father and historian of the primitive church. **Antherus:** Anterus, bishop of Rome (d. 236)
who recorded acts of the martyrs. **Phileas:** Egyptian bishop (d. ca. 307) who recorded the
persecution of Christians 264–266. **Nicephorus:** Byzantine historian (ca. 1256–ca. 1335)
who wrote a church history in twenty-three volumes.

Line 9. **Fabianus...Rome:** bishop of Rome (236–250) who ordered notaries to compile the
acts of the martyrs.

Line 12. **notaireys:** margin.

Line 13. **Platina, Polydorus:** emended from "Platina Polydorus". **Platina:** Bartolomeo Platina
(1421–1481), Italian humanist who wrote *Liber de vita Christi ac de vitis summorum pontificum
omnium* (*Life of Christ and Lives of All the Greatest Popes*) (1479). **Polydorus:** Poydore Vergil
(1470?–1555?), Italian humanist who published *Anglica Historia* (*History of England*) in
1534. **Masseus:** possibly Mattheus or Matthew Paris, thirteenth-century historian who wrote
the *Chronica Majora* (*Greater Chronicle*), which Bale consulted elsewhere.

tendome over, so wele as were than. Now are the true Christyanes vexed
of the syttynge Byshoppes for their Christen beleve, so wele as than.
Now are they revyled, ponnyshed, imprysoned, and have all evyll spo-
20   ken agaynst them for Christes verytees sake. Math. 5. so wele as than.

And what can be more confortable to the sufferers, than to knowe
the ernest constancye of their troubled companyons in that kyngedome of pacyence? Apo. 1. or to marke in them the stronge workynge of
faythe, and beholde the myghtye mageste of God in their agonyes? what
though they were afore, synners of the worlde. Saynt Bernarde sayth in
hys homelyes upon Salomons cantycles, that the godlye sufferaunce of
martyrs hath geven as good erudycyon to the christen churche, as ever
ded the doctryne of the sayntes. Than is it mete that some be sterynge,
and not that all men in these dayes be ydell, concernynge that godlye
30   offyce. Manye have suffered in thys realme of late years, by the bolde
callynge on of Antichristes furyouse advocates, whose lattre confessyons, causes, and answers, are a great deale more notable and godlye, if
they be ryghtlye wayed, than ever were the confessyons, causes and
answers of the olde canonysed martyrs, whych in the popes Englysh
churche have had so manye solempnytees, servyces, and sensynges.
Manye have also most desperatlye recanted through their most wycked
persuasyons and threttenynges, in whose vayne recantacyons are both to
be seane, their blasphemyes agaynst God, and manyfest treasons agaynst
their kynge.
40   Now in conferrynge these martyrs, the olde with the newe, and the

---

Line 17. **martyrs**: margin.

Line 21. **sufferers.**: margin.

Line 25. **Saynt Bernarde**: Bernard, abbot of Clairvaux (1090–1153), theologian and church
father. **Bernardus.**: margin.

Line 28. **mete**: fitting. **sterynge**: stirring; busy.

Line 30. **offyce**: function; here, of recording martyrdoms.

Line 31. **Barnes and other**: margin.

Line 32. **causes**: charges.

Line 36. **Recanters**: margin.

Lines 40–41. **conferrynge**: comparing. **Now…Christes**: Bale drew legends of "good" and
"bad" English martyrs from various sources, both historical and unhistorical, including
chronicles, saints' lives, and martyrologies; see Introduction, pages xxxiv–xxxv.

popes with Christes. I seclude first of all the Brytayne churche, or the prymatyve churche of thys realme, whych never had autoryte of the Romysh pope. Her martyrs in dede were agreable to that Christ spake afore in the Gospell concernynge hys martyrs, wherby we shuld knowe them, as we evydentlye fynde in the lyves of Emerita kynge Lucyes syster, Amphibalus, Albanus, Aaron, Julius, Dionothus, and soch other. I sende yow forth (sayth he) as shepe amonge wolves. Men shall delyver ye up in their counsels and synagoges. Ye shall be brought before rulers and kynges, and be hated of all men in a maner for my names sake, Mathei 10. Cast not afore in your myndes what answere to make. For I in that houre shall geve ye both utteraunce and wysdome, whych all your adversaryes shall not be hable to withstande, Luce 21. They shall excommunycate yow or condempne yow for heretykes. Yea, they shall brynge yow in soche hate of the world, that who so ever kylleth yow, wyll thynke he doth God great good servyce. And thys shall they do bycause they knowe ryghtlye neyther the father nor yet me, Joan. 16.

Manye other lyke sentences left the lorde Jesus Christ in hys holye Gospell, that we shuld alwayes by them dyscerne hys true martyrs, from the popes and Mahometes counterfett martyrs. In England here sens the first plantacyon of the popes Englysh churche, by Augustyne and other Romysh monkes of Benettes superstycyon, ii. kyndes of martyrs hath bene, One of monasterye buylders and chaunterye founders,

50

60

Line 41. **seclude:** exclude.

Line 42. **Brytayne churche.:** margin.

Line 45. **kynge Lucyes:** in legends, Lucius was the first Christian king of Britain (ca. 180).

Line 46. **Amphibalus:** the cleric who converted Saint Alban. **Albanus:** Saint Alban of Verulam (fl. third century), first British martyr. **Aaron, Julius:** legendary martyrs of Caerleon-on-Usk (d. ca. 305). **Dionothus:** abbot of Bangor (d. 603) who resisted the Roman Bishop Augustine's rule and was killed with 1200 monks by King Ethelfrid.

Line 47. **he:** Jesus; see Matt. 10:16–22.

Line 47. **Christ.:** margin.

Line 50. **afore:** ahead of time.

Line 52. **Byshoppes.:** margin.

Line 61. **Benettes:** Saint Benedict's. **Englysh churche.:** margin.

Line 62. **chaunterye:** chapel.

whom the temporall prynces and secular magistrates have dyverslye
done to deathe, sumtyme for dysobedyence, and sumtyme for manyfest
treason, as we have of Wallenus of Crowlande, Thomas of Lancastre,
Rycharde Scrope, Becket and soch other. The ymages of these have bene
sett up in their temples, lyke the olde goddes of the paganes, and have
had ther vygyls, holye dayes, ryngynges, sacryfysynges, candels, offer-
ynges, feastynges, and moch a do besydes, as they had. The other sort
70   were preachers of the Gospell, or poore teachers therof in corners, whan
the persecucyon was soche, that it myght not be taught abroade. And
these poore sowles, or true servauntes of God, were put to deathe by the
holye spyrytuall fathers Byshoppes, prestes, monkes, chanons, and fry-
ers. for heresye and lollerye, they saye. These Christen martyrs were
never solempnysed of them. No, they had not so moch as a penye dyrge
or a grote masse of Requiem, nomore than had Johan Baptyst and
Steven amonge the Jewes. But they have bene holden for condempned
heretykes ever sens.

Who ever hearde anye goodnesse yet reported of Dionothus with hys
80   M. and CC. companyons, whom Augustyne caused to be slayne at
Westchestre in hys churches begynnynge, bycause they wolde not
preache as he ded apoynt them, nor baptyse after the Romysh maner,

Line 65. **Wallenus of Crowlande:** Wallene of Crowland Abbey in Lincolnshire. **Thomas of Lancastre:** earl of Lancaster (1277?–1322) who was executed for treason against Edward II. **Martyrs:** margin.

Line 66. **Rycharde Scrope:** archbishop of York, who was beheaded in 1405 for treason against Henry IV. **Becket:** Saint Thomas à Becket (1118–1170), archbishop of Canterbury, who was murdered by Henry II's knights.

Line 68. **vygyls:** prayers at a nocturnal service, especially for the dead. **ryngynges:** ringing bells for canonized martyrs.

Line 70. **Other martyrs.:** margin.

Line 73. **chanons:** clergy living in a religious community run according to the canons (rules) of the church.

Line 74. **lollerye:** Lollardy; fourteenth-century religious, dissenting movement associated with Wycliffe's followers.

Lines 75–76. **penye...Requiem:** the usual phrases are "mass-penny" and "dirge-groat"; a groat or silver coin was paid for singing the dirge and the mass-penny offered for the mass for the souls of the dead. **No dyrge:** margin.

Line 80. **Augustyne.:** margin.

neyther yet hallowe the eastre feast as they ded. Manye a blessed creature, both men and women, have bene brent sens Johan Wycleves tyme
and afore, for onlye dysclosynge the pharysees yokes and teachynge the
Gospels lyberte. And then have that bawdye bloudye Synagoge of
Sathan dyffamed, blasphemed, condempned, execrated and cursed to
hell as most detestable heretykes and dogges. Where as if they were of
Christ, they ought (in case they were their haters or enemyes) to suffre
them, to saye wele of them, to do them good, and to praye for them.   90
Math. 5. Luce 6. and not thus to use more tyrannye over them, than
ever ded Saracene, Turke, Tyraunt or devyll. A great dyfference is there
of the martyrs whom they make, from the martyrs whom they
canonyse. Of them whom they dampne, from them whom they worshypp. Yea, so great a dyfference or dyversyte betwyn them (if ye marke
them wele) as is betwixt golde and dyrt, or lyght and darkenesse.

The martyrs, whose deathes they have procured by all ages of their
bloudthurstye church, harkened unto Christ, healde of ryghtousnesse,
and sought their lorde God in sprete, Esa. 51 but the martyrs for the
most part, whom they have with so manye latyne wawlynges, torches   100
and candell burnynges, magnyfyed in their temples, harkened to the
pope, healde of hys unryghtousnesse, and sought out hys superstycyouse ydolatryes. In the conferrynge of their olde canonysed martyrs,
with our newlye condempned martyrs here, Anne Askewe and her other
iii. companyons, with soch lyke, their dyfference wyll be moch more
easelye perceyved. First lete us begynne with Thomas Becket, whych
was so gloryouse a martyr and precyouse advocate of theirs, that they

---

Line 84. **Wycleve.**: margin.
Line 87. **dyffamed**: defamed.
Line 89. **Suffre.**: margin.
Line 93. **Dyfference of martyrs.**: margin.
Line 97. **Martyrs**: margin.
Line 98. **healde of**: held with; maintained allegiance to.
Line 100. **wawlynges**: harsh cries; wails.
Line 103. **Compare**: margin.
Line 106. **Becket.**: margin.

made hys bloude equall with Christes bloude and desyred to clyme to
heaven therby. Manye wonderfull myracles coulde that mytred patrone
110 of theirs do in those dayes, whan the monkes had fryre Bakons bokes
and knewe the bestowynge of fryre Bongayes mystes but now he can do
non at all. Thys Becket in all hys floryshynge doynges, harkened to the
pope, defended hys pompouse kyngedome, supported hys churches excesse, and wretchedlye dyed for the synnefull lybertees of the same.
Anne Askewe and her sort, gave dylygent hede to their lorde Jesus
Christ, sought the kyngedome of heaven in daylye repentaunce,
myghtelye detested all ydolatrouse worshyppynges, and in conclusyon
suffered most tryumphaunt deathe for the same.

Concernynge other martyrs. As Wenefryd, otherwyse called Bony-
120 face an Englysh monke and archebyshopp of Magunce was slayne con-
firmynge neophytes, or professyng hys newlye baptysed brode to the
Romysh popes obedyence. There was founde aboute hym a casket full
of rellyckes or dead mennys bones, whan he was put to deathe in the
yeare of our lorde, 755. Anne Askewe and her felyshypp, had non other
rellyckes aboute them, whan they stode at the stake to be brent in
Smythfelde. but a bundell of the sacred scriptures enclosed in ther
hartes, and redye to be uttered agaynst Antichristes ydolatryes. Saynt
Clare of Orchestre contemnynge lawfull marryage, made hym selfe an
ydell prest, and was byheaded in hys owne gardene by procurement of a
130 woman. S. Clytanke of Southwales, was in lyke case stabbed in with a

---

Line 109. **mytred:** wearing a mitre, a bishop's hat. **myracles:** margin.

Line 110. **fryre Bakon:** Friar Roger Bacon (1214?–1294), Franciscan friar, philosopher, and scientist who was suspected of heresy and necromancy.

Line 111. **bestowynge:** employment. **fryre Bongayes mystes:** Friar Thomas Bungay (fl. 1290), Franciscan friar popularly supposed to be a magician.

Line 115. **Ryght martyrs.:** margin.

Lines 119–20. **Wenefryd...Bonyface:** Saint Boniface (680–754), preacher and founder of monasteries under Pope Gregory II; martyred in Germany. **Bonifacius Anglus:** margin.

Line 120. **slayne:** emended from "flayne".

Lines 127–28. **Saynt Clare:** English hermit at Rouen where he was killed. **Clarus.:** margin.

Line 130. **S. Clytanke:** Clitancus, king of south Wales, who was killed by a jealous retainer as he prayed. **Clitancus:** margin.

dagger, bycause a yonge mayden loved hym. The onlye true honoure of God was it, and no wordlye cause, that Anne Askewe and her companye dyed for. Saynt Edwyne beynge wele armed, was slayne in battayle at Hatfelde in the North, and S. Edwarde rydynge a Huntynge in the forest of Warham in the weast, was kylled upon hys horse in drynkynge a cuppe of wyne. And all thys was done for the kyngedomes of thys worlde. The martyrdome of Anne Askewe and her Bretherne, was neyther in battelynge nor huntynge, rydynge nor drynkynge, but in that ryght course whych Christ prescrybed unto hys dyscyples undre the cruell Byshoppes, for hys onlye glorye.   140

Saynct Cadock of Cowbridge a Byshopp, was pearced through with a speare, as he stode at hys Masse at one of the clocke at after none, bycause he wolde be of the order of martyrs. Saynt Elphege archebyshopp of Caunterburye was stoned to deathe of the Danes, bycause he wolde not paye them thre. M. Marke, in the yeare of our lorde. M. and xii. Of soch martyrs, moch doubted Lanfrancus, whych succeded hym in that offyce about a iiii. score years after, and dysputed therof with Anselmus. The cause of Anne Askewe and her companyons, was neyther madnesse nor moneye, but the onlye sekynge of their lorde God a ryght. As Saynt Indract with other devoute pylgrymes of Rome   150

Line 132. **wordlye:** worldly.

Line 133. **Saynt Edwyne:** king of the Northumbrians who was killed in 633 at Hatfield Chase by the Mercians and Welsh. **Edwinus:** margin.

Line 134. **S. Edwarde:** King Edward the Martyr who was killed in 979 in the forest of Wareham, Dorset. **Edwardus.:** margin.

Line 138. **drynkynge:** emended from "drykynge".

Line 141. **Saynct Cadock of Cowbridge:** a Welsh monk who became a bishop and was killed ca. 580. **Cadocus.:** margin.

Line 143. **Saynt Elphege:** archbishop of Canterbury (954–1012); imprisoned during the Danish invasion, he refused to pay 3,000 marks ransom, was stoned, and then murdered by his godson.

Line 146. **Lanfrancus:** Lanfranc (ca. 1005–1089), archbishop of Canterbury and church reformer. **Lanfrancus.:** margin.

Line 148. **Anselmus:** Saint Anselm (1033–1109), theologian and archbishop of Canterbury.

Line 150. **Saynt Indract:** Irish pilgrim to Saint Patrick's shrine at Glastonbury who was murdered by retainers of the West Saxon king. **Indractus:** margin.

laye in bed in their inne at Shapwyck by Glastenbury, their throtes were cut in the nyght for moneye, whych was reckened to be in their pylgrymes scryppes. Saynt Juthware a vyrgyne was byheaded also, for layenge fresh chese or cruddes whether ye wyll, to her brestes. The cause of Anne Askewe and her other fellawes, conferred with Christes scriptures, semeth a farre other matter. Hewalde the blacke and Hewalde the whyght ii. Englysh monkes, goynge from place to place with cruettes, chalyce, and superaltare, to do their daylye sacryfyces, were done to deathe in Frislande by the bowers of the cuntraye for teachynge a
160   straunge relygyon, and are worshypped at Coleyne for martyrs. For bearynge about Christes testament, whych is most heavenlye treasure, and for spredynge the wholsom doctryne therof, was Anne Askewe and her sort brent by the prestes procurement, yet axe they no honour for it.

Osytha runnynge awaye from her husbande, by the intysement of ii. monkes bycame a professed nonne, and was murthered of the Danes. Wenefryda by counsell of a prest, dysdaynouslye refusynge the marryage of a prynce christened, lost her head for it. Maxentia also played a

---

Line 153. **scryppes:** scrips; small wallets or bags. **Saynt Juthware:** seventh-century saint whose legend recounts that she was advised by her stepmother to lay cheese on her breasts; she was then accused of being pregnant and lactating and beheaded by her brother. **Juthwara.:** margin.

Line 154. **cruddes:** curds; fermented milk. **whether...wyll:** whichever of the two you want.

Lines 155–56. **scriptures:** emended from "sriptures".

Lines 156–57. **Hewalde...whyght:** two English monks killed in 690; their names reflected their hair color. **cruettes:** small vessels to hold wine or water for use in the celebration of the Eucharist. **Hewaldi duo.:** margin.

Line 158. **superaltare:** portable stone slab consecrated as an altar.

Line 159. **Frislande:** Friesland, province in the Netherlands. **bowers:** peasants.

Line 161. **Anne Askewe.:** margin.

Line 163. **axe:** ask.

Line 164. **Osytha:** queen of the East Saxons (ca. 700) who founded a convent by the river Colne; in her legend, she was beheaded by marauding Danes. **Ositha:** margin.

Line 166. **Wenefryda:** Saint Winifred (d. ca. 650); her legend recounts that when she was beheaded, water gushed where her head fell and that Saint Beuno restored her to life. **dysdaynouslye:** disdainfully. **Wenefrida.:** margin.

Line 167. **Maxentia:** king of Scotland's daughter; her legend recounts her refusal of the pagan prince Maxentius, who pursued her to France and beheaded her. **Maxentia.:** margin.

part not all unlyke to thys. Soch pylde popysh martyrdomes, compared to the martyrdome of Anne Askewe and her faythfull cumpanye, is as is rustye yron compared to pure sylver. S. Wyllyam of Rochestre a Scotte, leavynge both wyfe and howsholde, ydellye to trudge on pylgrymage, was strycken in the head with an axe, of hys owne companyon by the waye. Saynt Thomas of Dover a monke was soch a wone, as was slayne of the frenche men for hydynge the churches jewels, crosses, chalyces and copes. No soch lyght corruptyble vanytees were they, that Anne Askewe and her constaunt bretherne dyed for, but for the precyouse veryte of God. Yonge S. Wyllyam of Norwych, yonge S. Robert of Burye, yonge S. Hugh of Lyncolne, yonge S. Melor of Cornewayle, yong S. Kenelme of Glocestre, yonge S. Eldrede of Ramsaye and hys brother, with soch other lyke, were but verye babes (they saye) and were martyred of the Jewes and of other enemyes. Wherfor their martyrdomes shall be but babysh in comparyson of these, the veryte havynge by them so small furtheraunce.

Foillanus and hys iii. bretherne, goynge homeward in the nyght, after they had wele banketed with S. Gertrude and her nonnes, were kylled

---

Line 170. **S. Wyllyam:** Saint William of Rochester (d. 1201) whose legend recounts his murder by his servant on the way from Rochester to Canterbury. **Guilhelmus.:** margin; William (Latin).

Line 173. **Saynt Thomas:** Saint Thomas of Dover (d. 1295), a Benedictine monk murdered in a French raid; miracles were said to occur at his tomb. **Thomas.:** margin.

Lines 177–81. **Yonge...enemyes:** Bale refers to medieval stories of murdered children in which Jews were often accused of the killing. These unhistorical accounts appear to be connected to the local cults centered on the child. **S.:** saint.

Line 177. **S. Wyllyam:** a twelve-year-old child said to have been killed in Norwich in 1144; Jews were accused of the murder. **S. Robert:** according to legend, a boy crucified in Bury St. Edmund's on Good Friday, 1181. **Yonge Sayntes.:** margin.

Line 178. **S. Hugh:** boy said to have been killed in Lincoln in 1255; Jews were accused of the murder. **S. Melor:** according to legend, a fourteen-year-old killed by his uncle, the usurping duke of Cornwall.

Line 179. **S. Kenelme:** son of King Coenwulf (796–821); according to legend, the seven-year-old king of Mercia was killed by his tutor who was bribed by Kenelm's sister Cynefrith. **S. Eldrede:** Ethelred, a prince of Kent who was murdered in 640 with his brother, Ethelbricht, by their cousin's counsellor; their bodies were later removed to Ramsey Abbey in Huntingdonshire.

Line 184. **Foillanus:** Saint Foyllan, an Irish monk and instructor of Saint Gertrude; he built a monastery in France and was murdered nearby ca. 655. **Foillanus:** margin.

in a wood of one murtherer, and their horses solde in the next market
towne. Justinanus, S. Davyes ghostlye father in Wales, was slayne in a
gardene of hys iii. monkes, bycause he compelled them to do more
laboure than he wolde do hys selfe. After Kilianus was come home from
190 Rome, he was murthered in hys selle with other holye pylgrymes by a
woman, as they laye there a slepe in the nyght. Saynt Ursula also and
her she pylgrymes, with their chaplaynes, nurses, and suckynge babes,
were but homelye handeled at Coleyne of the hunnes and pyctes (if that
legende be true) as they were commynge homewardes from Rome.
Compare me Anne Askewe and her comdempned cumpanye, with
these clowted, canonysed, solempnysed, sensed, mattensed, and massed
martyrs, and tell me by the Gospels tryall, whych of them seme most
Christenlyke martyrs. Yea, brynge saynt Edmonde of Burye. S. Fremunde of Dunstable, S. Ethelbert of Herforde, S. Oswalde of Gloces-
200 tre, S. Oswyne of Tynmoth, and Saynt Wynstane of Evesham (whych
are the best of the Englysh martyrs) to the touche stone of Gods worde,
and ye shall fynde their martyrdomes and causes full unlyke to theirs
whom the Byshoppes murther now apace in Englande. In all these

---

Line 187. **Justinanus:** Justinian, sixth-century priest of Brittany who was Saint David's
spiritual advisor; he was killed by his servants and buried in Saint David's, Wales. **Justinanus.:**
margin.

Line 189. **Kilianus:** Saint Kilian, an Irish missionary, murdered ca. 689 by a newly converted
queen. **Kilianus.:** margin.

Line 191. **Saynt Ursula:** in medieval chronicles, daughter of Dionotus, king of Cornwall
(fourth century); her legend recounts that she was one of 11,000 virgins killed at Cologne.
Ursula.: margin.

Line 196. **clowted:** patched up or botched. **Prove the spretes.:** margin.

Line 198. **saynt Edmonde:** Edmund the Martyr (849–869), an East Anglian king killed by
Danes at Bury in Suffolk.

Lines 198–99. **S. Fremunde:** King Offa's son who saved the Mercians from the Danes but was
killed by a traitor in 866. **S. Ethelbert:** king of the East Angles killed in 794 by Offa's queen.
S. Oswalde: holy king of Northumberland (604–642) who was killed by Penda, king of
Mercia.

Line 200. **S. Oswyne:** gentle King Oswin of Northumberland who was killed by his cousin
Oswy in 651. **Saynt Wynstane:** a king of the marches (d. 850); his legend recounts that he was
murdered by his cousin Berhtric. **Edmundus Fremundus and other.:** margin.

Line 202. **fynde:** emended from "fynhe".

Line 203. **apace:** swiftly.

Englysh martyrs reherced here afore, ye shall fynde verye fewe coloures
or yet tokens, that Christ sayd hys martyrs shuld be knowne by, unlesse
ye take pylgrymages, pompes rellyckes, women, battels, huntynges,
ydelnesse, monkeryes, moneye, treasure, worldlye kyngedomes, contempt of marryage, superstycyons and soch other vanytees for them.
And than wyll I saye, and not lye in it, that ye are moch better overseane
than lerned in the scriptures of God, as your olde blynde bludderynge   210
predecessours hath bene. Ye wyll axe me here, if I recken Englande than
all barren of Christen martyrs? Naye marry do I not, For I knowe it
hath had good store sens the popes faythe came first into Englande
to the Gospels obscuracyon, though their names be not knowne to
all men. Great tyrannye was shewed by the heythnysh emprours and
kynges at the first preachynge of the Gospell in the prymatyve churche
of the Brytaynes, by the cruell callynge on of the pagane prestes. But
nothynge lyke to that hath bene shewed sens in the Englysh churche by
the spirytuall tyraunt of Rome and hys mytred termagauntes, at the
provocacyon of ther oyled swylbolles and blynd Balaamytes. For they   220
most cruellye brent those innocentes, whych ded but only reade the testament of God in their mother tunge, and do not yet repent them of
that myschefe but contynewe therein.

If ye marke wele these ii. examynacyons of Anne Askewe, ye shall
fynde in her and in her other iii. companyons, besydes other whom the
Byshoppes in our tyme and afore hath brent, the expresse tokens that

---

Line 204. **coloures:** identifying devices or badges.

Line 204. **Tokens.:** margin.

Line 206. **pompes rellyckes:** an alternative reading, "popes rellyckes," results if "pōpes" in the
basetext is emended to "popes".

Line 208. **the autor:** margin.

Line 210. **bludderynge:** blundering (?); see *OED.* Cf. "bloderynge," page 28.

Line 211. **Good store.:** margin.

Line 216. **Brytannysh.:** margin.

Line 219. **Englysh.:** margin.

Line 219. **mytred termagauntes:** savage bullies wearing bishops' hats.

Line 220. **Balaamytes:** in Num. 22–24, Balaam's ass sees God's angel before Balaam does.

Line 225. **Tokens.:** margin.

Christ sealeth hys martyrs with. They apered as shepe amonge wolves.
They were throwne in stronge preson. They were brought forth into
counsels and synagoges. Their answers were out of Gods sprete (as herin
230 apereth) and not out of their owne. They were revyled, mocked,
stocked, racked, execrated, condempned, and murthered, as is sayd
afore, By a spirytualte also, as he promysed they shuld be, Math. 23.
and 24. Yea, those spirytuall tyrauntes besydes their mortall malyce
upon the innocent bodyes, have most blasphemouslye uttered in their
spyghtfull sermons and writynges, that their sowles are dampned, as is
to be seane in the bokes of wynchestre and Peryn. But lete them be ware
least they dampne not their owne wretched sowles. For full sure we are
by Christes stronge promes, Luce 12. That their sowles they can not
harme with all their popes blacke curses. Full swetelye rest they now in
240 the peace of God, where their slaunderouse and malycyouse judgementes can not hurte them at all. Sapi. 3. Lete those Epycures pygges
dampne them with as manye blasphemouse lyes as they can ymagyne,
for other armour they have not. And we shall on the other syde
canonyse them agayne with the myghtye wordes and promyses of
Christ, whych they shall never be hable to resist. The father of our lorde
Jesus Christ, graunt the lyght of hys worde so to sprede the worlde over
that the darke mystes of Sathan maye clerelye be expelled, to the specyall confort of hys redemed churche, and glorye of hys eternall name.

Amen.

Line 229. **Answers:** margin.

Line 232. **Tyrauntes.:** margin.

Line 236. **Wynchestre:** margin.

Line 236. **Peryn.:** margin.

Line 241. **Epycures:** followers of Epicurus, a Greek philosopher (342?–270 B.C.); used loosely to mean those without religious faith. **epycures pygges.:** margin.

Line 246. **Lyght.:** margin.

THE LATTRE EXAMINACION

of the worthye servaunt of God mastres Anne Askewe
the yonger doughter of Sir Wyllyam Askewe knyght
of Lyncolne shyre, latelye martyred in Smithfelde
by the wycked Synagoge of Antichrist.

The censure or judgement of Johan Bale therupon,
after the sacred Scriptures and Chronycles.

Christ wylled hys most dere Apostle and secretarye Saynt Johan the
Evangelist, to sygnyfye by writynge to the oversear or preacher of the
congregacyon of Pergamos, that there onlye are hys faythfull members   10
murthered, where Sathan inhabyteth or holdeth resydence. And for
example he bryngeth forth hys constaunt witnesse Antipas, whych was
there most cruellye slayne of that Synagoge of hys, for confessynge the
veryte, Apoca. 2. That Behemoth (sayth Job) that Levyathan, that
Sathan, regneth as a most myghtye kynge over all the spirytuall chyldren of pryde. Job 42. A murtherer (sayth Christ to the spirytualte of
the Jewes) and a blasphemouse lyar, is that father of yours, and hath
bene from the worldes begynnynge Joan. 8. These maners hath he not
yet left, but contynueth them styll in hys wycked posteryte.

In the prymatyve churche (as testyfyeth Bedas) they persecuted the   20
heares of Christes head, whych were so pure as the whyte wolle that is
apte to receyve all colours, Apoca, 1. They slewe those true belevers
whych hys worde and sprete had depured from all false worshyppynges,
and made fytt for all trybulacyons to be suffered for hys names sake. In

---

Line 8. **S. Johan.:** margin.
Line 10. **Pergamos:** Pergamum, associated with idolatry. See Rev. 2: 12–17.
Line 16. **Sathan.:** margin.
Line 16. **spirytualte:** group of religious people.
Line 21. **Christes heares.:** margin.
Line 23. **depured:** cleansed, purified.

these lattre dayes they meddele with his fete, whych are lyke unto
brasse, burnynge as it were in an whote furnace, Apo. 1. For they that
beleve now agreably to hys worde, and not after ther corrupted and
cursed customes, are consumed in the fyre. As here after wyll apere by
thys godlye woman Anne Askewe, whych with other more was brent at
30 London in the yeare of our lorde a M. D. XLVI. For the faythfull testymonye of Jesu agaynst Antichrist. Whose lattre handelynge here
foloweth in course, lyke as I receyved it in coppye, by serten duche merchauntes commynge from thens, whych had bene at their burnynge,
and beholden the tyrannouse vyolence there shewed. First out of the
preson she wrote unto a secrete frynde of hers, after thys maner folowynge.

Anne Askewe.

I do perceyve (dere frynde in the lorde) that thu art not yet persuaded
throughlye in the truthe concernynge the lordes supper, bycause Christ
40 sayd unto hys Apostles. Take, eate. Thys is my bodye whych is geven for
yow. In gevynge forth the breade as an outwarde sygne or token to be
receyved at the mouthe, he mynded them in a perfyght beleve to
receyve that bodye of hys whych shuld dye for the people, or to thynke
the deathe therof, the onlye helthe and salvacyon of their sowles. The
breade and the wyne were left us, for a sacramentall communyon, or a
mutuall pertycypacyon of the inestymable benefyghtes of hys most precyouse deathe and bloud shedynge. And that we shuld in the ende
therof, be thankefull togyther for that most necessarye grace of our
redempcyon. For in the closynge up therof, he sayd thus. Thys do ye, in

Line 25. **Christes fete.**: margin.
Line 26. **burnynge**: emended from "burynge".
Line 28. **Fyre.**: margin.
Line 32. **Coppye.**: margin.
Line 39. **Christ.**: margin.
Line 42. **mynded**: reminded, exhorted.
Line 44. **helthe**: spiritual well-being; salvation.
Line 45. **Breade.**: margin.

remembraunce of me. Yea, so oft as ye shall eate it or drynke it, Luce 22.   50
and 1. Corinth. 11. Els shuld we have bene forgetfull of that we ought
to have in daylye remembraunce, and also bene altogyther unthankefull
for it.

Johan Bale.

Agreable is thys womannis doctryne here, to the scriptures of both testamentes. Wherin these wordes Edere & Bibere, to eate and to drynke,
are oft tymes spirytuallye taken for Credere, to beleve or receyve in faythe. The poore (sayth David) shall eate and be satisfyed. All that seke to
please the lorde shall prayse hym, and their sowles shall never perysh.
Psal. 21. They that eate me (sayth the veryte of God) shall hungre more   60
and more, and they that drincke me shall thirst more desyerously for
me. Eccles. 24. Onlesse ye eate the fleshe of the sonne of man (sayth
Christ) and drynke hys bloude, ye can have no lyfe in yow, Joan. 6.
These scriptures expounde the doctours spirytuallye, yea, the papistes
and all. Where as the other iii. Evangelistes, Mathew, Marke, and Luke,
sheweth nothynge els of the lordes supper but the playne historie, S.
Johan writynge last of them all, manyfesteth there the whole complete
doctryne and full understandynge therof after Christes owne instruccyons and meanynge. Requyred is it there, that the true receyvers
therof, be taught of God, and lerned of the heavenlye father and not of   70
synnefull mennes customes.

The worke of God, or that pleaseth God, is not there the puttynge of
breade into the mouthe and bellye, but to beleve or exactlye to consydre, that Christ dyed for us to clense us from synne, to joyne us into one
mystycall bodye, and to geve us the lyfe everlastynge. And that there is
non other but he that can procure us that lyfe. For that whych entereth

---

Line 50. **Remembre**: margin.
Lines 56–57. **Edere...Credere**: Latin verbs, which Bale translates. **Edere & Bibere.**: margin.
Line 60. **Beleve.**: margin.
Line 64. **doctours**: scholars.
Line 65. **Evangelystes.**: margin.
Line 67. **Doctryne.**: margin.
Line 73. **Faythe.**: margin.

the mouthe, feadeth onlye the bodye. But that entereth faythe, feadeth
the sowle. I am the lyvynge breade (sayth he) whych came downe from
heaven. He onlye that beleveth in me, hath the lyfe everlastynge, Joan.
80 6. The sprete is it that quyckeneth, the fleshelye understandynge, or
onlye mouthe eatynge, profyteth nothynge at all. Here wyll an
obstynate papyst paraventure saye, that we attrybute nothynge to the
corporall communyon. Yeas, we reverentlye, graunt, that ryghtlye
mynystred after Christes instytucyon, it both confirmeth our faythe in
the necessarye consyderacyons of hys deathe, and also sturreth up that
brotherlye Christen love whych we ought to have towards our neyber,
besydes that thys faythfull woman hath spoken here of it afore. And
these are the onlye frutes whych he requireth of us in that supper or sacramentall metynge.

90   *Anne Askewe.*

Therfor it is mete, that in prayers we call unto God, to grafte in our
foreheades, the true meanynge of the holye Ghost concernynge thys
communyon. For S. Paule doth saye that the letter slayeth. The sprete is
it onlye that geveth lyfe. 2. Cor. 3. Marke wele the vi. chaptre of Johan,
where all is applyed unto faythe. Note also the fort chaptre of S. Paules
first epistle to the Corynthes, and in the ende therof ye shall fynde
playnelye, that the thynges whych are seane are temporall, but they that
are not seane are everlastynge. Yea, loke in the third chaptre to the
Hebrues, and ye shall fynde that Christ as a sonne and no servaunt,
100 ruleth over hys howse (whose howse are we, and not the dead temple) if
we holde fast the confydence and rejoysynge of that hope to the ende.

Line 78. **Christ.**: margin.

Line 80. **quyckeneth:** receives life.

Line 83. **Communyon.**: margin.

Line 86. **Love.**: margin.

Line 93. **Letter.**: margin.

Line 99. **Christ.**: margin.

Lines 98–103. **Yea, loke...Psalm. 94:** the words of Heb. 3:7–8 are based on Ps. 94 (Ps. 95 in
the King James version). **whose...temple:** Christians are a spiritual community of believers;
see Heb. 3:6.

Wherfor as sayth the holye Ghost. To daye if yow shall heare hys voyce, harden not your hartes, &c, Psalm. 94.

Johan Bale.

By the fore heades understande she the hartes or myndes of men, for so are they taken of S. Johan, Apoc. 7. and 22. I can not thynke, but herin she had respect unto the plate of fyne golde whych the lorde commaunded to be sett upon Aarons foreheade, for the acceptacyon of the people of Israel, Exodi. 2. For here wolde she all mennys hartes to be endued and lyghtened with the most pure sprete of Christ, for the understandynge of that most holye and necessarye communyon, the corrupted dreames and fantasyes of synnefull men sett a part. She knewe by the syngular gyft of the holye Ghost, that they are lyenge masters, procurers of ydolatrye, and most spyghtfull enemyes to the sowle of man, that applyeth that offyce to the corruptyble lyppes, whych belongeth to an uncorrupted faythe, so settynge the creature that is corruptyble breade, in place of the creator Christ both God and man, Roma. 1. lamentynge it with the ryghtouse, at the verye hartrote. And in thys she shewed her selfe to be a naturall membre of Christes mystycall bodye. 1. Cor. 12. relygyouslye carefull for her Christen bretherne and systerne, least they shuld take harme of the popes masmongers.

Anne Askewe.
The summe of my examynacyon afore the kynges
counsell at Grenewyche.

Your request as concernynge my preson fellawes, I am not hable to

---

Line 105. **Foreheades.**: margin.
Line 109. **Hartes.**: margin.
Line 110. **endued...with**: possessed of.
Line 114. **spyghtfull**: emended from "spyghfull".
Line 115. **Lyars**: margin.
Line 116. **creature**: creation.
Line 118. **hartrote**: heart-root; the bottom of the heart.
Line 119. **A membre.**: margin.
Line 121. **masmongers**: mass-mongers; contemptuous term for Roman Catholics.
Line 125. **Companyons.**: margin.

satysfye, bycause I hearde not their examynacyons. But the effect of
myne was thys I beynge before the counsell, was asked of mastre kyme.
I answered, that my lorde chancellour knewe all redye my mynde in
that matter, They with that answere were not contented, but sayd, it
130 was the kynges pleasure, that I shuld open the matter to them. I
answered them playnelye, that I wolde not so do. But if it were the kynges pleasure to heare me, I wolde shewe hym the truthe. Then they
sayd, it was not mete for the kynge with me to be troubled. I answered,
that Salomon was reckened the wysest kynge that ever lyved, yet mys-
lyked not he to heare. ii. poore common women, moch more hys grace
a symple woman and hys faythfull subject. So in conclusyon, I made
them non other answere in that matter.

Johan Bale.

Concernynge mastre Kyme, thys shuld seme to be the matter. Her
140 father Sir Wyllyam Askewe knyght and hys father olde mastre Kyme,
were sumtyme of famylyaryte and neybers within the countye of Lyncolne shyre. Wherupon the seyd Sir Wyllyam, covenaunted wyth hym
for lucre, to have hys eldest doughter marryed with hys sonne and heyre
(as an ungodlye maner it is in Englande moch used amonge noble
men). And as it was her chaunce to dye afore the tyme of marryage, to
save the moneye he constrayned thys to supplye her rowme. So that in
the ende she was compelled agaynst her wyll or fre consent to marrye
with hym. Notwithstandynge the marryage ones past, she demeaned
her selfe lyke a Christen wyfe, and had by hym (as I am infourmed) ii.

Line 127. **mastre kyme:** Thomas Kyme, Askew's husband. See Introduction, page xix.

Line 130. **open:** reveal or disclose.

Line 130. **Kyme.:** margin.

Line 134. **Salomon:** see 1 Kings 3:16 ff. **Solomon:** margin.

Line 139. **Kyme.:** margin.

Line 143. **lucre:** gain, profit.

Line 144. **An use.:** margin.

Line 146. **constrayned...rowme:** forced Anne to take her place.

Line 148. **demeaned:** behaved.

Line 149. **Marryed:** margin.

chyldren. In processe of tyme by oft readynge of the sacred Bible, she   150
fell clerelye from all olde superstycyons of papystrye, to a perfyght
beleve in Jhesus Christ. Wherby she so offended the prestes (as is to be
seane afore) that he at their suggestion, vyolentlye drove her oute of hys
howse. Wherupon she thought her selfe free from that uncomelye
kynde of coacted marryage, by thys doctryne of S. Paule 1. Cor. 7. If a
faytfull woman have an unbelevynge husbande, whych wyll not tarrye
with her, she may leave hym. For a brother or syster is not in subjeccyon
to soch, specyallye where as the marryage afore is unlawfull. Upon thys
occasyon (I heare saye) she sought of the law a dyvorcement from hym,
namelye and above all, bycause he so cruellye drove her out of hys   160
howse in despyght of Christes veryte. She coulde not thynke hym worthye of her marryage whych so spyghtfullye hated God the chefe autor
of marryage. Of thys matter was she first examyned (I thynke) at hys
instaunt laboure and sute.

Anne Askewe.

Then my lorde chauncellour asked me of my opynyon in the sacrament. My answere was thys. I beleve, that so oft as I in a Christen congregacyon, do receyve the breade in remembraunce of Christes deathe,
and with thankes gevynge accordynge to hys holye instytucyon, I
receyve therwith the frutes also of hys most gloryouse passyon. The   170
Byshopp of wynchestre bad me make a dyrect answere. I sayd, I wolde
not synge a newe songe to the lorde in a straunge lande.

Line 151. **papystrye:** papistry; Reformers' hostile term for Roman Catholicism.
Line 153. **Exyled.:** margin.
Line 154. **uncomelye:** unseemly; improper.
Line 155. **coacted:** enforced.
Line 159. **Dyvorcement.:** margin.
Line 162. **A beast.:** margin.
Line 164. **instaunt:** urgent.
Line 167. **Sacrament.:** margin.
Line 171. **Wynchestre.:** margin.
Line 172. **synge…lande:** cf. Ps. 137:4.

Johan Bale.

Dyrect ynough was thys answere after Christes syngle doctryne, but not after the popes double and covetouse meanynge for hys oyled queresters advauntage. And here was at hande hys generall advocate or stewarde, to loke upon the matter, that nothynge shuld perysh perteynynge to the mayntenaunce of hys superstycyouse vayne glorye, if anye craftye polycye myght helpe it. What offended thys godlye Christen woman here, 180 eyther in opynyon or faythe, the cruell and vengeable tyrauntes? But that ye must (as David sayth) temper your tunges with venemouse wordes to destroye the innocent. Psal. 63. Coulde yow have brought in agaynst her a matter of more daunger concernynge your lawes, to depryve her of lyfe, ye wolde have done it, soch is your gostlye charyte. But be sure of it, as hawtye as ye are now, the harde plage therof wyll be yours, whan the great vengeaunce shall fall for shedynge of innocentes bloude. Mathei 23.

Anne Askewe.

Then the Byshopp sayd, I spake in parables. I answered it was best for 190 hym. For if I shewe the open truthe (quoth I) ye wyll not accept it. Then he sayd I was a paratte. I tolde hym agayne, I was ready to suffre all thynges at hys handes. Not onlye hys rebukes, but all that shuld folowe besydes, yea, and that gladlye. Then had I dyverse rebukes of the counsell, bycause I wolde not expresse my mynde in all thynges as they wolde have me. But they were not in the meane tyme unanswered for all that, whych now to rehearce, were to moche. For I was with them there

---

Line 175. **Answere.**: margin.
Line 175. **queresters**: choristers; singers.
Line 179. **Tyraunt.**: margin.
Line 180. **vengeable**: destructive.
Line 184. **Daunger.**: margin.
Line 184. **gostlye**: spiritual.
Line 185. **plage**: plague.
Line 189. **Parables**: margin.
Line 191. **paratte**: parrot.
Line 193. **Rebukes.**: margin.

above fyve houres. Then the clerke of the counsell conveyed me from
thens to my ladye Garnyshe.

Johan Bale.

Most commonlye Christ used to speake in darke symylytudes and para-   200
bles, whan he perceyved hys audyence rather geven to the hearynge of
pharysaycall constytucyons and customes, than to hys heavenlye veryte,
Math. 13. Mar. 4. Luce 7. Whych rule thys woman beynge hys true
dyscyple, forgote not here, in commenynge with thys proude Byshopp,
whom she knewe to be alwayes a most obstynate withstander of that
wholsom veryte of hys. And as concernynge mockes and scornefull
revylynges, they have bene ever in that generacyon of scorners more
plenteouse than good counsels to the ryghtwyse. And therfor as a name
after their condycyons, it is unto them appropryate of the holye Ghost
in manye places of the scriptures. In the lattre dayes (sayth Judas the   210
apostle) shall come mockers, walkynge in ungodlynesse all after their
owne lustes. These are they whych separate themselves from the common sort by a name of spyrytualtie, beynge in conversacyon beastlye,
and havynge no sprete that is godlye. But derelye beloved (sayth he)
grounde your selves surelye upon our most holye faythe, &c.

Anne Askewe.

The next daye I was brought agayne before the counsell. Then wolde
they nedes knowe of me, what I sayd to the sacrament. I answered that I
alredye had sayd that I coulde saye. Then after diverse wordes, they bad

---

Line 197. **v. houres.**: margin.

Line 198. **my ladye Garnyshe:** "garnish" is slang for the money jailors extorted from new
prisoners (earliest *OED* citation: 1592); thus "my ladye Garnyshe" is Askew's ironic term for
prison.

Line 200. **Parables:** margin.

Line 202. **pharysaycall constytucyons:** hypocritcal regulations; "Pharisee" is always a nega-
tive term in pre-modern biblical commentary.

Line 205. **Wynchestre.**: margin.

Line 208. **Mockers:** margin.

Line 214. **Hypocrytes.**: margin.

Line 218. **Sacrament.**: margin.

220 me, go by. Then came my lorde Lyle, my lorde of Essexe, and the
Byshopp of wynchestre requyrynge me ernestlye, that I shuld confesse
the sacrament to be fleshe, bloude and bone. Then sayd I to my lorde
Par and my lorde Lyle, that it was great shame for them to counsell contrarye to their knowlege. Wherunto in fewe wordes they ded saye, that
they wolde gladlye all thynges were wele.

Johan Bale.

Always have the worldelye governours shewed more gentylnesse and
faver to the worde of God, than the consecrate prestes and prelates. As
we have for example in the olde lawe, that Ezechias the kynge of Juda
230 wolde in no case at their callynge on, put Micheas the true prophete
unto deathe, whan he had prophecyed the destructyon of Samaria for
their ydolatrye, and for the tyrannye of their prynces and false prophetes, Miche 1. and 3. Neyther wolde the prynces at the prestes headye
exclamacyons, murther Hieremye for the lordes veryte preachynge, but
mercyfullye delyvered hym out of their malycyouse handes, Hieremye
26. Pylate in lyke case, concernynge the newe lawe, pleated with the
Jewes spirytualte, to have saved Christ from the deathe, Math. 27. Joan.
18. So ded the captayne Claudius Lisias delyver Paule from their mortall malyce, after that the hygh prest Ananias had commaunded hym to
240 be smytten, and hys retynewe conspyred hys deathe, Acto. 23. At the

---

Line 220. **my lorde Lyle:** John Dudley, viscount Lisle (1502?–1553), a privy councillor and
later duke of Northumberland. **my lorde of Essexe:** William Parr (1513–1571), earl of Essex,
brother of Queen Katherine Parr and a privy councillor.

Line 221. **Wynchestre.:** margin.

Lines 222–23. **my lorde Par:** the earl of Essex.

Line 224. **Godlye.:** margin.

Line 227. **Prynces.:** margin.

Line 229. **Ezechias:** Hezekiah, king of Judah.

Line 230. **Micheas:** Micah, the Old Testament prophet. **Micheas.:** margin.

Line 233. **headye:** violent.

Line 234. **hieremye.:** margin.

Line 236. **pleated:** pleaded. **Pylate.:** margin.

Line 238. **Lisias:** margin.

prestes onlye provocacyon was it, that the heythnysh emprours so grevouslye vexed and tormented the Christen belevers in the prymatyve churche, as testyfyeth Egesyppus, Clemens Alexandrinus, Eusebius, and other olde hystoryanes.

Anne Askewe.

Then the Byshopp sayd, he wolde speake with me famylyarlye. I sayd, so ded Judas whan he unfryndelye betrayed Christ. Then desyered the Byshopp to speake with me alone. But that I refused. He asked me, whye? I sayd, that in the mouthe of two or thre wytnesses everye matter shuld stande, after Christes and Paules doctryne. Math. 18. and 2. Cor. 13.

250

Johan Bale.

Ded she not (thynke yow) hytt the nayle on the head, in thus tauntynge thys Byshopp? yeas. For as great offence doth he to Christ, that geveth one of hys belevynge members unto deathe, as ded he that betrayed first hys owne bodye. That ye have done unto those lyttle ones (shall he saye at the lattre daye) whych have beleved in me, ye have done unto myne owne persone, Math. 25. Who so toucheth them (sayth Zacharye) shall touche the apple of the lordes owne eye. Zacha. 2. But thys beleveth not that perverse generacyon.

260

Anne Askewe.

Then my lorde chauncellour beganne to examyne me agayne of the sacrament. Then I axed hym, how longe he wolde halte on both sydes? Then wolde he nedes knowe, where I founde that? I sayd in the scripture 3. Reg. 18. Then he went hys waye.

Line 242. **Cesares.**: margin.

Line 248. **Wynchestre.**: margin.

Line 254. **Treason.**: margin.

Line 258. **Christes.**: margin.

Line 262. **Sacrament.**: margin.

Line 263. **halte...sydes:** waver between two opinions, a common reference to 1 Kings 18:20.

Johan Bale.

Of Helias the prophete were these wordes spoken, to the people of
Israel, soch tyme as they halted betwyne ii. opynyons or walked
unryghtlye betwyne the true lyvynge God, and the false God Baal as we
270 do now in Englande betwyne Christes Gospell and the popes olde rot-
ten customes. We slenderlye consydre with S. Paule, that Christ wyll
have no felyshypp or concorde with Belial, lyght with darkenesse,
ryghtwysnesse with unryghtwysnesse, the temple of God with ymages,
or the true belevers with the infydels, 2. Corinth. 6. For all our newe
Gospell, yet wyll we styll beare the straungers yoke with the unbelevers,
and so become neyther whote nor colde, that God maye spewe us out of
hys mouthe as unsaverye morsels. Apoc. 3. Saynge unto us as to the
folysh vyrgynes. Verelye I knowe yow not. Mathei 25.

Anne Askewe.

280 Then the Byshopp sayd, I shuld be brente. I answered, that I had
serched all the scriptures yet coulde I never fynde there that eyther
Christ or hys Apostles put anye creature to deathe. Well, well, sayd I,
God wyl laughe your threttenynges to scorne, Psal. 2. Then was I commaunded to stande a syde.

Johan Bale.

Amonge other sygnes, that the holye scripture geveth us to knowe an
Antichrist by, it sheweth that he shall be an adversarye, 2. Thes. 2. An
unsacyable dogge, Esa. 56. A persuynge enemy, psa. 4. An enemye in
the sanctuarye, Psal 73. A ravenynge wolfe, Mat. 7. Luce 10. Joan. 10.
290 Acto. 20. And a most cruell murtherer, Dani. 11. Joan. 16. Apoc. 13.

Line 267. **Of Helias:** By Elijah.

Line 268. **Halte.:** margin.

Line 271. **slenderlye:** to a small extent.

Line 271. **Englande:** margin.

Line 276. **Tepidi.:** margin; lukewarm (Latin).

Line 280. **Brenne.:** margin.

Line 287. **antichrist:** margin.

Line 288. **unsacyable:** insatiable.

Line 289. **To brenne.:** margin.

Unto soche (sayth S. Johan) is it geven to vexe men with heate of fyre, Apo. 16. The wyckednesse of prestes (sayth Hiere.) shedeth innocentes bloude. Yea (saye they) ye must be brent, ye must dwell amonge the gentyles, Treno. 4. Or be committed to pryson of the worldlye powers, and so put unto deathe by them. We marvele not therfor though these partes be played of proude Byshoppes. Consyderynge the holye Ghost must be founde true in hys fore judgementes, and that some ther must be to do the feates. But trulye ded thys woman conclude with the prophecye of David, Psalme 2. That God whych dwelleth in heaven shall have their tyrannye in derysyon, and bringe all their wycked coun-   300
sels to naught, in the clere openynge of hys worde, have they never so manye paynted colours of false ryght wysnesse.

Anne Askewe.

Then came mastre Pagett to me with manye gloryouse wordes, and desyred me to speake my mynde to hym. I myght (he sayd) denye it agayne, if nede were. I sayd, that I wolde not denye the truthe. He asked me, how I coulde avoyde the verye wordes of Christ. Take, eate. Thys is my bodye, whych shall be broken for yow. I answered, that Christes meanynge was there, as in these other places of the scripture. I am the dore, Joan. 10. I am the vyne, Joan. 15. Beholde the lambe of God,   310
Joan. 1. The rocke stone was Christ. 1 Cor. 10. and soch other lyke. Ye maye not here (sayd I) take Christ for the materyall thynge that he is sygnyfyed by. For than ye wyll make hym a verye dore, a vyne, a lambe, and a stone, cleane contrarye to the holye Ghostes meanynge. All these in dede do sygnyfye Christ, lyke as the breade doth hys bodye in that place. And though he ded saye there. Take, eate thys in remembraunce of me. Yet ded he not byd them hange up that breade in a boxe, and make it a God, or bowe to it.

Line 295. **Prestes.**: margin.

Line 300. **God lawheth.**: margin.

Line 304. **mastre Pagett:** William Paget (1505–1563), one of Henry VIII's principal secretaries and a close advisor. See Introduction, page xxviii. **Pagett.**: margin.

Line 308. **Christes meanyng:** margin.

Line 313. **Sygnyfye.**: margin.

Line 316. **Remembraunce.**: margin.

Johan Bale.

320 Moche a do is here made, and manye subtyle wayes are sought out, to
brynge thys woman into their corrupted, and false beleve, that the corruptyble creature made with handes, myght stande in place of the eternall creator or maker God and man for the prestes advauntage. But all is
in vayne. In no case wolde he so accept it. Nothyng lesse mynded
Christ, than to dwell in the breade, or to become a feadynge for the
bodye, whan he sayd. Take, eate. Thys is my bodye. For a contrarye
doctryne he taught hys dyscyples the yeare afore hys last supper, as we
have in the vi. chaptre of Johan. Where as he declareth hys flesh to be a
spirytuall meate, hys bloude a spirytuall drynke, and both then to be
330 receyved in faythe, the breade and the wyne remaynynge as sygnes of
hys everlastynge covenaunt. Reason is it, that he rather be judged the
receyver whych lyveth in that refeccyon, than he whych lyveth not
therby. Whych is the sowle and not the bodye, What neaded Christ to
have geven to those bodyes a newe bodylye feadynge, whych were suffycyentlye fed afore with the passe over lambe? If he had not ment therin
some other maner of thynge?

But he suffycyentlye ynough declareth hys owne meanynge, Luce 22.
Where he commaundeth us to do it in hys remembraunce, and not to
make hym agayne by blowynge upon the breade. Thys sacramentall
340 eatynge and drynkynge in hys remembraunce, S. Paule more largely
declareth, 1, Cor, 11. So oft (sayth he) as ye shall eate of that breade and
drynke of that cuppe, ye shall shewe the lordes deathe tyll he come. If ye
ernestlye marke that lattre clause (tyll he come) ye shall wele perceyve
that hys bodylye presence in the breade, is utterlye denyed there. More
over in the afore sayd xxii. chaptre of Luke, bycause we shuld not be to

---

Line 322. **Idolatrye.**: margin.
Line 324. **Not in breade.**: margin.
Line 329. **spirytuall:** margin.
Line 332. **refeccyon:** refection; spiritual refreshment.
Line 333. **the eater.**: margin.
Line 339. **Remembraunce.**: margin.
Line 343. **Tyll he come.**: margin.

scrupulose. Christ sheweth what that wyne and breade of hys supper were, yea, as he left them there, even in these wordes. I saye unto yow (sayth he) that hens forth I shall not drynke of thys frute of the vyne (or eate of thys frute of wheate) tyll the kyngedome of God become, or tyll I drynke it newe with yow in my fathers kyngedome, Math 26. Marci 14. Here calleth it he the juse of the grape or frute of the vyne, and not the bloude yssuynge from hys bodye. Yet is that cuppe (as S. Paule sayth) the partakynge of Christes bloude, and the breade that we breake there, the partakynge of Christes bodye, 1. Corint. 10. But that is in faythe and sprete, as afore in Johan.

Anne Askewe.

Then he compared it unto the kynge, and sayd, that the more hys magestees honour is set forth, the more commendable it is. Then sayd I, that it was an abhomynable shame unto hym, to make no better of the eternall worde of God, than of hys slenderlye conceyved fantasye. A farre other meanynge requyreth God therin, than mannys ydell wytte can devyse, whose doctryne is but lyes without hys heavenlye veryte. Then he asked me, if I wolde commen with some wyser man? That offer, I sayd, I wolde not refuse. Then he tolde the counsell. And so went I to my laydes agayne.

Johan Bale.

Not all unlyke is thys Pagett here, unto those graye fryres whych made of Christ but a fygure or shaddowe to their first Patrone S. Frances, as we fynde in the hystorye of hys ydolatrouse feast, and also in the boke of conformytees of Frances to Christ, written by an Italysh fryre called Bartholomeus Pisanus. In Frances (they saye) is expressed the full sygni-

350

360

370

Line 348. **Frute of the vyne.**: margin.

Line 353. **Partakynge.**: margin.

Line 358. **Pagett.**: margin.

Line 361. **Idell wytte.**: margin.

Line 367. **graye fryres**: Franciscan friars.

Line 368. **S. frances**: margin.

Line 371. **Bartholomeus Pisanus**: Bartholomew of Pisa (1262–1347), Dominican theologian, preacher, and author.

fycacyon of Christ, by reason of hys woundes. And Pagett here com-
pareth Christes presence in the sacrament, to the kynges presence, I
wote not where. And as great pleasure (I thynke) he doth the kynge
therin, as though he threwe dust in hys face or salte in hys eyes, but that
soch flatterynge Gnatoes must do their feates, though they be most
blasphemouse. Neyther heade nor tayle hath thys wytlesse comparyson
of hys, to make good hys enterpryse with thys woman. And moch
doubt it is, whether he maketh here Christ a shaddowe to the kynge, or
380   the kynge a shaddowe to Christ. But he shulde seme rather to take
Christ for the shaddowe. O gracelesse papystes, whan wyll ye be godlye
wyse? Thus to your owne dampnacyon ye worke the workes of Sathan
in deceyvableness, amonge them that perysh for not lovynge the veryte,
2 Thes. 2.

Anne Askewe.

Then came to me doctor Coxe, and doctor Robynson. In conclusyon
we coulde not agree. Then they made me a byll of the sacrament, wyllynge me to set my hande therunto, but I wolde not. Then on the son-
daye I was sore sycke, thynkynge no lesse than to dye. Therfor I desyred
390   to speake with Latymer it wolde no be. Then was I sent to Newgate in
my extremyte of syckenesse. For in all my lyfe afore, was I never in soch
payne. Thus the lorde strengthen yow in the truthe. Praye, praye praye.

Johan Bale.

What an hurlye burlye is here, for thys newe beleve? that Christ shuld
dwelle in the breade, whych is mannys creature and not gods, Christ is

---

Line 373. **A comparyson.**: margin.

Line 376. **Gnatoes:** Gnato, the parasite in Terence's play, *Eunuchus.*

Line 380. **Christ a shaddow:** margin.

Line 386. **doctor Coxe:** Richard Cox (1500–1581), humanist scholar and Reformer in Katherine Parr's circle. **doctor Robynson:** probably Thomas Robinson or Robertson (fl. 1520–1561), archdeacon of Leicester in the diocese of Lincoln. **Coxe and Robynson.**: margin.

Line 387. **byll:** formal written document.

Line 390. **Latymer:** Hugh Latimer (1485?–1555), Reformist preacher, closely associated with Katherine Parr's circle, especially the duchess of Suffolk. **Newgate:** prison for those charged with criminal offences in the city of London. **newgate:** margin.

Line 395. **creature:** creation. **In breade.**: margin.

the lyvynge breade whych came from heaven, Joan. 6. But that is not
suffycyent (saye the prestes) unlesse ye beleve also, that he is that dead
breade whych came from the waffer bakers. And therunto must ye set
your owne hande writynge, els wyll it not be allowed in the spirytuall
courte. For he that speaketh great thynges and blasphemyes (whych is
Antichrist) makynge warre with the sayntes, wyll have it so, Apo. 13. In
the Apostles tyme, and manye yeares after, it was ynough for a christen
mannys ryghtwysnesse, to beleve with the hart, that Jesus is the lorde,
and that God raysed hym up from the dead. Roma. 10. But now we
must beleve that he commeth downe agayn at the wyll of the prestes, to
be inpaned or inbreaded for their bellyes commonwelthe, lyke as he
afore came downe, at the wyll of hys heavenlye father, to be incarnated
or infleshed for our unyversall sowles helth. And unto thys we must set
our hande writynge, that we maye be knowne for Antichristes cattell.
Els shall we to stynkynge Newgate by their spirytuall appoyntment, be
we never so sycke, and within a whyle after, to the fyre in Smythfelde.
For Christes membre must tast with hym both esell and gall.

Anne Askewe.

The confessyon of me Anne Askewe, for the tyme I was in
Newgate, concernynge my beleve.

I fynde in the Scriptures (sayth she) that Christ toke the breade, and
gave it to hys dyscyples, saynge. Eate, Thys is my bodye, whych shall be
broken for yow, meanynge in substaunce hys owne verye bodye, the
breade beynge therof an onlye sygne or sacrament. For after lyke maner
of speakynge, he sayd, he wolde breake downe the temple, and in iii.
dayes buylde it up agayne, sygnyfyenge hys owne bodye by the temple,
as S. Johan declareth it. Joan. 2. And not the stonye temple it selfe. So

Line 398. **A waffer**: margin.
Line 401. **antichrist**: margin.
Line 406. **inpaned**: impaned; embodied in bread. **Inpaned**: margin.
Line 410. **newgate.**: margin.
Line 412. **esell**: eisell; vinegar. **gall**: bitter bile.
Line 416. **Breade.**: margin.
Line 421. **Temple.**: margin.

that the breade is but a remembraunce of hys death, or a sacrament of
thankes gevynge for it, wherby we are knytt unto hym by a communyon of Christen love. Although there be manye that can not perceyve
the true meanynge therof, for the vayle that Moses put over hys face
before the chyldren of Israel, that they shuld not se the clerenesse therof,
Exo. 34. and 2. Cor. 3. I perceyve the same vayle remayneth to thys
daye. But whan God shall take it awaye, than shall these blynde men se.

430   *Johan Bale.*

Ye wyll saye paraventure, that the symylytudes here of breade and of the
temple, are not lyke. For he blessyd the breade with thankes gevynge. So
wyll ye saye, an other tyme for your pleasure and advauntage, that he
blessyd the temple also, and called it both the howse of hys father and
also the howse of prayer. I praye ye, be as good here to your market
place, as ye are to your sale wares therin, for your onlye bellyes sake. For
the one wyll not do wele to your commodyte in ydelnesse, without the
other. But take good hede of it, if ye lyst. For Christ hath alredye called
one of them an howse of merchaundyse and a denne of theves, by rea-
440 son of your unlawfull occupyenge therin, Joan. 2. and Luce. 19. He
hath also promysed to overthrowe it, Math. 24. and not to leave one
stone therof standynge upon an other, Marci 13. Bycause ye have not
regarded the tyme of your vysytacyon, or not accepted hys eternall
worde of helthe. A warnynge myght the turnynge over of your monas-
teryes have bene unto yow, if ye were not, as ye are altogyther blynde.

I cannot thynke the contrarye, but he calleth the other also, as ye
handle it now a dayes in the popes olde toyes of conveyaunce, the
abhomynacyon of desolacyon, or soch an abhomynable ydoll as subver-

---

Line 424. **wherby**: emended from "wherhy".

Line 426. **Moses vayle.**: margin.

Line 434. **Blessed**: margin.

Line 438. **Temple.**: margin.

Lines 444–45. **turnynge...monasteryes**: confiscation of church properties when the English
church separated from Rome. **warnyng**: margin.

Line 447. **toyes of conveyaunce**: trifles of expression; cunning devices.

Line 448. **abhomynacyon of desolacyon**: unchristian practices; see Mark 13:14. **The masse.**:
margin.

tynge Christes true relygyon, wyll be your fynall destruccyon both here
and in the worlde to come. For ydolles are called abhomynacyon, all the   450
Scriptures over. Yet shall it endure (sayth Daniel) sumwhere, unto the
ende of all, Daniel 9. Wherby ye maye wele perceyve, that it comprehendeth not onlye the tryumphaunt stremers of Tyberius, or golden
ymages of Caligula whych both prevented the subversyon of Hierusalem, but some other ydoll els whych shuld contynewe. And it foloweth
in the Gospell texte, that he shuld sytt in the holye place for the tyme of
hys contynuaunce, Mathei 24. And not in the paganes temples. Tell me
if your Masses be done anye where els, than in your hallowed sanctu-
aryes, upon your sanctyfyed aulters, and in your holye ornamentes and
consecrate cuppes? Neyther maye anye do them, unlesse they be anoyn-   460
ted therunto of your Byshoppes and sorcerers.

Not without the holye place (sayth Christ) is that abomynacyon, but
in it, Math. 24. Antichrist (sayth S. Paule) shall sytt, not without, but
within the verye temple of God. 2. Thessalon. 2. The papacye is not
without, but within the verye churche of Christ, what though it be no
part therof, Apoca. 11. Therfor it shall be mete that we be ware, and
separate our selves from them at the admonyshmentes of hys holye
doctryne, least we be partakers with yow in their promysed dampnacyon, Apoca. 18. By the vayle over Moses face, she meaneth the blynde
confydence that manye men yet have in olde Jewysh ceremonyes and   470
beggerlye tradycyons of men, as S. Paule doth call them, Gala. 4.
Wherby the veryte of God is sore blemyshed. The spirytuall knowlege,
whych cometh by the clere doctryne of the Gospell, mynystreth no soch

---

Line 450. **Idolles.**: margin.

Line 453. **Tyberius**: Tiberius, Roman Emperor A.D. 14–37. **Tyberius**: margin.

Line 454. **Caligula**: Roman Emperor A.D. 37–41. **subversyon**: overthrow. **Caligula**: margin.

Line 458. **Masses**: margin.

Line 459. **holye ornamentes**: communion vessels.

Line 462. **antichrist**: margin.

Line 466. **Therfor**: emended from "Thefor".

Line 467. **Shurne them.**: margin. **Shurne**: shun.

Line 470. **the vayle**: margin.

impedymentes of darkenesse. But all thynges are clerelye seane to them whych are endued ther with. They can be deceyved by non of Sathans subtyle convayers, but perceyveth all thynges, whych have obtayned the pure eyes of faythe.

Anne Askewe.

480 For it is playnelye expressed in the hystorye of Bel in the Bible, that God dwelleth in nothynge materyall. O kynge (sayth Daniel) be not deceyved Daniel 14. For God wyll be in nothynge that is made with handes of men. Acto. 7. Oh what styffnecked people are these, that wyll alwayes resyst the holye Ghost. But as their fathers have done, so do they, bycause they have stonye hartes. Written by me Anne Askewe, that neyther wyshe deathe, nor yet feare hys myght, and as merye as one that is bowne towardes heaven. Truthe is layed in pryson, Luce 21, The lawe is turned to wormewood, Amos 6. And there can no ryght judgement go forth, Esaie 59.

Johan Bale.

490 Marke here how gracyouslye the lorde kepeth promyse with thys poor servaunt of hys. He that beleveth on me (sayth Christ) out of hys bellye shall flowe ryvers of lyvynge water, Joan. 7. Neyther lasheth thys woman out in her extreme troubles, language of dispayre nor yet blasphemouse wordes agaynst God with the unbelevynge, but uttereth the scriptures in wonderfull habundaunce to hys lawde and prayse. She rebuketh here the most pestylent vyce of ydolatrye. Not by olde narracyons and fables, but by the most pure worde of God, as ded Daniel and Steven. And in

---

Line 474. **Darkenesse.**: margin.

Line 477. **Syght.**: margin.

Line 480. **Daniel.**: margin.

Line 482. **styffnecked**: proud.

Line 485. **Strength.**: margin.

Line 486. **bowne**: bound; headed.

Line 490. **Promes.**: margin.

Line 496. **Faythe.**: margin.

the ende she sheweth the stronge stomacke of a most Christen martyr, in that she is neyther desyerouse of the deathe, neyther yet standeth in feare of the vyolence or extremyte therof. What a constancye was thys of a woman, frayle, tendre, yonge and most delycyouslye brought up? But that Christes sprete was myghtye in her who bad her be of good chere, For though the tyrauntes of thys worlde have power to slee the bodye, yet have they no power over the sowle, Mathei 20. Neyther have they power in the ende to demynysh one heare of the heade, Luce 21.

    She faynteth not in the myddes of the battayle, 1. Cor. 9. But persevereth stronge and stedefast to the verye ende, Math. 10. Not doubtynge but to have for her faythfull perseveraunce, the crowne of eternall lyfe, Apoc. 2. So merye am I (sayth she good creature, in the myddes of Newgate) as one that is bowne towardes heaven. A voyce was thys of a most worthye and valeaunt witnesse, in the paynefull kyngedome of pacyence, Apoca. 1. She faythfullye reckened of her lorde God, that he is not as men are, fyckle, Numeri 23. But most sure of worde and promyse, Psalme 144. And that he wolde most faythfullye kepe covenaunt with her, whan tyme shuld come, Apoca. 2. She had it most groundedlye planted in her hart, that though heaven and earthe ded passe, yet could not hys wordes and promes passe by unfulfylled Luc. 21. Ashamed maye those carnall Helchesytes be, whych have not onlye denyed the veryte of their lorde God, but also most shamefullye blasphemed and dishonoured both it and themselves for the pleasure of a yeare or ii. to dwell styll in thys fleshe. They consydre not, that he, with whome they mocke, hath power to sende them to helle, for their blasphemye, Luce 12. They shall not fynde it a matter lyght, for their

Line 500. **A martyr**: margin.

Line 501. **delycyouslye**: luxuriously.

Line 503. **Tyrauntes**: margin.

Line 506. **stedefast.**: margin.

Line 512. **Valeaunt.**: margin.

Line 517. **Faythe.**: margin.

Line 518. **Helchesytes**: Elkesaites (100–400 A.D.), a sect that followed both Jewish and Christian doctrine. **Helchesytes.**: margin.

inconstancye to be vometed out of the mouthe of God, as unsaverye morsels, Apoca. 3. Neyther shall they prove it a Christmas game, to be denyed of Christ before hys heavenlye father and hys angels, for denyenge here hys veryte, Math. 10.

Anne Askewe.

Oh forgeve us all our synnes and receyve us gracyouslye. As for the workes of our handes, we wyll nomore call upon them. For it is thu lorde that arte our God. Thu shewest ever mercye unto the fatherlesse. Oh, if they wolde do thys (sayth the lorde) I shuld heale theyr sores, yea with all my harte wolde I love them. O Ephraim, what have I to do with ydolles anye more. Who so is wyse, shall understande thys. And he that is ryghtlye enstructed, wyll regarde it. For the wayes of the lorde are ryghteouse. Soch as are godlye wyll walke in them. And as for the wycked, they wyll stomble at them, Osee 14.

Johan Bale.

All these wordes alleged she, out of the last chaptre of Oseas the prophete, where as he prophecyed the destruccyon of Samaria for the onlye vyce of ydolatrye. In the worde of the lorde, she declareth her selfe therin, to detest and abhorre that vyce above all, and to repent from the hart, that she hath at anye tyme worshypped the workes of mennys handes, eyther stone, wode, breade, wyne, or anye soch lyke, for the eternall lyvynge God. Consequentlye she confessyth hym to be her onlye God, and that she had at that tyme trust in non other els, neyther for the remyssyon of her synnes, nor yet sowles comfort at her nede. And lyke soch a wone as is unfaynedlye converted unto the lorde, she axeth of the spirytuall Ephraimytes in hys worde, what she hath anye

---

Line 526. **Inconstaunt.**: margin.

Line 529. **Prayer.**: margin.

Line 533. **Ephraim**: one of the twelve tribes of Israel; see Hosea 14:8. **ephraim.**: margin.

Line 535. **ryghtlye**: emended from "ryghlye".

Line 540. **Oseas.**: margin.

Line 544. **idolatrye.**: margin.

Line 549. **Ephraimytes.**: margin.

more to do with ydolles? or whye they shuld so tyrannouslye enforce her   550
to the worshypynge of them? consyderynge that he so ernestlye abhor-
reth them. Fynallye ii. sortes of people she reckeneth to be in the
worlde, and sheweth the dyverse maner of them. The one in the sprete
of Christ obeyeth the worde, the other in the sprete of errour contemp-
neth it. And lyke as S Paule doth saye. To the one part is it, the savour of
lyfe unto lyfe and to the other, the savour of deathe unto deathe. 2.
Corinth. 2.

Anne Askewe.

Salomon (sayth S. Steven) buylded an howse for the God of Jacob.
Howbeyt the hyest of all dwelleth not in temples made with handes. As   560
sayth the prophete, Esa. 66. Heaven is my seate and the earthe is my
fote stole. What howse wyll ye buylde for me? sayth the lorde, or what
place is it that I shall rest in? hath not my hande made all these thynges?
Acto. 7. Woman beleve me (sayth Christ to the Samarytane) the tyme is
at hande that ye shall neyther in thys mountayne nor yet at Hierusalem
worshypp the father. Ye worshypp ye wote not what, but we knowe
what we worshypp. For salvacyon commeth of the Jewes. But the houre
commeth, and now is, wherin the true worshyppers shall worshypp the
father in sprete and veryte, Joan. 4. Laboure not (sayth Christ) for the
meate that perysheth, but for that endureth into the lyfe everlastynge,   570
whych the sonne of man shall geve yow. For hym god the father hath
sealed, Joan. 6.

Johan Bale.

Here bringe she iii. stronge testymonyes of the newe testament, to confirme her owne Christen beleve therwith, and also both to confute and
condempne the most execrabyle heresye and false fylthye beleve of the

---

Line 552. **ii. sortes.**: margin.
Line 559. **S. Steven.**: margin.
Line 563. **Temple.**: margin.
Line 567. **worshypp**: margin.
Line 570. **Meate.**: margin.
Line 574. **3. bulwerkes.**: margin.

papystes. The first of them proveth, that the eternall God of heaven, wyll neyther be wrapped up in a clowte, nor yet shutte up in a boxe. The seconde declareth, that in no place of the earthe, is he to be sought, 580 neyther yet to be worshypped, but within us, in sprete and veryte. The thirde of them concludeth, that Christ is a feadynge for the sowle and not for the bodye. More over he is soch a meate, as neyther corrupteth, mouldeth, nor perysheth, neyther yet consumeth or wasteth awaye in the bellye. Lete not the Romysh popes remnaunt in Englande thynke, but in condempnynge the faythe of thys godlye woman, they also condempne the veryte of the lorde, unlesse they can discharge these iii. textes of the scripture with other iii. more effectuall. As I thynke, they shall not, nisi ad Calendas Grecas. If they allege for their part, the saynge of Christ, Math. 24. Lo here is Christ, or there is Christ. They 590 are confounded by that whych foloweth. Wherin he ernestlye chargeth hys faythfull folowers not to beleve it, callynge the teachers of soch doctryne, false anoynted, deceyvable prophetes, and sorcerouse workemen. Marci. 13.

Anne Askewe.

The summe of the condempnacyon of me Anne Askewe, at yelde hawle.

They sayd to me there, that I was an heretyke and condempned by the lawe, if I wolde stande in my opynyon. I answered that I was no heretyke, neyther yet deserved I anye deathe by the lawe of God. But as concernynge the faythe whych I uttered and wrote to the counsell, I wolde 600 not (I sayd) denye it, bycause I knew it true. Then wolde they nedes knowe, if I wolde denye the sacrament to be Christes bodye and bloude:

Line 578. **clowte:** cloth.

Line 584. **Romystes:** margin.

Line 588. **nisi...Grecas:** unless on the Greek Calends (Latin); since the Greeks did not use calends (the first of the month) to reckon time, the meaning is "never."

Line 589. **Lo, here, Se there.:** margin.

Line 592. **sorcerouse:** pertaining to sorcery.

Line 595. **yelde hawle:** Guildhall.

Line 596. **Heretyke:** margin.

Line 601. **Sacrament.:** margin.

I sayd, yea. For the same sonne of God, that was borne of the vyrgyne Marie, is now gloriouse in heaven, and wyll come agayne from thens at the lattre daye lyke as he went up, Acto. 1. And as for that ye call your God, is but a pece of breade. For a more profe therof (marke it whan ye lyst) lete it lye in the boxe but iii. monthes, and it wyll be moulde, and so turne to nothynge that is good. Wherupon I am persuaded, that it can not be God.

Johan Bale.

Christ Jesus the eternall sonne of God, was condempned of thys gener-   610
acyon for a sedicyouse heretyke, a breaker of their sabbath, a subverter of their people, a defyler of their lawes, and a destroyer of their temple or holye churche, Joan. 7. Luce 23. Mathei 26. Marci 14. and suffered deathe for it at ther procurement, by the lawe than used. Is it than anye marvele, if hys inferiour subject here, and faythfull membre do the same, at the cruell callynge on and vyolent vengeaunce of their pos-teryte? No, no, the servaunt must folowe her mastre, and the fote her heade, and maye be founde in that poynte no frear than he, Joan. 13. Saynt Augustyne dyffynynge a sacrament, calleth it in one place, a sygne of an holye thynge. In an other place a vysyble shappe of an invysyble   620
grace. Whose offyce is to instructe, anymate, and strengthen our faythe towardes God, and not to take it to it self, and so depryve hym therof. Christes bodye and bloude are neyther sygnes nor shaddowes, but the verye effectuall thynges in dede, sygnyfyed by those fygures of breade and wyne. But how that drye and corruptyble cake of theirs shuld become a God, manye men wondre now a dayes in the lyght of the

---

Line 604. **the lattre daye:** Day of Judgment.

Line 606. **Moulde in the boxe.:** margin.

Line 607. **nothynge:** emended from "nothyge".

Line 610. **Christ condempned:** margin.

Line 615. **Membre:** margin.

Line 619. **Sacrament.:** margin.

Line 624. **no sygnes:** margin.

Line 625. **cake:** communion wafer.

Gospell, lyke as they have done afore tyme also. And specyallye whye the wyne shuld not be accepted and set up for a God also so wele as the breade, consyderynge that Christ made so moche of the one as of the

630 other.

Anne Askewe.

After that they wylled me to have a prest. And than I smyled. Then they asked me, if it were not good? I sayd, I wolde confesse my fawtes to God. For I was sure that he wolde heare me with faver. And so we were condempned without a quest.

Johan Bale.

Prestes of godlye knowlege she ded not refuse. For she knewe that they are the massengers of the lorde, and that hys holye wordes are to be sought at ther mouthes, Mala. 2. Of them she instauntlye desyred to be

640 instructed, and it was denyed her, as is written afore. What shuld she than els do, but returne unto her lorde God? in whome she knewe to be habundaunce of mercye for all them whych do from the hart repent, Deutro. 30. As for the other sort of prestes, she ded not amys to laugh both them and their maynteners to scorne. For so doth God also, Psalme 2. And curseth both their absolucyons and blessynges, Mala. 2. A thefe or a murtherer shuld not have bene condempned without a quest, by the lawes of Englande. But the faythfull members of Jesus Christ, for the spyght and hate that thys worlde hath to hys veryte, must have an other kynde of tyrannye added therunto, besydes the unrygh-

650 touse bestowynge of that lawe. Wo be unto yow (sayth the eternall God of heaven by hys prophete) or dampnacyon be over your heades, that make wycked lawes, and devyse cruell thynges for the poore oppressed

---

Line 627. **the wyne.**: margin.

Line 633. **Confessyon:** margin.

Line 635. **condempned...quest:** according to law, presentment by a quest (jury) should have preceded condemnation; see Introduction, page xxvi.

Line 637. **Teachers:** margin.

Line 642. **Belles prestes.:** margin.

Line 648. **Tyrannye:** margin.

Line 652. **Wycked lawes.:** margin.

innocentes. Esaie 10. Wo unto hym that buyldeth Babylon with bloude, and maynteyneth that wycked cytie styll in unryghtwysnesse, Abacuch 2. Nahum. 3. Ezech. 24.

Anne Askewe.

My beleve whych I wrote to the counsell was thys. That the sacramentall breade was left us to be receyved with thankes gevynge, in remembraunce of Christes deathe, the onlye remedye of our sowles recover. And that therby we also receyve the whole benefyghtes and frutes of hys most gloryouse passion.

660

Johan Bale.

We reade not in the Gospell, that the materyall breade at Christes holye supper, was anye otherwyse taken of the Apostles, than thus. Neyther yet that Christ our mastre and saver requyred anye other takynge of them. If so manye straunge doubtes had bene therin, and so hygh dyffycultees, as be moved and are in controversye amonge men now a dayes both papystes and other, they coulde no more have bene left undyscussed of hym, than other hygh matters were. The dyscyples axed here neyther how nor what as doubtlesse they wolde have done, if he had mynded them to have taken the breade for hym. They thought it ynough to take it in hys remembraunce, lyke as he than playnelye taught them, Luce 22. The eatynge of hys fleshe and drynkynge of hys bloude therin, to the relevynge of their sowles thirst and hunger, they knewe to perteyne unto faythe accordynge to hys instruccyons in the vi. of Johan. What have thys godlye woman than offended, whych neyther have denyed hys incarnacyon nor deathe in thys her confessyon of faythe, but most firmelye and groundedlye trusted to receyve the frutes of them both.

670

Line 659. **Remembraunce:** margin.

Line 659. **recover:** recovery.

Line 660. **benefyghtes:** emended from "henefyghtes".

Line 670. **Apostles.:** margin.

Line 673. **Eatynge:** margin.

Line 676. **have:** has.

Line 678. **The summe of beleve.:** margin.

Anne Askewe.

680 Then wolde they nedes knowe, whether the breade in the boxe were God or no? I sayd. God is a sprete, and wyll be worshypped in sprete and truthe, Joan. 4. Then they demaunded. Wyll you planelye denye Christ to be in the sacrament? I answered that I beleved faythfullye the eternall sonne of God not to dwell there. In witnes wherof I recyted agayne the hystorye of Bel, and the ix. chaptre of Daniel, the vii. and xvii. of the Actes, and the xxiiii. of Mathew, concludynge thus. I neyther wyshe deathe, nor yet feare hys myght, God have the prayse therof with thankes.

Johan Bale.

690 Amonge the olde ydolaters, some toke the sunne, some the mone, some the fyre, some the water, with soch other lyke for their Goddes, as witnesseth Diodorus Siculus, Herodotus, Plynius, Lactantius and dyverse autours more. Now come our dottynge papystes here, wadynge yet more deper in ydolatrye, and they must have breade for their God, yea, a waffer cake whych is scarse worthye to be called breade. In what sorowfull case are Christen people now a dayes? that they maye worshypp their lorde and redemer Jhesus Christ in no shappe that hys heavenlye father hath set hym forth in, but in soch a shappe onlye as the
700 waffer baker hath ymagyned by hys slendre wytte. Gods creatures were they whom the ydolaters toke for their Goddes, but thys cake is onlye the bakers creature, for he alone made it breade, if it be breade. And so moch is it a more unworthye God than the other. Farre was it from

---

Line 681. **breade...boxe:** communion wafer in the pyx.
Line 682. **O beastlye ydolaters.:** margin.
Line 686. **O constaunt martyr.:** margin.
Line 691. **Olde ydolaters.:** margin.
Line 693. **Diodorus Siculus:** Greek historian (first century B.C.). **Herodotus:** Greek historian (484?–ca. 430 B.C.). **Plynius:** Pliny the Younger (ca. 61–113), author of the *Epistolae* (*Letters*), a record of contemporary Roman society. **Lactantius:** Latin rhetorician and theologian (ca. 240–320).
Line 695. **newe ydolaters.:** margin.
Line 700. **A waffer:** margin.

Christ to teache hys dyscyples to worshypp soch a God, eyther yet to
have hym self honoured in soch a symylytude. Nothynge is here spoken
agaynst the most holye table of the lorde, but agaynst that abhomynable
ydoll of the prestes, whych hath most detestablye blemyshed that most
godlye and wholsom communyon.

A gloryouse witnesse of the lorde ded thys blessyd woman shewe her
self, in the answere makynge to thys blasphemouse beggerye, whan she   710
sayd, that god was a sprete and no waffer cake, and wolde be worshipped in sprete and veryte, and not in superstycyon and juglynge of
the ydoll prestes. Godlye was she to denye Christes presence in that execrable ydoll but moch more godlye to geve her lyfe for it. Her alleged
scriptures prove, that God dwelleth not in temples, but a fowle
abhomynacyon in hys stede, as is shewed afore. In that she feareth not
the power of deathe, she declareth her self a most constaunt martyr
praysynge her lorde God for hys gyft. She called to remembraunce the
promyses of her lorde Jhesus Christ, that they shuld se no deathe whych
observed hys worde, Joan. 8. Agayne they that beleved on hym, shuld   720
joyfullye passe through from deathe unto lyfe, Joan. 5. And upon these
promyses, she most strongelye trusted. She consydered also with Peter,
that Christ had swallowed up deathe, to make us the heyres of everlastynge lyfe, 1. Petri 3. More over that he had overthrowne hym whych
sumtyme had the rule of deathe, Hebre. 2. And also taken awaye the
sharpe stynge of the deathe it self, Osee 13.

Line 705. **self**: emended from "felf".
Line 706. **The supper.**: margin.
Line 709. **Answere**: margin.
Line 712. **juglynge**: conjuring; trickery.
Line 713. **An ydoll.**: margin.
Line 714. **alleged**: quoted.
Line 717. **Deathe.**: margin.
Line 722. **Promyses**: margin.

Anne Askewe.

My lettre sent to the lorde Chauncellour.

The lorde God, by whome all creatures have their beynge, blesse yow
730 with the lyght of hys knowlege, amen. My dutye to your lordshyppe
remembred &c. It myght please yow to accepte thys my bolde sute as
the sute of one, whych upon due consyderacyons is moved to the same
and hopeth to obtayne. My request to your lordeshypp is only, that it
may please the same to be a meane for me to the kynges magestie, that
hys grace maye be certifyed of these fewe lynes whych I have written
concernynge my beleve. Whych whan it shall be trulye conferred with
the harde judgement geven me for the same, I thynke hys grace shall
wele perceyve me to be wayed in an uneven payer of balaunces. But I
remytt my matter and cause to almyghtye god, whych ryghtlye judgeth
740 all secretes. And thus I commende your lordeshypp to the governaunce
of hym, and felyshypp of all sayntes. Amen. By your handemayde Anne
Askewe.

Johan Bale.

In thys byll to the chauncellour, apereth it playne all frowarde affeccyons sequestred, what thys woman was. She is not here dejected with
the desperate, for unryghtouse handelynge, mournynge, cursynge, and
sorowynge, as they do commonlye. But standynge up strongelye in the
lorde, most gentyllye she obeyeth the powers, she blesseth her vexers
and persuers and wysheth them the lyght of Gods necessarye knowlege,

---

Line 728. **lorde Chauncellour:** Sir Thomas Wriothesley (1505–1550), lord chancellor who
became first earl of Southampton in 1547; he was a prominent conservative determined to stop
the Reformers.

Line 729. **To the Chauncellour.:** margin.

Line 734. **The kyng:** margin.

Line 736. **conferred:** compared.

Line 738. **payer:** pair.

Line 739. **To God.:** margin.

Line 744. **frowarde:** ardent.

Lines 744–45. **affeccyons:** feeling. **sequestered:** set aside.

Line 745. **Stronge.:** margin.

Luce 6. She consydereth the powers to be ordayned of God, Roman- 750
orum 13. And though their autoryte be sore abused, yet with Christ
and hys Apostles, she humblye submytteth herself to them, thynkynge
to suffer undre them as no yll doer but as Christes true servaunt, 1. Pet.
4. Notwithstandynge she layeth forth here both before chauncellour
and kynge, the matter wherupon she is condempned to deathe, that
they accordynge to their bounde dewtye, myght more ryghtlye waye it,
3. Regum 10. Not that she coveted therby to avoyde the deathe, but to
put them in remembraunce of their offyce concernynge the swerde,
whych they ought not vaynelye to mynystre, Roma, 13. and that they
shuld also be without excuse of ignoraunce in the great daye of reck- 760
enynge, for permittynge soch vyolence to be done, Roma. 2. In the
ende yet to make all sure, she commytteth her cause and quarell to God,
wherin she declareth her onlye hope to be in hym, and no man, Psalm.
145.

Anne Askewe.

My faythe brevelye written to the kynges grace.

I Anne Askewe of good memorie although God hath geven me the
breade of adversyte and the water of trouble, yet not so moch as my
synnes have deserved, desyre thys to be knowne to your grace. That for
as moch as I am by the lawe condempned for an evyll doer, Here I take 770
heaven and earthe to recorde, that I shall dye in my innocencye. And
accordynge to that I have sayd first, and wyll saye last, I utterlye abhorre
and detest all heresyes. And as concernynge the supper of the lorde, I
beleve so moch as Christ hath sayd therin, whych he confirmed wyth
hys most blessyd bloude. I beleve also so moch as he wylled me to
folowe and beleve, and so moch as the catholyck churche of hym doth

---

Line 750. **Obedyent.**: margin.
Line 755. **Her matter.**: margin.
Line 758. **remembraunce**: emended from "remembyaunce". **swerde**: sword; punishment.
Line 759. **Their offyce.**: margin.
Line 762. **To god.**: margin.
Line 768. **Trouble.**: margin.
Line 773. **Heresyes**: margin.

teache. For I wyll not forsake the commaundement of hys holye lyppes.
But loke what God hath charged me with hys mouthe, that have I
shutte up in my harte. And thus brevelye I ende, for lacke of lernynge.
780 Anne Askewe.

Johan Bale.

In thys she dyschargeth her self to the worlde agaynst all wrongefull
accusacyons and judgementes of heresye, what though it be not
accepted to that blynde worlde, unto whome the lorde sayd by hys
prophete. Your thoughtes are not my thoughtes, neyther yet are your
wayes my wayes. But so farre as the heavens are hyer than the earthe, so
farre do my wayes excede yours, and my thoughtes yours, Esa. 55. Heresye is not to dyssent from the churche of Rome in the doctryne of
faythe, as Lanfrancus in hys boke de Eucharistia adversus Berengarium,
790 and Thomas walden in hys worke of sermons, Ser. 21. dyffyneth it. But
heresye is a voluntarye dyssentynge from the veryte of the scriptures of
God, and also a blasphemouse depravynge of them, for the wretched
bellyes sake, and to maynteyne the pompes of thys worlde. Thus is it
dyffyned of S. Hierome in commentariis Hiere. S. Augustyne and Isidorus agreynge to the same, Consydre than whether he be the thefe that
sytteth upon the benche, or he that standeth at the barre? The popysh
clergye that condempneth, or the innocent that is condempned? Atha-

---

Line 778. **Faythe.**: margin.

Line 782. **dyschargeth**: clears; acquits. **Dyscharge.**: margin.

Line 788. **Heresye.**: margin.

Line 789. **Lanfrancus...Berengarium**: Lanfranc (1005–1089), archbishop of Canterbury,
wrote (ca. 1070) *De Sacramento Corporis et Sanguinis Christi* (*Concerning the Sacrament of the
Body and Blood of Christ*) against Berengar of Tours who had argued that the eucharist was a
symbol rather than the real body and blood of Christ.

Line 790. **Thomas walden**: Thomas Walden, also known as Thomas Netter (d. 1430), a
Carmelite author who opposed Wycliffe and Hus.

Line 790. **dyffyneth**: emended from "Dyffyneth".

Line 791. **What it is.**: margin,

Lines 794–95. **S. Hierome**: Saint Jerome (ca. 341–ca. 420), Latin Church Father.
commentariis... Isidorus: the two Latin Church Fathers, Augustine (354–430) and Isidore of
Seville (560–636), in their commentaries on Jerome.

Lines 795–96. **he...benche**: the judge. **he...barre**: the prisoner.

Line 797. **Who is the heretyke.**: margin.

nasius in hys boke de fuga adversus Arrianos, calleth them the heretykes, whych seketh to have the Christen belevers murthered as ded the
seyd Arryanes. Thys godlye woman, hyr innocencye to clere, laboureth   800
not here to an inferyour membre of the realme, but to the head therof,
the kynges owne persone. Whome she beleveth to be the hygh mynyster
of God, the father of the lande, and upholder of the people, Sapi. 6.
that he myght faythfullye and ryghtlye judge her cause. But who can
thynke that ever it came before hym? Not I, for my part.

Anne Askewe.

The effect of my examynacyon and handelynge, sens my departure from
Newgate.

On tewesday I was sent from newgate to the sygne of the crowne where
as mastre Ryche and the Byshopp of London with all their power and   810
flatterynge wordes went aboute to persuade me from God. But I ded
not exteme their glosynge pretenses. Then came there to me Nicolas
Shaxton, and counselled me to recant as he had done. Then I sayd to
hym, that it had bene good for hym, never to have bene borne with
manye other lyke wordes.

Lines 797–98. **Athanasius:** Egyptian theologian (ca. 293–373), chief orthodox Christian
defender against the heresy of Arianism.

Line 798. **de fuga adversus Arrianos:** Athanasius wrote *Orations against the Arians* and *Apology
for his Flight;* Bale combines the Latin titles. Arians were followers of Arius, a heretic who
declared that Christ was not of the same substance or essence as God.

Line 803. **the kynge:** margin.

Line 807. **departure:** emended from "depature".

Line 809. **the sygne of the crowne:** an inn identified by the sign over its door.

Line 810. **mastre Ryche:** Richard Rich (1496?–1567), member of the conservative court faction; see Introduction, page xxvii. **Ryche.:** margin.

Line 812. **exteme:** esteem.

Line 813. **Nicolas Shaxton:** Nicholas Shaxton (1485?–1556), former bishop of Salisbury,
condemned for heresy on the same day as Askew; see Introduction, pages xxii–xxiii. **Shaxton:**
margin.

Line 814. **it...borne:** cf. Matt. 26:24.

Johan Bale.

After that Christ had ones overcommen Sathan in the desart, where he
had fasted longe tyme, Math. 4. We reade not in the scriptures that he
was moch assaulted or vexed of the worlde, the fleshe, and the fyende,
820   whych are reckened the common enemyes of man. But yet we fynde in
the Gospell, that these iii. ghostlye enemyes, the prelates, the prestes,
and the lawers, or the Byshoppes, pharysees, and scrybes, never left hym
afterwarde, tyll they had throughlye procured hys deathe. Marke it (I
desyre yow) if it be here anye otherwyse wyth hys dere membre. What
other enemyes tempteth here Anne Askewe, than the Byshopp of London, mastre Ryche, and doctor Shaxton, besydes the great Cayphas of
Wynchestre with hys spyghtfull (I shuld saye) spirytuall rable, or who
els procureth her deathe? Ye wyll thynke paraventure, concernynge mastre Ryche, that though he be an enemye, yet is he no spirytuall enemye,
830   bycause he is not anoynted with the popes grese. But than are ye moch
deceyved. For it is the sprete (of blasphemye, avaryce, and malyce) and
not the oyle, that maketh them spirytuall. And whereas they are anoynted in the hande with oyle, he is in the hart anoynted with the sprete of
Mammon, betraynge with Judas at the Byshoppes malycyouse callynge
on, the poor innocent sowles for moneye, or at the least for an amby-
cyouse faver.

    O Shaxton, I speake now unto the and (I thynke) in the voyce of
God. What devyll bywytched the to playe thys most blasphemouse
part? as to become of a faythfull teacher, a temptynge sprete? Was it not
840   ynough, that thu and soch as thu art, had forsaken your lorde God and

---

Line 817. **Sathan.**: margin.

Line 821. **3. ghostlye enemyes.**: margin.

Line 826. **Cayphas:** in Matthew 26:57, the high priest to whom Christ was brought; here, the bishop of Winchester.

Line 827. **rable:** rabble; crowd.

Line 827. **Wynchestre.**: margin.

Line 830. **grese:** disparaging reference to holy oil used to anoint priests.

Line 830. **spirytuall:** margin.

Line 834. **Mammon:** devil of covetousness. **Mammon:** margin.

Line 837. **Shaxton.**: margin.

troden hys veryte most unreverentlye undre your fete, but with soch
feates (as thys is) thu must yet procure the a more deper, or double
dampnacyon? Ryghtlye sayd thys true servaunt of God, that it had bene
better for the and thy fellawes, that ye never had bene borne. Ye were
called of God, to a most blessyd offyce. If ye had bene worthye that
vocacyon (as ye are but swyne, Mathei 7.) ye had persevered faythfull
and constaunt to the ende, Mathei 10. and so have worthelye receyved
the crowne therof, Apoca. 2. But the love of your beastlye fleshe, hath
verye farre in yow overwayed the love of the lorde Jesus Christ. Ye now
shewe what ye are in dede, even waverynge reedes with everye blast   850
moved, Luce 7. Yea verye faynt harted cowardes and hypocrytes, Apo. 3.
Ye abyde not in the shepe folde as true shepeherdes, but ye flee lyke
hyrelynges, Joan. 10. Had ye bene buylded upon the harde rocke, as ye
were on the fyckle sande, Math. 7. neyther Romysh floodes nor Englysh
wyndes had over throwne yow. But now loke onlye, after your deser-
vynge, for thys terryble judgement of God. For them (sayth S. Paule)
whych voluntarylye blaspheme the truthe, after they have receyved the
Gospell in faythe and in the holye Ghost, remayneth no expyacyon of
synne, but the fearfull judgement of hell fyre. For a mocke have they
made of the sonne of God, Hebreo. 6. and 10.   860

Anne Askewe.

Then mastre Riche sent me to the tower, where I remayned tyll thre of
the clocke. Then came Riche and one of the counsell, chargynge me
upon my obedyence, to shewe unto them, if I knewe man or woman of
my secte. My answere was, that I knewe none, Then they asked me of

---

Line 841. **Double.**: margin.
Line 845. **Unworthy**: margin.
Line 851. **Hypocrytes.**: margin.
Line 857. **Judgement.**: margin.
Line 862. **tower**: the Tower of London.
Line 862. **Ryche.**: margin.
Line 865. **my secte**: Reformers.

my ladye of Sothfolke, my ladye of Sussex, my ladye of Hertforde, my
ladye Dennye, and my ladye Fizwyllyams. I sayd, if I shuld pronounce
anye thynge agaynst them, that I were not hable to prove it.

Johan Bale.

870   Never was there soche turmoylynge on the earthe, as is now a dayes for
that wretched blynde kyngedome of the Romysh pope. But trust upon
it trulye, ye terryble termagauntes of hell, There is no practyse, there is
no wysdome, there is no counsell, that can agaynst the lorde prevayle,
Proverb. 21. Ye loke to be obeyed in all devylyshnesse. But ye consydre
not, that where God is dyshonoured by your obedyence, there
belongeth non to yow, Acto. 5. Ye have moch a do here with sectes, as
though it were a great heresye, ryghtlye to beleve in our lorde Jesus
Christ, after the Gospell and not after your Romysh father. But where
was ever yet a more pestylent and devylysh secte, than is that Sodomy-
880   tysh secte, whom ye here so ernestlye maynteyne with tyrannye and
myschefe? How gredylye seke yow the slaughter of Gods true servauntes, ye bloudthurstye wolves? as the holye Ghost doth call yow.
Psal. 25. If the vertuouse ladyes and most noble women, whose lyves ye
cruellye seke in your madde ragynge furye, as ravyshynge lyons in the
darke, Psal. 9. have throwne of their shulders for Christes easye and
gentyll burdene, Mathei 11, the popes uneasye and importable yoke,

---

Line 866. **my ladye of Sothfolke:** Catherine Brandon, duchess of Suffolk (1519/20–1580), a
Reformist patron and friend of Katherine Parr.   **my ladye of Sussex:** Anne Radcliffe, countess
of Sussex.   **my ladye of Hertforde:** Anne Stanhope, countess of Hertford (1497–1587), one of
Katherine Parr's circle and wife of Edward Seymour, afterwards Protector Somerset.

Line 867. **my ladye Dennye:** Lady Joan Denny, wife of Henry VIII's privy councillor, Sir
Anthony Denny.   **my ladye Fizwyllyams:** possibly Jane Ormond, third wife and widow of Sir
William FitzWilliam (d. 1534), a member of Henry VIII's Privy Council, and grandfather of
Anne Cooke Bacon. **Christen ladyes.:** margin.

Line 870. **Babylon.:** margin.

Line 875. **Obedyence.:** margin.

Lines 879–80. **Sodomytysh:** Sodom-like; see Gen. 19 and Rev. 11:8. **A secte.:** margin.

Line 883. **Ladyes.:** margin.

Line 886. **importable:** unbearable.

Luce 11. Happye are they that ever they were borne. For therby have they procured, a great quyetnesse and helthe to their sowles. For Christes worde is quycke, and bryngeth nothynge els to the sowle but lyfe, Hebreo. 4. The popes olde tradycyons and customes, beynge but the wysdome of the fleshe, are verye poyson and deathe, Roma. 8. 890

Anne Askewe.

Then sayd they unto me, that the kynge was infourmed, that I coulde name, if I wolde a great nombre of my secte. Then I answered, that the kynge was as wele deceyved in that behalfe, as dyssembled with in other matters.

Johan Bale.

Great Assuerus, kynge of the Perseanes and Medes, was infourmed also, that the servaunt of God Mardocheus was a traytour, whych neverthe-lesse had dyscovered ii. traytours a lyttle afore, and so saved the kynges lyfe, Hester 3. But Haman that false counseller, whych so infourmed the kynge, was in the ende proved a traytour in dede (as I doubt it not but some of these wyll be founde after thys) and was worthelye hanged for it, so fallynge into the snare that hys selfe had prepared for other, Psal. 7. Albertus Pyghius, Cochleus, Eckius, and soch other pestylent papystes, have fylled all Christendome with raylynge bokes of our kynge, for renouncynge the Romysh popes obedyence, but therof ye infourme not hys grace. No, neyther excuse ye, nor yet defende ye hys godlye acte in that behalfe. But ye are (as apereth) verye well contented, that he be yll spoken of for it. 910

Line 889. **Helthe.**: margin.

Line 893. **The kyng**: margin.

Line 899. **Mardocheus**: Mordecai; see Esther 2:5 ff. **Mardocheus.**: margin.

Line 903. **Haman.**: margin.

Line 905. **Albertus Pyghius**: Pighius (1490–1542), Dutch Catholic theologian. **Cochleus**: Johannes Cochlaeus (1479–1552), theologian, author of polemical tracts opposing Luther. **Eckius**: Johann Eck (1486–1543), theologian, opponent of Luther. **Papystes**: margin.

Line 909. **Craftye.**: margin.

It is not a yeare a go, sens our wynchestre was at Utrecht in hollande
(where as the seyd Pyghius dwelt, and was for hys papystrye in great
autoryte) I knowe certaynlye, the man there was moch more easye to
please in that cause, than in an other slevelesse matter of hys owne concernynge Martyne Bucer. Hys gallauntes also warraunted there (I
knowe to whome) that the Romysh pope, by the Emprours good helpe,
shuld within fewe yeares have in Englande, as great autoryte as ever he
had afore. I doubt not but sumwhat they knewe of their masters good
conveyaunce, but of thys is not the kynge infourmed. I coulde write
here of manye other mysteryes, concernynge the observaunt fryres and
other raungynge Rome ronners, what newes they receyve wekelye out of
Englande from the papystes there, and in what hope they are put, of
their returne thydre agayne. For I have seane ther braggynge letters
therof, sent from Emeryck to Frislande, and from the cuntraye of
Coleyne into Westphalye. Of thys and soch other conveyaunces, the
kynge is not yet infourmed, but (I trust) he shall be.

Anne Askewe.

Then commaunded they me to shewe, how I was maynteyned in the
Counter, and who wylled me to stycke by my opynyon. I sayd that
there was no creature, that therin ded strengthen me. And as for the
helpe that I had in the Counter, it was by the meanes of my mayde. For
as she went abroade in the stretes, she made to the prentyses, and they
by her ded sende me moneye. But who they were, I never knewe.

920

930

Line 912. **Pyghius.**: margin.
Line 914. **slevelesse:** sleeveless; vain, unprofitable.
Line 915. **Martyne Bucer:** continental Reformer (1491–1551), mediator between Luther and Zwingli. **gallauntes:** men of fashion and pleasure. **Bucer.**: margin.
Line 920. **observaunt fryres:** Franciscan friars following the earliest rules of the order. **Observauntes.**: margin.
Line 924. **Emeryck** Emmerich, town in Germany. **Frislande:** Friesland, province in the Netherlands.
Line 924. **Letters.**: margin.
Line 925. **Coleyene:** Cologne, city in Germany.
Line 925. **Westphalye:** Westfalen, state in Germany.
Line 930. **to accuse.**: margin.
Line 932. **prentyses:** apprentices.

Johan Bale.

Joseph was in pryson undre Pharao the fearce kynge of Egypte, yet was he favourablye handeled and no man forbydden to consort hym, Gene. 39. Whan Johan Baptist was in stronge duraunce undre Herode the tyraunt of Galile, hys dyscyples ded frelye vysytt hym, and were not rebuked for it, Math. 11. Paule beynge emprysoned and in cheanes at Rome, undre the most furyouse tyraunte Nero, was never blamed for   940 sendynge hys servaunt Onesimus abroade, nor yet for writynge by hym to hys fryndes for socour, Philem. 1. Neyther yet was Philemon troubled for relevynge hym there by the seyd Onesimus, nor yet hys olde frynde Onesipherus, for personallye there vysytynge hym, and supportynge hym with hys moneye, lyke as he had done afore also at Ephesus. Now conferre these storyes and soch other lyke, with the present handelynge of Anne Askewe and ye shall wele perceyve our Englysh rulers and judges in their newe Christyanyte of renouncynge the pope, to excede all other tyrauntes in all crueltye, spyght and vengeaunce. But loke to have it no otherwyse, so longe as mytred prelates are of counsell.   950 Be ashamed cruell beastes, be ashamed, for all Christendome wondereth on your madnesse above all.

Anne Askewe.

Then they sayd, that there were dyverse gentylwomen, that gave me moneye. But I knewe not their names. Then they sayd that there were dyverse ladyes, whych had sent me moneye. I answered, that there was a man in a blewe coate, whych delyvered me ,x, shyllynges, and sayd that

---

Line 936. **consort:** keep company with. **Joseph.:** margin.
Line 937. **duraunce:** imprisonment.
Line 939. **Paule.:** margin.
Line 941. **Onesymus.:** margin.
Line 947. **Judges.:** margin.
Line 950. **of counsell:** advisors.
Line 951. **Prelates:** margin.
Line 954. **Gentyllwomen.:** margin.

my ladye of Hertforde sent it me. And an other in a vyolet coate ded
geve me viii. shyllynges, and sayd that my ladye Dennye sent it me.
960 Whether it were true or no, I can not tell. For I am not suer who sent it
me, but as the men ded saye.

Johan Bale.

In the tyme of Christes preachynge what though the holye clergye wer
than not pleased therwith, but judged it (as they do styll to thys daye)
most horryble heresye, yet serten noble women, as Marye Magdalene,
Joanna the wyfe of Chusa Herodes hygh stewarde, Susanna, and manye
other folowed hym from Galile, and mynystred unto hym of their substaunce, concernynge hys bodylye nedes Luce 8. These with other more,
after he was by the seyd clergye done to most cruell deathe for the veryte
970 preachynge, both prepared oyntmentes and spyces to anoynte hys
bodye, Luce 24. and also proclamed abroade hys gloryouse resurrec-
cyon to hys Apostles and other, Joan. 20 contrarye to the Byshoppes
inhybycyon, Acto. 4. Yet reade we not that anye man or woman was
racked for the accusement of them. A woman amonge the Macedo-
nyanes, dwellynge in the cytie of Thyatira, and called Lydia by name, a
purple seller verye rytche in merchaundyse, receyved Paule, Sylas, and
Timothe with other suspected bretherne in to her howse and
habundauntly releved them there. Act. 16. yet was she not troubled for
it. In lyke maner at Thessalonica, a great nombre of the Grekes and
980 manye noble women amonge them, beleved Paules forbydden
doctryne, and resorted boldelye both to hym and to Sylas, Acto. 17. yet
were they not cruellye handeled for it.

Be ashamed than ye tyrauntes of Englande, that your horryble tyran-

---

Line 958. **Ladyes.**: margin.
Line 962. **Christ.**: margin.
Line 966. **Noblewomen.**: margin.
Line 972. **Byshoppes**: emended from "Byhoppes".
Line 974. **accusement**: accusation.
Line 975. **Lydia.**: margin.
Line 979. **Noble women.**: margin.
Line 983. **Tyrauntes**: margin.

nyes shuld excede all other, Jewes or Gentyles, turkes or Idolaters. More
noble were these women here rehearced, for thus relevynge Christ and
hys members, than for anye other acte, eyther yet degre of nobylyte. For
whereas all other have peryshed, these shall never perysh, but be con-
served in the most noble and worthye scriptures of God, the tyrannouse
Byshoppes and prestes with their tyrannouse maynteners there condempned. A through Christen charyte is not lightlye terryfyed, with the   990
tempestes of worldlye afflicyons nomore than true faythe is changed in
men that be Christenlye constaunt. Soch can not chose but consydre,
that it is both gloryouse to be afflicted for Christ, 1. Petri 3. and also
most merytoryouse to releve them here in their afflyccyons, Math. 25.
Unto that Christen offyce hath Christ promysed the lyfe everlastynge at
the lattre daye, where as Masse hearynge is lyke to remayne without
rewarde, except it be in helle for ydolatrye and blasphemye. Not unto
them that in pryson vysyteth murtherers and theves (if ye marke wele
the texte) is thys rewarde promysed. For they are not there allowed for
Christes dere members, but unto them that releve the afflicted for hys   1000
verytees sake.

Anne Askewe.

Then they sayd, there were of the counsell that ded maynteyne me. And
I sayd, no. Then they ded put me on the racke, bycause I confessed no
ladyes nor gentyllwomen to be of my opynyon, and theron they kepte
me a longe tyme. And bycause I laye styll and ded not crye, my lorde
Chauncellour and mastre Ryche, toke peynes to racke me their owne
handes, tyll I was nygh dead.

Johan Bale.

Nicodemus, one of the hygh counsell, was sore rebuked amonge the   1010

Line 989. **Prelates.**: margin.

Line 991. **Faythe.**: margin.

Line 996. **Masse hearynge**: margin.

Line 1004. **racke**: an instrument of torture, a frame with a roller at each end to which the victim's wrists and ankles were tied; the joints were stretched by rotating the rollers.

Line 1005. **the racke**: margin.

Line 1010. **Nicodemus.**: margin.

senyours of the Jewes, for defendyng Christes innocencye, whan they
went aboute to slee hym, Joan. 7. And therfor it is no newe thynge that
Christes doctryne hath supportacyon amonge the counsels of thys
worlde. All men be not of one corrupted appetyte, nor yet of one ungracyouse dyete. Christ promysed hys dyscyples, that they in one
howsholde shuld fynde both hys enemyes and fryndes. I am come
(sayth he) to set man at varyaunce agaynst hys father, and the doughter
agaynst her mother, and the doughter in lawe agaynst the mother in
lawe. He that loveth hys father or mother, hys sonne or doughter, hys
1020 prynce or governour, above me, he is not mete for me, Math. 10. I feare
me thys wyll be judged hygh treason. But no matter. So longe as it is
Christes worde, he shall be also undre the same judgement of treason.
Lete no man care to be condempned with hym, for he in the ende shall
be hable to rectyfye all wronges.

   Marke here an example most wonderfull, and se how madlye in their
ragynge furyes, men forget themselves and lose their ryght wittes now a
dayes. A kynges hygh counseller, a Judge over lyfe and deathe, yea, a
lorde Chauncellour of a most noble realme, is now become a most vyle
slave for Antichrist, and a most cruell tormentoure. Without all dys-
1030 cressyon, honestye, or manhode, he casteth of hys gowne, and taketh
here upon hym the most vyle offyce of an hangeman and pulleth at the
racke most vyllanouslye. O Wrisleye and Riche ii. false christianes and
blasphemouse apostataes from God. What chaplayne of the pope hath
inchaunted yow, or what devyll of helle bewytched yow to execute upon
a poore condempned woman, so prodygyouse a kynde of tyrannye?
Even the verye Mammon of inyquyte, and that insacyable hunger of

---

Line 1016. **Fryndes.**: margin.
Line 1020. **mete**: suitable.
Line 1021. **hygh treason.**: margin.
Line 1026. **Frenesye.**: margin.
Line 1029. **A tourmentour.**: margin.
Line 1030. **casteth...gowne**: removed his outer robe.
Line 1032. **Wrisleye and Riche.**: margin.
Line 1033. **apostataes**: apostates (Latin); those who forsake their religious faith.
Line 1036. **Mammon.**: margin.

avarice, whych compelled Judas to betray unto deathe hys most lovynge master, Joan. 12. The wynnynges were not small that ye reckened upon, whan ye toke on ye that cruell enterpryse, and wolde have had so many great men and women accused. But what els have ye wonne in the ende, than perpetuall shame and confusyon? God hath suffered yow so to dyscover your owne myscheves, that ye shall nomore be forgotten of the worlde, than are now Adonisedech, Saul, Hieroboam, Manasses, Olophernes, Haman, Tryphon, Herode, Nero, Trajanus, and soche other horryble tyrauntes.

And as concernynge the innocent woman, whom yow so cruellye tormented. Where coulde be seane a more clere and open experyment of Christes dere membre, than in her myghtye sufferynges? lyke a lambe she laye styll without noyse of cryenge, and suffered your uttermost vyolence, tyll the synnowes of her armes were broken, and the strynges of her eys peryshed in her heade. Ryght farre doth it passe the strength of a yonge, tendre, weake, and sycke woman (as she was at that tyme to your more confusyon) to abyde so vyolent handelynge, yea, or yet of the strongest man that lyveth. Thynke not therfor but that Christ hath suffered in her, and so myghtelye shewed hys power, that in her weakenesse he hath laughed your madde enterpryses to scorne, Psalm. 2. Where was the feare of God, ye tyrauntes? Where was your christen professyon, ye helle houndes? Where was your othe and promes to do true justyce, ye abhomynable perjures, whan ye went aboute these cursed feates? More fytt are ye for swyne kepynge, than to be of a pryncts counsell, or

---

Line 1040. **wretches**: margin.

Lines 1043–44. **Adonisedech**: Adonizedec, king of Jerusalem; see Josh. 10. **Saul**: king of Isreal who disobeys God in 1 Sam. 15–16. **Hieroboam**: Jeroboam, king of Israel who turns to idolatry in 1 Kings 12–14. **Manasses**: Manasseh, the wicked king of Judah in Pr. of Man. **Olophernes**: Holofernes, Assyrian general in Jth 2 ff. **Tryphon**: general of the Syrian army 150–145 B.C.; see 1 Macc. 12:39 ff. **Trajanus**: Trajan, Roman Emperor A.D. 98–117. **Tyrauntes**: margin.

Line 1047. **A lambe.**: margin.

Line 1050. **synnowes**: sinews or tendons, nerves. **strynges**: nerves.

Line 1052. **Tyrauntes**: margin.

Line 1054. **Christ.**: margin.

Line 1059. **perjures**: perjurers. **Perjures**: margin.

yet to governe a Christen commen welthe. If Christ have sayd unto them whych do but offende hys lytle ones that beleve in hym, that it were better they had a mylstone tyed aboute thyir neckes, and were so throwne into the bottom of the see, Luce 17. What wyll he saye to them that so vyllaynouslye pull at the racke in ther myschevouse malyce? These are but warnynges take hede if ye lyst, for a full sorowfull plage wyll folowe hereafter.

Anne Askewe.

Then the lyefetenaunt caused me to be loused from the racke. Inconty-
1070 nentlye I swounded, and then they recovered me agayne. After that I sate ii. longe houres reasonynge with my lorde Chauncellour upon the bare floore, where as he with manye flatterynge wordes, persuaded me to leave my opynyon. But my lorde God (I thanke hys everlastynge goodnesse) gave me grace to persever, and wyll do (I hope) to the verye ende.

Johan Bale.

Evermore have the olde modye tyrauntes, used thys practyse of devylysh-nesse. As they have perceyved themselves not to prevayle by extreme handelynges they have sought to prove masteryes by the contrarye.
1080 With gaye glosynge wordes and fayre flatterynge promyses, they have craftelye cunpassed the servauntes of God, to cause them consent to their wyckednesse. And in thys temptynge occupacyon, are Wrisleye and Riche verye connynge. Notwithstandynge they shall never fynde the chosen of God, all one with the forsaken reprobates. The electe ves-

---

Line 1063. **A mylstone.**: margin.

Line 1069. **lyefetenaunt**: the lieutenant of the Tower, Sir Anthony Knevet. See Textual Introduction, page liv. **Unlosed.**: margin.

Lines 1069–70. **Incontynentlye**: immediately. **swounded**: swooned.

Line 1071. **reasonynge**: holding a discussion.

Line 1074. **Persever.**: margin.

Line 1077. **modye**: moody; haughty. **Practyse.**: margin.

Line 1080. **glosynge**: flattering.

Line 1081. **cunpassed**: compassed; besieged.

Line 1082. **Temptacyon**: margin.

sels holde the eternall God for their most specyall treasure, and have hym in soch inteire love, that they had moch lever to lose themselves, than hym. The wicked desperates have the voluptuouse pleasures of thys vayne worlde so dere, that they had lever to forsake God and all hys workes, than to be sequestred from them. Thys godlye yonge woman referreth prayse unto her lorde God, that he hath not left her in thys paynefull conflycte for hys verytees sake, but persevered stronge with her, beynge in hope that he wolde so styll contynewe with her, to the verye ende, as without fayle he ded.

Manye men sore wondre now a dayes that Wrisleye whych was in my lorde Cromwels tyme so ernest a doer agaynst the pope, is now becomen agayne for hys pedlarye wares so myghte a captayne. But they remembre not the common adage, that honour changeth maners, and lucre judgementes. These great ynne kepers (they saye) had lever to have one good horse man to hoste, than vi. men on fote, specyallye if they weare velvet whodes or fyne rochettes. What els foloweth Christ but beggerye and sorowes whych are verye hatefull to the worlde? Where fatnesse is cawte of everye mannys laboure, there is yet sumwhat to be loked for, If hys christen zele be soch, that he wyll have no she heretykes unponnyshed lete hym do first of all, as we reade of dyverse ryghtfull governers amonge the heythen. Lete hym serche hys owne howse wele. Paraventure he maye fynde aboute my ladye hys wyfe, a rellyck of no lyttle vertu, a practyse of Pythagoras, or an olde midwyves blessynge,

---

Line 1086. **lever:** rather. **3. sortes.:** margin.

Line 1091. **Prayse.:** margin.

Line 1094. **Wrisleye:** margin.

Line 1095. **Cromwels tyme:** in the 1530s when Thomas Cromwell was Henry VIII's chief advisor and architect of the English Reformation.

Line 1098. **ynne kepers.:** margin.

Line 1100. **whodes:** hoods.

Line 1102. **fatnesse:** luxury. **cawte:** caught; attained.

Line 1103. **Profyght:** margin.

Line 1106. **my ladye.:** margin.

Line 1107. **Pythagoras:** Greek philosopher (ca. 580–ca. 500 B.C.) to whom early modern writers attributed the idea of the transmigration of souls.

whych she carryeth closelye on her, for preservacyon of her honoure.
Her opynyon is (folke saye) that so longe as she hath that upon her, her
1110 worldlye worshyp can never decaye. I praye God thys provysyon in
short space deceyveth her not as it hath done pope Silvester the seconde,
and as it ded of late years Thomas wolsye our late Cardynall. Thys heresye goeth neyther to the racke nor the fyre, to Newgate nor yet Smythfelde, as contynuallye doth the pore Gospell.

Anne Askewe.

Then was I brought to an howse, and layed in a bed, with as werye and
payneful bones, as ever had pacyent Job, I thanke my lorde God therof.
Then my lorde Chauncellour sent me worde if I wolde leave my opynyon, I shuld want nothynge. If I wolde not, I shuld fourth to Newgate,
1120 and so be burned. I sent hym agayne worde, that I wolde rather dye,
than to breake my faythe. Thus the lorde open the eyes of their blynde
hartes, that the truthe maye take place. Fare wele dere frynde, and
praye, praye, praye.

Johan Bale.

Beholde in thys last parcell, most evydent sygnes of a Christen martyr
and fayth full witnesse of God, besydes that went afore. She allegeth not
in all thys longe processe, lyenge legendes, popysh fables, nor yet olde
wyves parables, but the most lyvelye autorytees and examples of the
sacred Byble. She putteth her selfe here in remembraunce, not of des-
1130 perate Cayne, nor yet of sorowfull Judas, but of most pacyent Job, for
example of godlye sufferaunce. For Anguysh and payne of her broken

---

Line 1110. **Honoure:** margin.

Line 1111. **pope Silvester:** Gerbert of Aurillac (ca. 945–1003), pope 999–1003; legends
attributed his great learning to magical or devilish powers.

Line 1112. **Thomas wolsye:** Thomas Wolsey (ca. 1475–1530), cardinal, lord chancellor, and
chief advisor to Henry VIII, 1515–1529. **cardynall:** margin.

Line 1118. **A tyraunt.:** margin.

Line 1121. **Swete woman.:** margin.

Line 1125. **A martyr:** margin.

Line 1129. **Gods creature.:** margin.

joyntes and broused armes and eyes, she curseth not the tyme that ever she was borne, as the maner of the unfaythfull is. But she hyghlye magnyfyeth and prayseth God for it. Neyther was she perverted with flatterynge promyses, nor yet overcommen with terryble threttenynges of deathe. Neyther doubted she the stynke of Newgate, nor yet the burnynge fyer in Smythfelde. But coveted rather deathe of her bodye for the syncere doctryne of Christ, than lyfe of the same undre the ydolatrouse doctryne of the Romysh pope. She desyred God to take mercye of her enemyes, and exhorted all Christen people instauntlye to praye 1140
for them. If these be not the frutes of a true belever, what other frutes els can we axe?

Anne Askewes answere unto Johan Lassels letter.

Oh frynde most derelye beloved in God. I marvele not a lyttle, what shuld move yow, to judge in me so slendre a faythe, as to feare deathe, whych is the ende of all myserye. In the lorde I desyre yow, not to beleve of me soch wyckednesse. For I doubt it not, but God wyll perfourme hys worke in me, lyke as he hath begonne.

Johan Bale.

I wolde but knowe of them whych are common readers of chronycles 1150
and Sayntes lyves, where they ever redde of a more fervent and lyvelye faythe than was in thys godlye yonge woman. As lyght a matter estemed she deathe, as ded Eleazarus that aunclent senyour, or yet the vii. Machabees with their most worthye mother, 2. Mach. 6. and 7. For she sayd, that it was but the ende of all sorowes. She reckened not with the covet-

---

Line 1134. **Christes servaunt.**: margin.

Line 1136. **doubted:** feared.

Line 1141. **A verye Saynt.**: margin.

Line 1143. **Johan Lassels:** John Lassells; Reformer from Nottinghamshire and an attendant of the King's Chamber who was condemned with Askew. See page 154.

Line 1145. **Deathe.**: margin.

Line 1150. **Chronycles.**: margin.

Line 1153. **Eleazarus:** see 2 Macc. 6:18.

Line 1154. **Deathe.**: margin.

ouse man, the remembraunce therof bytter, Eccle. 14. But with the ryghteouse she thought it a most redye and swyfte passage unto lyfe, Joan. 5. The feare of deathe judged she great wyckednesse in a Christen belever, and was in full hope that God wolde not suffre her to be trou-
1160 bled therwith. For whye, deathe loseth us no lyfe, but bryngeth it in unto us lyke as the harde wynter bryngeth in the most plesaunt somer. Who can thynke, whan the sunne goeth downe, that it utterlye so pery-sheth? Death unto the ryghteouse belever, is as a profytable harvest, whych after sweate and labour bryngeth in most dylectable frutes. Non otherwyse thought it Anne Askewe, than a verye entraunce of lyfe, whan she had it thus in desyre, and faythfullye trusted with Paule, that God wolde fynysh in her that he than begonne to hys owne glorye. Philippen. 1.

Anne Askewe.

1170 I understande, the counsell is not a lyttle dyspleased, that it shulde be reported abroade, that I was racked in the towre. They saye now, that they ded there, was but to fear me. Wherby I perceyve, they are ashamed of their uncomelye doynges, and feare moch least the kynges mageste shulde have infourmacyon therof. Wherfor they wolde no man to noyse it. Well, their crueltye God forgeve them. Your hart in Christ Jesu. Fare wele, and praye.

Johan Bale.

Hypocrytes and tyrauntes wolde never be gladlye knowne abroade, for that they are in dede. But for that they are not, they loke alwayes to be
1180 gloryouslye noysed. Wrisleye and Ryche wolde yet be judged of the

---

Line 1160. **No feare.**: margin.
Line 1163. **Harvest.**: margin.
Line 1164. **sweate**: emended from "fweate".
Line 1171. **Racked.**: margin.
Line 1172. **fear**: frighten.
Line 1173. **uncomelye**: improper.
Line 1175. **noyse**: report. **No noyse**: margin.
Line 1178. **Wrisleye and Ryche.**: margin.

worlde, ii. sober wyse men, and verye sage counsellers. But thys tyrannouse example of theirs, maketh a most manyfest shewe of the contrarye. Yea, and the God of heaven wyll have it so knowne to the unyversall worlde, to their ignomynye and shame. So is he wonte to rewarde all cruell Apostataes, as he rewarded Julianus, for their wylfull contempt of hys veryte. The martyr of Christ for her pacyent sufferaunce shall leave here behynde her a gloryouse report, where as these forsworne enemyes and pursuers of hys worde, have purchased themselves a perpetuall infamye by their cruelte and myschefe. In excuse of their madnesse, they saye, they ded it only to feare her. Is it not (thynke yow) a propre frayenge playe, whan our armes and eyes are compelled to leave their naturall holdes? Ye ment no lyght dallyaunce, whan ye wolde have had so manye gret women accused, and toke the hangemannys offyce upon your owne precyouse personnes. O tormentours and tyrauntes abhomynable. Ye feare least your temporall and mortall kynge shuld knowe your madde frenesyes. But of the eternall kynge, whych wyll ryghtlye ponnysh yow for it, with the devyll and hys angels (unlesse ye sore repent it) ye have no feare at all. It is so honest a part, ye have played, that ye wyll not have it noysed. But I promyse yow, so to dyvulge thys unsemelye facte of yours in the latyne, that all christendome over, it shall be knowne what ye are.

Anne Askewe.

I have redde the processe, whych is reported of them that knowe not the truthe, to be my recantacyon. But as sure as the lorde lyveth. I never ment thynge lesse, than to recant. Notwithstandynge thys I confesse, that in my first troubles, I was examyned of the Byshopp of London

1190

1200

Line 1185. **Julianus:** Flavius Claudius Julianus or Julian the Apostate (332–363), Roman Emperor who abjured Christianity and promoted paganism. **Julianus:** margin.

Line 1189. **an excuse:** margin.

Line 1191. **frayenge:** frightening.

Line 1195. **Tyrauntes:** margin.

Line 1199. **No noyse:** margin.

Line 1203. **processe:** proceedings.

Line 1206. **Of Cayphas.:** margin.

aboute the sacrament. Yet had they no graunte of my mouth but thys. That I beleved therin, as the worde of God ded bynde me to beleve. More had they never of me.

₁₂₁₀   *Johan Bale.*

In the ende of her first examynacyon, is thys matter treated of more at large. Here do she repete it agayne, onlye to be knowne for Christes stedefast membre, and not Antichristes. To the voyce of hym she faythfullye obeyed, but the voyce of that Romysh monstre and other straungers she regarded not, Joan. 10. As she perceyved whan she was before the Byshopp of London, that all passed styll, after their olde tyrannye, and nothynge after the rules of scripture, she suspected their doctryne more than afore, and thought them non other than Christ warned hys dyscyples to be ware of, Luce 12. Wherupon she throughlye covenaunted ₁₂₂₀ with her self, never to denye hys veryte afore men at their callynge on, least he shuld agayne denye her before hys eternall father. Mathei 10. For if the confessynge therof bryngeth salvacyon, as saynt Paule sayth it doth, Roman. 10. The denyenge therof on the other syde, must nedes brynge in dampnacyon.

Anne Askewe.

Then he made a coppye, whych is now in prynt, and requyred me to sett therunto my hande. But I refused it. Then my ii. suertyes ded wyll me in no wyse to stycke therat. For it was no great matter, they sayd. Then with moch a do, at the last I wrote thus, I Anne Askewe do beleve ₁₂₃₀ thys if Gods worde do agre to the same, and the true catholick churche,

---

Line 1213. **Christes martyr.**: margin.

Line 1216. **after**: according to.

Line 1216. **Bonner.**: margin.

Line 1219. **Wolves.**: margin.

Line 1222. **salvacyon.**: margin

Line 1227. **suertyes**: sureties; guarantors.

Line 1227. **Hande writynge**: margin.

Johan Bale.

Commonlye is it spoken of popysh prestes, that in doynge their false feates, they sytt in Gods stede. Thys poynt folowed the bludderynge Byshopp of London here, whych for their olde fantasyed superstycyon, laboured in thys woman to dysplace the syncere veryte of the lorde. But so surelye was she buylded upon the harde rocke, that neyther for enmyte nor fryndeshypp, wolde she ones remove her fote, Mathei 7. Neyther anguyshe, trouble, torment, nor fyre, coulde separate her from that love of her lorde God Roma. 8 Though she were for hys sake rebuked and vexed, and also appoynted as a shepe to be slayne, Psal. 43, Yet ded she strongelye through hym overcome, and have (I doubt it not) obtayned the crowne of lyfe, Apoca. 2.

1240

Anne Askewe.

Then the Byshopp, beynge in great dyspleasure with me, bycause I made doubtes in my writynge, commaunded me to pryson. Where I was a whyle. But afterwardes by the meanes of fryndes, I came out agayne. Here is the truthe of that matter. And as concernynge the thynge that ye covete most to knowe, Resort to the vi. of Johan, and be ruled alwayes therby. Thus fare ye wele. Quoth Anne Askewe.

Johan Bale.

1250

In all the scriptures we reade not, that eyther Christ or yet hys Apostles commaunded anye man or woman to pryson for their faythe, as thys tyraunt Byshopp ded here. But in dede we fynde that Christes holye Apostles, were oft tymes cruellye commaunded to pryson of the same spyghtfullye spirytuall generacyon, Acto. 4. 5. 12. 16. Christ wylled hys true belevers to loke for non other at their spirytuall handes, than

---

Line 1232. **Gods stede.**: margin.
Line 1236. **Buylded.**: margin.
Line 1239. **A lambe.**: margin.
Line 1245. **Pryson.**: margin.
Line 1248. **Eucharystye.**: margin.
Line 1251. **Pryson.**: margin.
Line 1255. **Christ.**: margin.

enprysonmentes and deathe, Mathei 10. Joan. 16. And therfor sayd
Peter unto hym. I am redye to go with the, lorde, both into pryson and
to deathe, Luce 22. Paule greatlyecomplayneth of hys enprysonmentes
1260 and scourgynges by them, 2. Corinth, 11. Dyverse in the congregacyon
of Smyrna were enprysoned by that fearce synagoge of Sathan, Apoca.
2. Esaye prophecyenge the condycyons of the spirytuall Antichrist,
sayth amonge other, that he shulde holde men captyve in preson, Esaie
14. Ezechiel reporteth that he shuld churlyshlye checke, and in cruelte
rule, Ezechie. 34. Zacharye sheweth that he shuld eate up the fleshe of
the fattest, Zacharie 11. Daniel declareth that he shuld persecute with
swerde and fyre. Daniel 11. And saynt Johan verefyeth that he shuld be
all dronke with the bloude of the witnesses of Jesu, Apoca. 17. And
therfor in these feates, hys Byshoppes do but their kyndes.
1270 Thus endeth the lattre examynacyon.

The confessyon of her faythe whych Anne Askewe
made in Newgate afore she suffered.

I Anne Askewe, of good memorye, although my mercyfull father hath
geven me the breade of adversyte, and the water of trouble, yet not so
moch as my synnes hath deserved, confesse my selfe here a synner
before the trone of hys heavenlye mageste desyerynge hys eternall mercye. And for so moch as I am by the lawe unryghtouslye condempned
for an evyll doer concernynge opynyons, I take the same most mercyfull
God of myn, whych hath made both heaven and earthe, to recorde, that
1280 I holde no opynyons contrarye to hys most holye worde.

Line 1260. **Smyrna.**: margin.

Line 1262. **antichrist:** margin.

Line 1267. **with fyre:** margin.

Line 1269. **do...kyndes:** act according to their natures.

Line 1272. **suffered:** suffered death.

Lines 1273–74. **although...trouble:** cf. Isa. 30: 20. **Trouble.:** margin.

Line 1278. **Condempned.:** margin.

Line 1279. **both:** emended from "hoth".

Johan Bale.

What man of sober dyscressyon, can judge thys woman yll, indyfferentlye but markynge thys her last confessyon? Not a fewe of most evydent
argumentes are therin, to prove her the true servaunt of God. Her
wyttes were not ones dystracted, for all her most tyrannouse handelynges. She was styll of a perfyght memorye, accountynge her empryson-
mentes, revylynges, rackynges, and other tormentes, but the breade of
adversyte and the water of trouble, as ded David afore her, Psalm. 79.
As the lovynge chylde of God, she receyved them without grudge, and
thought them deserved on her partye. She toke them for hys hande of   1290
mercye, and gave most hygh thankes for them. She mekelye confessed
her selfe in hys syght a synner, but not an haynouse heretyke, as she was
falselye judged of the world. In that matter she toke hym most stronglye
to witnesse, that though in faythe she were not agreable to the worldes
wylde opynyon, yet was she not therin contrarye to hys heavenlye
truthe. She had afore that proved their spretes conferrynge both their
judgements, 1. Joan. 4. and perceyved them farre unlyke, Esaie 55.

Anne Askewe.

And I trust in my mercyfull lorde, whych is the gever of all grace, that
he wyll gracyouslye assyst me agaynst all evyll opynyons, whych are con-   1300
trarye to hys blessyd veryte. For I take hym to witnesse, that I have, do,
and wyll do unto my lyves ende, utterlye abhorre them to the uttermost
of my power. But thys is the heresye whych they report me to holde,
that after the prest hath spoken the wordes of consecracyon, there
remayneth breade styll.

Johan Bale.

Consydre without frowarde, parcyall or wylfull affeccyon, the poyntes

---

Lines 1282–83. **indyfferentlye.** unconcernedly.
Line 1283. **prove her:** margin.
Line 1288. **Frutes of faythe.:** margin.
Line 1293. **Obedyent to God.:** margin.
Line 1300. **No heretyke.:** margin.
Line 1303. **Breade.:** margin.
Line 1307. **frowarde:** bold. **affeccyon:** biased feeling.

herin contayned, and than judge of what harte or conscyence they have
rysen. The hope of thys woman was onlye in God. Hym she confessed
1310 to be of all grace the gever. Alone in hys mercye she trusted. She
instauntlye desyred hym to defende her from all errours. She abhorred
all heresyes. She detested mennys superstycyouse invencyons. And most
firmelye cleaved to hys eternall worde. If these with those that went
afore, be not frutes of true christyanyte, or of a perfyght membre of
Gods eleccyon, what frutes wyll we demaunde? S. Paule sayth No man
can confesse that Jesus is the lorde (as she hath done here) but in the
holye Ghost, 1. Corinth. 12. David also specifyeth that the lorde never
forsaketh them whych call upon hys name, and put their trust in hym,
Psal. 9. And as touchynge the prestes consecracyon, whych is soch a
1320 charme of inchauntement as maye not be done but by an oyled offycer
of the popes generacyon, she ded godlye to reject it in that clowtynge
kynde. For in all the Byble is it not that anye man can make of a drye
waffer cake, a newe saver a newe redemer, a newe Christ, or a newe
God, No though he shuld utter all the wordes and scriptures therin.

Anne Askewe.

But they both saye, and also teache it for a necessarye artycle of faythe,
that after those wordes be ones spoken, there remayneth no breade. but
even the selfe same bodye that hynge upon the crosse on good frydaye,
both fleshe, bloude, and bone. To thys beleve of theirs, saye I naye. For
1330 then were our commen Crede false, whych sayth that he sytteth on the
ryght hande of God the father almyghtye, and from thens shall come to

---

Line 1308. **Prove yet:** margin.

Line 1311. **instauntlye:** urgently.

Line 1314. **Frutes of faythe.:** margin.

Line 1319. **Consecracyon.:** margin.

Lines 1321–22. **clowtynge kynde:** clumsily patched-together form.

Line 1323. **Waffer.:** margin.

Line 1328. **Breade.:** margin.

Line 1330. **our commen Crede:** the Apostles' Creed, a statement of Christian belief.

Line 1331. **Shall come.:** margin.

judge the quyck and the dead. Loo, thys is the heresye that I holde, and for it must suffer the deathe.

Johan Bale.

Of Antichrist reade we in the scriptures, that he and hys oyled Apostles shuld do false myracles, Math. 24. 2. Thes. 2. and Apoca. 13. We fynde also in the same selfe places, that he shuld exalte hymselfe above all that is called God, or that is worshypped as God. Who ever hearde of so great a wondre? that a drye cake myght become a God to be wor-shypped? A myracle were thys above all the myracles that ever were   1340 wrought, and a worke above all the workes that ever were done, if it were true as it is most false. Though our eternall God created heaven and earthe in the first begynnynge, and fourmed all other creatures, Gene, 1. Yet reade we not of hym, that he made of hys creatures anye newe God to be worshypped. In that poynt are our oyled Antichristes afore hym. And where as he rested whollye in the seventh daye, from that offyce of creacyon, Gene. 2. and never toke it upon hym sens that tyme, as testyfyeth Johan Chrisostome, Augustyne, Hierome, Bedas, Alcuinus, and all ther other doctors. Yet wyll they take upon them to create everye daye a fresh, and whan their olde God stynketh in the   1350 boxe, remove hym out of the waye, and put a newe in hys rowme. yea, they can make of breade (whych is but mannys corruptyble creature, and ordayned onlye to be eate) soch a God as shall stande checke mate with the great God of heaven, and paraventure deface hym also. Oh blasphemouse wretches and theves. Be ones ashamed of your abhomy-nable blyndenesse, and submytt your selves to a just reformacyon.

Line 1335. **antichrist:** margin.

Line 1341. **Myracle:** margin.

Line 1345. **No God.:** margin.

Line 1348. **Johan Chrisostome:** Saint John Chrysostom (ca. 347–407), patriarch of Constan-tinople, author of numerous scriptural commentaries. **Doctors.:** margin.

Line 1349. **Alcuinus:** Alcuin (ca. 732–804), Anglo-Latin scholar.

Line 1349. **doctors:** scholars.

Line 1350. **Moulde in the boxe.:** margin.

Line 1352. **whych:** emended from "wkych".

Line 1355. **Godmakers.:** margin.

Anne Askewe.

But as touchynge the holye and blessyd supper of the lorde, I beleve it
to be a most necessarye remembraunce of hys gloryouse sufferynges and
1360 deathe. More over I beleve as moch therin, as my eternall and onlye
redemer Jesus Christ wolde I shuld beleve. Fynallye I beleve all those
scriptures to be true. whom he hath confirmed with hys most precyouse
bloude.

Johan Bale.

No godlye instytucyon nor ordynaunce of Christ, do thys faythfull
woman contempne, but reverentlye submytteth herself therunto, in the
kynde that he ded leave them. She protesteth here to beleve so moch, as
can be shewed by the scriptures of both testamentes. And what is more
to be requyred of a Christen belever? Onlye ded she in conscyence
1370 refuse and abhorre, the ydell observacyons, the paganes superstycyons,
the sorcerers inchauntmentes, and the most parellouse ydolatryes,
whych the Romysh pope and hys clergye have added to their Masse for
covetousnesse. In thys (I suppose) she remembred the wordes of saynt
Paule, 1. Corinth 2. My talkynge (sayd he) and my preachynge, was not
with persuasyble or entysynge wordes of mannys corrupt wysdome, but
in utteraunce of the sprete and of power, that your faythe shuld not
stande in the wysdome of men, but in the power of God. For that (sayth
Christ) whych semeth hygh and holye afore men, is fylthye abhomynacyon before God, Luce 16.

1380   ### Anne Askewe.

Yea, and as S. Paule sayth, those scriptures are suffycyent for our
lernynge and salvacyon, that Christ hath lefte here with us. So that I

Line 1358. **The supper.**: margin.
Line 1361. **Scriptures.**: margin.
Line 1365. **ordynaunce**: dispensation.
Line 1366. **Without Masse.**: margin.
Line 1370. **observacyons**: practices. **Idolatryes.**: margin.
Line 1375. **Mannys wysdome**: margin.
Lines 1381–82. **S. Paule…salvacyon**: see Rom. 16:4. **Scriptures.**: margin.

beleve, we nede no unwritten verytees to rule hys churche with. Therfor loke what he hath layed unto me with hys owne mouthe, in hys holye Gospell, that have I with Gods grace, closed up in my harte. And my full trust is (as David sayth) that it shall be a lanterne to my fote steppes, Psalme 118.

Johan Bale.

Styll are these frutes of inestymable wholsomnesse, declarynge thys woman a most perfyght and innocent membre of Jesus Christ. In thys whole processe (marke it hardelye) she ronneth not for socour to the muddye waters or broken pyttes of the Phylistynes, Hieremye 2. Whych are the corrupt doctrynes and tradycyons of men. But she seketh to the verye welsprynge of helthe, and fountayne of salvacyon, Joan. 4. All unwritten verytees left she to those waverynge wanderers whych wyll eternallye perysh with them. And in the verytees written, appoynted she to journaye amonge the true Christen belevers towardes the lande ever-lastynge. In all her affayres most fyrmelye she cleaveth to the scriptures of God, whych geveth both sprete and lyfe, Joan. 6. As the harte in the forest desyreth the plesaunt water brokes, so longed her sowle and was desyerouse of the manyfest glorye of her eternall God, Psal. 41. If her porcyon be not in the lande of the lyvynge, Psal. 141. Yea, if she be not allowed a cytezen with the Sayntes, Ephe. 1. And her name regestred in the boke of lyfe, Apoca. 20. Yt wyll be harde with manye. But certayne and sure I am, that with Marye Marthaes systre, soch a sure part have she chosen, as wyll not be taken awaye from her, Luce 10.

1390

1400

Line 1384. **Hope.**: margin.

Line 1387. **Psalme 118**: Psalm 119 in the King James version; see verse 105.

Line 1390. **prove styll**: margin.

Line 1391. **hardelye**: assuredly.

Line 1396. **Frutes of faythe.**: margin.

Line 1401. **Her god.**: margin.

Line 1405. **A sure part.**: margin.

Anne Askewe.

There be some do saye, that I denye the Eucharystye or sacrament of
thankes gevynge. But those people do untrulye report of me. For I both
1410   saye and beleve it, that if it were ordered lyke as Christ instytuted it and
left it, a most syngular confort it were unto us all. But as concernynge
your Masse, as it is now used in our dayes, I do saye and beleve it, to be
the most abhomynable ydoll that is in the worlde. For my God wyll not
be eaten with tethe, neyther yet dyeth he agayne. And upon these
wordes, that I have now spoken, wyll I suffer deathe.

Johan Bale.

All the workes of God and ordynaunces of Christ, she reverentlye
admytted, as grounded matters of Christen beleve. But the Romysh
popes creatures wolde she in no case allowe to stande up checke mate
1420   with them. The Masse (whych is in all poyntes, of that fylthye Antichristes creacyon) toke she for the most execrable ydoll upon earthe.
And ryghtlye. For non other is the chylde to be reckened, than was hys
father afore hym, be he man or beast. The whelpe of a dogge, is non
other than a dogge, whan he cometh ones to hys age. Idolles (sayth
David) are lyke them that make them. So are they also whych put their
trust in them, Psalme 113. An ydoll doth Zacharye call that proude
slaughterouse shepehearde, Zacharye 11. Who then can denye hys prodygyouse ordynaunces to be the same? What other is the worke of an
ydolatrouse worker, than an execrable ydoll? And loke what propyrtees
1430   anye ydoll hath had, or feates hath wrought yet sens the worldes begynnynge, the popes prodygyouse Masse hath had and wrought the same,
with manye conveyaunces more.

Line 1408. **Eucharystye.**: margin.
Line 1413. **masse, an ydoll.**: margin.
Line 1418. **obedyence.**: margin.
Line 1421. **The Masse.**: margin.
Line 1424. **ydolaters**: margin.
Line 1428. **An ydoll.**: margin.
Line 1432. **conveyaunces**: cunning devices.

Of popes hath it receyved dysgysynges, instrumentes, blessynges, turnynges and legerdemaynes, with manye straunge observacyons borowed of the Jewes and paganes olde sacryfyces, besydes pardons for delyveraunce of sowles. Of monkes have it gotten a purgatorye after manye straunge apparycyons, with a longe ladder from thens to scale heaven with. It hath obtayned also, to be a remedye for all dyseases both in man and beast, with innumerable superstycyons els. Of unyversytees and their doctours, have it cawte all the subtyltees and craftye lernynges 1440 of the prophane phylosophers, to be defended by, as is to be seane in the workes of their sentencyoners, lyke as I have shewed in the mysterye of iniquyte, fo. 33. It serveth all wytches in their wytcherye, all sorcerers, charmers, inchaunters, dreamers, sothsayers, necromansers, conjures, crosse dyggers, devyll raysers, myracle doers, doggeleches, and bawdes. For without a masse, they can not wele worke their feates. The lawers lyke wyse, whych seke in Westmynstre hawle to gett most moneye by falsehede, can neyther be wele without it. It upholdeth vayne glorye, pryde, ambycyon, avaryce, glottonye, slouth, ydelnesse, hypocresye, heresye, tyrannye, and all other devylyshnesse besydes, It maynteyneth 1450 the spyrytuall souldyers of Antichrist, in all superfluouse lyvynge and wanton lecherouse lustes, with the chast occupyenges of Sodome and Gomor.

Line 1433. **instrumentes**: formal writings. **Popes.**: margin.

Line 1434. **turnynges**: perversions. **legerdemaynes**: deceptions.

Lines 1435–36. **pardons...sowles:** Roman Catholics could obtain pardons to gain release from Purgatory. **Monkes.**: margin.

Line 1441. **Universytees.**: margin.

Line 1442. **sentencyoners**: compilers of theological aphorisms.

Lines 1442–43. **mysterye of iniquyte:** Bale's *Mystery of inyquyte contayned within the heretycall genealogye of P. Pantolabus* (Antwerp, 1545).

Line 1444. **dreamers**: idle speculators. **sothsayers**: fortune tellers.

Line 1444. **the masse**: margin.

Line 1445. **doggeleches**: medical quacks.

Line 1447. **Westmynstre hawle:** the Great Hall of the Palace of Westminster in which the royal courts of justice met.

Line 1449. **Profytable.**: margin.

Line 1451. **Necessarye.**: margin.

Lines 1452–53. **Sodome and Gomor:** see Gen. 19; for their wickedness, God destroyed the two cities of Sodom and Gomorrah with fire and brimstone.

What other ghostlye frutes it hath I shall more largelye shewe in my boke called, The myracles of the Masse agaynst Peryne. Perchaunce some devoute Masse hearers wyll laye for the holynesse therof, that it contayneth both pystle and Gospell. Trulye that Epystle and that Gospell maye wele have a name of lyfe, as S. Johan sayth of the churche of Sardis, Apoca. 3. Yet is it in that offyce of massynge, non other than the dead or mortyfyenge letter. 2. Cor. 3. For the sprete that shuld quycken, is clerelye taken from it, So that nothynge els therof remayneth to the common people, but a dead noyse and an ydle sounde, as it is now in the Romysh language. Who can saye, but it was the scripture, that Sathan alleged unto Christ upon the pynnacle of the temple? Math. 4. Yet remayneth it there styll, after hys ungracyouse handelynge therof, as a false craftye suggestyon, a devylysh errour, or a shyelde of hys wyckednesse, and wyll do evermore. Where are the names of God, of hys Angels, and of hys sayntes, more ryfe, than amonge witches, charmers, inchaunters, and sorcerors? Yet can ye not saye, that they are amonge them to anye mannys salvacyon. as they wolde be in ryght handelynge. What it is that serveth an ydoll, lete godlye wyse men conjecture, whych are not all ignoraunt how Angell became a devyll.

1460 (margin)
1470 (margin)

Anne Askewe.

O lorde, I have more enemyes now, than there be heeres on my heade. Yet lorde lete them never overcome me with vayne wordes. But fyght thu lorde, in my stede. For on the cast I my care. With all the spyght they can ymagyne, they fall upon me whych am thy poore creature, Yet

---

Line 1455. **The myracles...Peryne:** *STC* does not list this title; perhaps after Peryn's conversion to Protestantism in 1547, Bale did not publish it. **myracles of the masse.:** margin.

Line 1459. **offyce of massynge:** the practice of celebrating mass.

Line 1460. **Dead letter.:** margin.

Line 1464. **Sathan.:** margin.

Line 1467. **Wytches.:** margin.

Line 1471. **An ydoll.:** margin.

Line 1474. **O...heade:** cf. Ps. 40:12. **heeres:** hairs. **Enemyes:** margin.

Line 1477. **hate them.:** margin.

swete lorde, lete me not set by them whych are agaynst the. For in the is
my whole delyght.

Johan Bale. 1480

O blessyd woman, and undoubted cytyzen of heaven. Truthe it is, that
thu hast had manye adversaryes, yea, and a farre greatter nombre of
them, than thu hast here reckened. And the more thu hast had, the
greatter is now thy vyctorye in Christ. The great bodye of the Beast thu
hast had to enemye. whych comprehendeth the malygnaunt muster of
Sathan on the one syde, and the erthly worshyppers of hys blasphemose
beastlynesse on the other syde, Daniel 11. Apo. 13. whose nombre is as
the sande of the see, infynyte, Apoc. 20. But consydre agayne, what
fryndeshypp thu hast gotten for it on the other part. Thu hast now to
frynde for thy faythfull perseveraunce agaynst those ydoll mongers, the 1490
sempyternall trynyte, the father, the sonne, and the holye Ghost, Joan
14. With the gloryouse multytude of Angels, the patriarkes, Prophetes,
Apostles and Martyrs, with all the elect nombre from ryghteouse Abel
hytherto. Thu hast also here upon earthe, and evermore shall have, the
faver of all them whych have not bowed to that fylthye Beast, whose
names are regestred in the boke of lyfe, Apo. 21. And as for thy ungodlye and cruell enemyes, as dust in the wynde the lorde wyll scattre them
from the face of the earthe, be they never so stowte and manye, Psal. 1.

Anne Askewe.

And lorde I hartelye desyre of the, that thu wylte of thy most mercyfull 1500
goodnesse, forgeve them that vyolence, whych they do and have done

---

Line 1482. **Adversaryes.**: margin.
Line 1484. **thy**: emended from "they".
Line 1484. **Beast**: the dragon of Rev. 12–13.
Line 1485. **Haters.**: margin.
Line 1489. **Fryndes.**: margin.
Line 1494. **Favorers**: margin.
Line 1497. **Northfolke.**: margin; Thomas Howard, third duke of Norfolk (1473–1554), privy
councillor and ally of Bishop Gardiner. See Introduction, page xxvii.

unto me. Open also thu their blynde hartes, that they maye herafter do that thynge in thy syght, whych is onlye acceptable before the. And to sett fourth thy veryte aryght, without all vayne fantasyes of synnefull men. So be it. O lorde, so be it. By me Anne Askewe.

Johan Bale.

Afore here she confessed with David that on God she had cast her care, and that in hym was all her hartes delyght. Psal. 60. She desyred hym also, never to fayle her in thys harde conflict, but stronglye to assist her, and in no case to permytt her to be overcommen of the flatterynge worlde, neyther yet to geve place to hys enemyes. And I doubt it not, but these are most evydent sygnes that she was hys faythfull servaunt. I knowe certaynlye, that all the power of helle, can not prevayle agaynst so ernest a faythe, Math. 16. For he hath so spoken it there, whych can not lye, Luce 21. and 1. Petri 2. In thys lattre part, she sheweth the nature of Christes lyvelye membre, and of a perfyght christen martyr in ii. poyntes first she desyreth God to forgeve her enemyes as Christ desyred hym in the tyme of hys passyon, Luce 23. And as holye Steven also ded for the tyme of hys deathe, Acto. 7. Secondlye she desyreth their hartes to be opened, that they maye trulye beleve and be saved, Acto. 16. Thys supernaturall affect of charyte had she only of the sprete of Christ, whych wylleth not the deathe of a frowarde synner, but rather that he be from hys wyckednesse turned, and so lyve Ezech. 33. Thus is she a Saynt canonysed in Christes bloude, though she never have other canonysacyon of pope, prest, nor Byshopp.

The destroyer shall be destroyed without handes. Daniel. 8.

Line 1502. **Prayer.**: margin.
Line 1508. **Swete woman.**: margin.
Line 1511. **Gods true servaunt.**: margin.
Line 1515. **Christes membre.**: margin.
Line 1520. **Charyte.**: margin.
Line 1521. affect: inward disposition.
Line 1523. **A Saynt.**: margin.

149

The Balade whych Anne Askewe made and sange whan she was in Newgate.

Lyke as the armed knyght
Appoynted to the fielde
With thys world wyll I fyght
And fayth shall be my shielde.

Faythe is that weapon stronge 5
Whych wyll not fayle at nede
My foes therfor amonge
Therwith wyll I procede.

As it is had in strengthe
And force of Christes waye 10
It wyll prevayle at lengthe
Though all the devyls saye naye

Faythe in the fathers olde
Obtayned ryghtwysnesse
Whych make me verye bolde. 15
To feare no worldes dystresse.

I now rejoyce in hart
And hope byd me do so
For Christ wyll take my part
And ease me of my wo. 20

Thu sayst lorde, who so knocke.
To them wylt thu attende
Undo therfor the locke
And thy stronge power sende.

More enmyes now I have. 25
Than heeres upon my heed
Lete them not me deprave
But fyght thu in my steed.

On the my care I cast
For all their cruell spyght 30

Lines 1-4. **armed knyght...shielde:** Askew recalls Eph. 6:11–18, Paul's injunction to "put on the whole armour of God...Above all, taking the shield of faith."

Line 2. **Appoynted:** equipped.

I sett not by their hast
For thu art my delyght.
    I am not she that lyst
My anker to lete fall
For everye dryslynge myst   35
My shyppe substáncyall.
    Not oft use I to wryght
In prose nor yet in ryme
Yet wyll I shewe one syght
That I sawe in my tyme.   40
    I sawe a ryall trone
Where Justyce shuld have sytt
But in her stede was one
Of modye cruell wytt.
Absorpt was rygtwysnesse   45
As of the ragynge floude
Sathan in hys excesse.
Sucte up the gyltelesse bloude.
    Then thought I, Jesus lorde
Whan thu shalt judge us all   50
Harde is it to recorde
On these men what wyll fall.
    Yet lorde I the desyre
For that they do to me
Lete them not tast the hyre   55
Of their inyquyte.

FINIS.

God save the kynge.

    God hath chosen the weake thynges of the worlde, to confounde
thynges whych are myghtye. Yea, and thynges of no reputacyon, for to
brynge to nought thynges of reputacyon, that no fleshe shuld presume in
hys syght. 1. Corinth. 1.

Line 55. **hyre:** payment.

The Conclusyon.

Thus hast thu (dylygent reader) the ende of these ii. examynacyons and answers of the most Christen martyr Anne Askewe, with other addycyons besydes. Marke in them the horryble madde furye of Antichrist and the devyll, how they worke in thys age by their tyrannouse members, to brynge the last vengeaunce swyftlye upon them. Afore tyme hath not bene seane, soch frantyck outrage as is now, the judges without all sober dyscressyon, ronnynge to the racke, toggynge, halynge, and pullynge therat, lyke tormentours in a playe. Compare me here Pylate with Wrisleye the hygh chauncellour of Englande, with Ryche and with other whych wyll be counted no small moates. And se how moch the pagane Judge excelleth in vertu and wysdome, the false christened Judge, yea, rather prodygyouse tyraunt. Whan Pylate had enquyred, what accusacyon the Jewes clergye had agaynst Christ, he perceyved they ded all of malyce, and refused to meddle therin. Joan. 18. In Wrisleye and Riche is no soch equyte. But they rather seke occasyon to accomplysh the full malyce of Antichrist.

Pylate shewed the accused all faver possyble. He examyned hym pryvatelye, he gave hym fryndelye wordes, he bad hym not feare to speake, he hearde hym with gentylnesse, he counselled with hym that he myght the more frelye suppresse their madde furye, and he promysed, they shuld do hym no wronge in case he wolde utter hys full mynde, Joan. 18. Farre contrarye to thys were Wrisleye and Ryche, whych not all ignoraunt of the Byshoppes beastlye errours, malycyouslye without all feare of God and shame of the worlde, executed upon thys godlye

Line 4. **antichrist:** margin.
Line 8. **halynge:** dragging.
Line 9. **tormentours in a playe:** in a Passion play in which Christ is mocked and beaten.
Line 9. **Compassyon.:** margin.
Line 11. **moates:** motes; trifles.
Line 13. **Pylate.:** margin.
Line 15. **Wrisleye:** margin.
Line 18. **Pylate.:** margin.
Line 23. **Wrysleye:** margin.

woman most terryble tyrannye. Pylate spake for the innocent, excused
hym, defended hym, layed fourth the lawe, pleated for hym sharpelye,
requyred them to shewe mercye, alleged for hym their custome,
declared hym an innocent and sought by all meanes to delyver hym,
Math. 27. These perjured magystrates Wrysleye and Ryche, not onlye
examyned thys innocent woman with rigour, but also hated her,
scorned her, revyled her, condempned her for an heretyke, and with
unspeakable tormentes sought to enforce her to brynge by accusacyon
other noble women and men to deathe.

More over Pylate wolde shede no innocent bloude, but laboured to
mytygate the Byshoppes furye, and instaunted them as they were
relygyouse, to shewe godlye faver, concludynge that he coulde by no
lawe of justice, judge hym worthye to dye Marci 15. These vengeable
tyrauntes Wrisleye and Riche insacyably thirsted, not only the innocent
bloude of thys faythfull servaunt of God, but also the bloude of the
noble duchesse of Sothfolke, the bloude of the worthye countesse of
Hertforde, and of the vertuouse countesse of Sussexe, the bloude of the
faythfull ladye Dennye, of the good lady Fizwyllyams, and of other godlye women more, soche wydowes and wyves as Paule, Peter, and Johan
commendeth in their epistles, besydes the bloude of serten noble men
of the kynges hygh counsell. And all at the spyghtfull callynge on of the
Byshoppes. Slacke eare gave Pylate to the prestes, he regarded not ther
dyspleasure, he detected their protervouse madnesse, by delayes he dyf-
ferred the sentence, and fynallye washed hys handes as one that was
clere from their tyrannye, Luce 23. Swyft eare gave Wrisleye and Ryche

Line 27. **Pylate.**: margin.
Line 30. **Wrisleye**: margin.
Line 35. **Pylate.**: margin.
Line 36. **instaunted**: urged.
Line 39. **Wrisleye**: margin.
Line 43. **Ladyes.**: margin.
Line 47. **Pylate.**: margin.
Line 48. **protervouse**: wayward, insolent.
Line 50. **Wrisleye and Ryche.**: margin.

with their wycked affynyte to the puffed up porkelynges of the pope
Gardyner, Bonner, and soch other, they folowed their cruell counsell,
they enprysoned her, judged her, condempned her, and racked her at
the last with their owne poluted bloudye tormentours handes, tyll the
vaynes and synnowes brast.

If ye marke the scriptures wele, ye shall easelye perceyve that Pylate
was not in fawte of Christes buffetynges, beatynges, scornynges, face
spyttynges, crownynge with thorne, and soch other extreme handelynges. But the malycyouse Byshoppes and prestes whych waged Judas to
betraye hym, hyred false wytnesses to accuse hym, monyed the multy-   60
tude to dyffame hym, fayned false matter agaynst hym, compelled the
lawe and terryfyed the judge, to have their full myschefe accomplyshed,
as our Byshoppes have done in thys cruell acte and soch other. Whan the
prestes wolde have blemyshed hys name by the ignomynyouse deathe
whych he suffered amonge theves on the crosse, Pylate proclamed it gloryouse unto all the worlde, writynge hys tytle in Hebrue, Greke, and
Latyne, Jesus of Nazareth kynge of the Jewes, and wolde not at their
instaunt callyng on, change it, Joan. 19. Wrisleye and Riche with their
ungracyouse affynyte, have in everye poynt folowed here the execrable
affectes of the prestes. Favorablye Pylate lycensed Joseph of Arymathye   70
to take downe Christes bodye, and to burye it, Math. 27. Wrisleye commaunded thys martyr of God with her faythfull companyons to be brent
to ashes. Pylate was ignoraunt of Gods lawes, and a pagane. Wrisleye and
Ryche knowe both the lawe and the Gospell, and are christyanes, the
more is it to their dampnacyon, to execute soch turkysh tyrannye.

Line 51. **porkelynges:** young pigs.
Line 55. **brast:** burst.
Line 56. **Pylate.:** margin.
Line 59. **waged:** paid.
Line 60. **monyed:** bribed. **Prestes.:** margin.
Line 63. **Pylate.:** margin.
Line 69. **ungracyouse affynyte:** wicked partnership. **Wrisleye:** margin.
Line 72. **Pylate.:** margin.
Line 73. **Wrisleye:** margin.

Now to conclude with Anne Askewe as the argument of thys boke requyreth. In the yeare of our lord a M. D. XLVI And in the monthe of Julye, at the prodygyouse procurement of Antichristes furyouse rem-naunt, Gardyner, Bonner, and soch lyke, she suffered most cruell deathe
80 in Smythfelde with her iii. faythfull companyons, Johan Lassels a gen-tylman whych had bene her instructour, Johan Adlam a tayler, and a prest so constaunt in the veryte agaynst the seyd Antichristes supersty-cyons as they, whose name at thys tyme I had not. Credyblye am I infourmed by dyverse duche merchauntes whych were there present, that in the tyme of their sufferynges, the skye abhorrynge so wycked an acte, sodenlye altered coloure, and the cloudes from above gave a thonder clappe, not all unlyke to that is written, Psal. 76. The elementes both declared therin the hygh dyspleasure of God for so tyrannouse a murther of innocentes, and also expreslye sygnyfyed hys myghtye hande
90 present to the confort of them whych trusted in hym, besydes the most wonderfull mutacyon whych wyll within short space therupon folowe. And lyke as the Centuryon with those that were with hym, for the tokens shewed at Christes deathe, confessed hym to be the sonne of God, Math. 27. So ded a great nombre at the burnynge of these mar-tyrs, upon the syght of thys open experyment, afferme them to be hys faythfull members.

Full manye a Christen hart have rysen and wyll ryse from the pope to Christ through the occasyon of their consumynge in the fyre. As the saynge is, of their ashes wyll more of the same opynyon aryse. Manye a
100 wone sayth yet both in Englande and Duchelande, also, O that woman

---

Line 76. **argument:** subject-matter.

Line 78. **Brent.:** margin.

Line 80. **iii...companyons:** see Introduction, pages xxii–xxiii.

Line 81. **Martyrs:** margin.

Line 85. **A sygne.:** margin.

Line 88. **Gods hande.:** margin.

Line 92. **Centurio:** margin.

Line 95. **experyment:** proof.

Line 98. **Christyanes.:** margin.

that woman O those men those men. If the popes generacyon and wycked remnaunt make manye more soch martyrs, they are lyke to marre all their whole market in Englande. It were best for them now a dayes to lete men be at lyberte for their holye fathers gaudysh ceremonyes, as they are for beare baytynges, cocke fyghtynges tennys playe, tables, tombelynge, daunsynge, or huntynge, who lyst and who maye. For as lyttle have those tradycyons of hys of the worde of God, in their prowdest outshewe, as they have. Here wyll some tender stomakes be greved, and report that in our headye hastynesse, we refuse to suffre with our weake bretherne accordynge to the doctryne of Paule. But I saye unto them, what so ever they be whych are so scrupulouse wanderers, that they most execrablye erre in so bestowynge the scriptures. For abhomynable is that tolleraunce of our brethernes weakenesse, where God is by ydolatrouse superstycyons, dysobeyed, dyshonoured, and blasphemed. A playne practyse were thys of Sathan in hypocresye to unholde all devylyshnesse.

On the other syde was there an other sort at the deathe of these blessyd martyrs, and they judged of thys alteracyon of the ayre and thonder clappe, as ded the Jewysh Byshoppes with their perverted multytude. Whych waggynge their heades, rayled, revyled, jangled, jested, scorned, cursed, mocked, and mowed at Christes precyouse sufferynges on the crosse, Math. 27. and Luce 23. These were the ydle wytted prestes at London and their beastlye ygnoraunt broodes, with olde superstycyouse bawdes and brethels, the popes blynde cattell. These

---

Line 101. **take hede:** margin.
Line 105. **Ceremonyes.:** margin.
Line 106. **tables:** backgammon.
Line 108. **outshewe:** display.
Line 108. **Tenderlynges.:** margin.
Line 112. **bestowynge:** applying.
Line 113. **Hypocresye.:** margin.
Line 117. **Papystes:** margin.
Line 121. **mowed:** made faces.
Line 122. **Prestes.:** margin.
Line 124. **brethels:** wretches. **Bawdes.:** margin.

cryed there lyke madde modye bedlemes, as they hearde the thonder,
They are dampned, they are dampned, their wyse preachers outasynge
the same at Paules crosse. In dede full nobyllye are they overseane in the
Byble that judge the thonders to sygnyfye dampnacyon. Thonder (sayth
the scripture) is the voyce of God, Eccle. 43. Thonder is the helpynge
130 power of the lorde, Job 26. and no dampnacyon. Christ called Johan
and James the sonnes of thonder, Marci 3. Whych betokened that they
shuld be ernest preachers, and no chyldren of dampnacyon. The lorde
by thonder, sheweth hys inscrutable workynge, Job 38. Moses receyved
the lawe, Helyas the sprete of prophecye, the Apostles the holye Ghost,
and all in thonder. What wycked sole wyll saye, they receyved so dampnacyon?

As the lambe had opened the first seale of the boke, the voyce that
went forth was as it had bene thonder, Apoca. 6. whych is no dampnacyon, but a sharpe callynge of people to Godwarde. The thonderynges
140 that apered whan the Angell fylled hys censer. Apoca. 8. were no dampnacyons but Gods ernest wordes rebukynge the worlde for synne. The
best interpretours do call those thonderynges whych came from the
trone of God. Apocal. 4. soche verytees of the scripture as terryfyeth
synners, and no dampnacyons. Neyther were the vii. thonderynges
whych gave their voyces, Apoc. 10. anye other than mysteryes at their
tymes to be opened, Eucherius Lugdunensis and other moralysers, call
thonders in the scripture, the voyces of the Gospell, and their lyght-
enynges, the clere openynges of the same. If thonder be a threttenynge
or a fearfull judgement of God (as in Psal. 103.) it is to them that abyde

---

Line 125. **bedlemes:** madmen (from the Bethlehem hospital for the insane).
Line 126. **outasynge:** shouting out.
Line 127. **overseane:** overseen; mistaken.
Line 128. **Thonders.:** margin.
Line 133. **Thonder.:** margin.
Line 138. **Apocal.:** margin.
Line 140. **censer:** vessel for burning incense.
Line 141. **Thonders.:** margin.
Line 146. **Eucherius Lugdunensis:** bishop of Lyons (d. ca. 449) and biblical exegete.
Eucherius: margin.

here, and not to them that depart from hens, A token is it also that the   150
horryble tyrauntes shall be as the meledust, that the wynde taketh
awaye sodenlye, Esaie 29. If plage do folowe of thonder, as it ded in
Egypt, whan Moses stretched forth hys rodde, Exodi 9, It shall lyght
upon them whych hath shewed the tyrannouse vyolence on the people
of God, as it ded upon pharao and hys cruell mynysters.

At the myghtye voyce whych was both sensyblye hearde and under-
standed of the Apostles from heaven, that the father was and wolde be
gloryfyed by Christ the people sayd nothynge but, It thondereth, Joan.
12. For nothynge els they understode therof. What Anne Askewe and
her companyons both hearde and se in thys thonder to their sowles con-   160
solacyon in their paynefull sufferynges, no mortall understandynge can
dyscerne. Onlye was it Steven (and paraventure a fewe dyscyples) that se
the heavens open whan he suffered, and not the cruell multytude whych
ranne upon hym with stones, Acto. 7. Lete beastlye blynde babbyllers
and bawdes with their charmynge chaplaynes than prate at large, out of
their malycyouse sprete and ydle braynes. We have in habundaunce the
veryte of Gods worde and promes, to prove them both saved and gloryfyed in Christ. For God ever preserveth them whych trust in hym, Psal.
16. All that call upon hys holye name, are saved, Johel. 2. What reason-
able man wyll thynke that they can be lost, whych have their lorde God   170
more dere than their owne lyves? No man shall be hable (sayth Christ)
to plucke my shepe out of my handes, but I wyll geve them eternall lyfe,
Joan. 10. Beleve (sayth Paule to the jayler at Philippos) on the lorde
Jesus Christ, and thu shall be saved and thy whole howsholde, Acto. 16.

Line 150. **For tyrauntes.**: margin.
Line 151. **meledust**: meal-dust; powder.
Line 153. **Northfolke.**: margin.
Line 157. **Marke wele.**: margin.
Line 160. **se**: saw.
Line 162. **S. Steven**: margin.
Line 165. **prate**: chatter.
Line 167. **gods worde.**: margin.
Line 171. **Not lost.**: margin.

They that seme in the syght of the unwyse to go into destruccyon, do rest in the peace of God, and are replenyshed with immortalyte, Sapien. 3. With other innumerable scriptures, to the prayse of God, whose name be gloryfyed worlde without ende, Amen.

FINIS.

God save the kynge.

180

Thus endeth the lattre conflict of Anne Askewe, latelye done to deathe by the Romysh popes malycyouse remnaunt, and now canonysed in the precyouse bloude of the lorde Jesus Christ

Imprented at Marpurg in the lande of Hessen, 16, die Januarii, anno 1. 5. 4. 7.

A table compendyouse of thys lattre boke.

God save the kynge.

The two examinations of the worthy servaunt of God, Maistris An Askew

FROM

John Foxe, *Actes and Monuments (1563)*

Title. John Foxe, the martyrologist, printed Askew's *Examinations* without Bale's commentary in his *Actes and Monuments of these latter and perillous dayes, touching matters of the Church, wherein are comprehended and described the great persecutions and horrible troubles, that have bene wrought and practised by the Romishe Prelates, speciallye in this Realme of England and Scotlande, from the yeare of our Lorde a thousande, unto the tyme nowe present.* See Introduction, page xxxiii.

The woodcut of Anne Askew's execution from John Foxe's *Actes and Monuments* (1563) by permission of the Huntington Library, San Marino, California.

issue of authorship

Here next foloweth the same yeare the true examinations of Anne Askew, which here thou shalt have gentle reder according as she wrote them with her own hande, at the instante desire of certaine faithfull men and women, by the which (if thou marke dilligently) the communications bothe of her, and of her examiners thou maist easelly perceive the tre by the frute and the man by his worke.

personal servant to God which elevates her in her piety

THE TWO EXAMINATIONS

of the worthy servant of God, Maistris An Askew, doughter of sir William Askew knight of Lincolneshire, martred in Smithfield for the Constante and faithfull testimonye of the truthe.

Similar to 87.10 Catherine

To satisfy your expectation, good people (saithe shee) this was my first examination in the yeare of our Lorde M. D. xlv. and in the moneth of March, first Christofer Dare examined me at Sadlers Hal, beyng one of the quest, and asked if I did not believe that the sacrament hanginge over the aultar was the very body of Christ really. Then I demaunded this question of him.

   Wherefore S. Steven was stoned to death. And he sayde, he coulde not tell. Then I aunswered, that no more would I assoyle his vain ques-

---

Lines 1–6. **Here...worke:** an address to the reader that also appears in the three editions of the *Examinations* without Bale's commentary. See Textual Introduction, page li.

Line 1. **same yeare:** Foxe dates the preceding story in 1546. See Introduction, page xxi.

Lines 2–3. **she...hande:** a quotation from Bale's *Summarium.* See Introduction, page xxxv.

Lines 10–11. **for...truthe:** a substitution for "by the Romysh popes upholders" in the title of previous editions.

Line 12. **The first examination of An askew:** margin.

Line 14. **Christofer Dare:** otherwise unidentified, one of twelve citizens appointed to the quest.

Line 14. **Sadlers Hal:** Saddlers Hall; headquarters of the Company of Saddlers in Wood Street near the Guildhall (destroyed in World War II).

Line 15. **quest:** body of persons appointed to hold an inquiry; see Introduction, page xxvi.

Line 19. **assoyle:** resolve.

20 tion. Secondly he saide that theire was a woman, which did testify, that
I should reade, how god was not in temples made with hands. Then I
shewed him the ,vii. and the .xvii. Cha of the actes of the Apostles, what
Steven and Paule had saide therein. Wherupon he asked me, how I
tooke those sentences? I aunswered that I woulde not throwe pearles
amonge swine, for accornes were good inough.

Thirdelye he asked me, wherefore I saide, that I had rather to reade
five lines in the bible, than to heare five masses in the temple, I confessed, that I said no lesse. Not for the dyspraise of either the Epistle or
Gospell, but bycause the one did greatly edify me, and the other noth-
30 inge at all. As saint Paule doth witnesse in the .xiiii. Chapter of his first
Epistle to the Corrinthians, where as he doth say. If the trumpet geveth
an uncertaine sounde, who wil prepare him selfe to the battaile.

Fourthly he layed unto my charge, that I shuld say. If an il priest
ministred, it was the devill and not God. My aunswere was, that I never
spake such thinge. But this was my sainge: That what soever he were
which ministred unto me, his ill condicions could not hurt my faith but
in spirite I received never the lesse, the body and bloude of christ. He
asked me, what I saide concerning confession? I aunswered him my
meaninge, which was as sainte James saieth, that every man ought to
40 knowledg his fautes to other, and the one to praye for the other. Sixtly
he asked me what I said to the kinges boke? And I answered him, that I
coulde saye nothinge to it, bycause I never saw it. Seventhly he asked
me if I had the sprite of God in me? I aunswered if I had not, I was but
reprobate or cast away. Then he said, he had sent for a priest, to examine
me, which was there at hand. The priest asked me, what I saide to the
sacrament of the aulter? And required much to knowe therein my
meaninge. But I desired him againe, to holde me excused concerninge
that matter. None other aunswere would I make him bycause I per-

---

Line 33. **il:** ill; evil.

Lines 39–40. **every man...other:** James 5:16.

Line 41. **the kinges boke:** *A Necessary Doctrine and Erudition for any Christen Man,* issued by
the king's authority 29 May 1543; it restored essential Roman Catholic doctrine as the official
national standard.

ceived him a papist. Eightly he asked me, if I did not think that private
masses did helpe soules departed: And saide, it was greate Idolatry to   50
beleve more in them, than in the death which Christ died for us. Then
they had me thence unto my Lorde Maire and hee examined me, as
they had before, and I aunswered him directly in al things as I answered
the quest afore. Besides this my lord mair laide one thinge unto my
charge which was never spoken of me but of them. And that was whether a mouse eatinge the hoste, received God or no? This question did I
never aske, but in dede they asked it of me, whereunto I made them no
aunswere but smiled. Then the bishops chaunceller rebuked me, and
sayde, that I was much to blame for uttring the scripturs. For S. Paul (he
said) forbode women to speak or to talke of the worde of God, I   60
answered him that I knew Paules meaninge as well as he, whiche is .i.
Corinthians .xiiii. that a woman ought not to speake in the congregation by the way of teaching. And then I asked him, how many women
he had sene, go into the pulpit and preach? He saide he never saw none.
Then I sayde, he ought to finde no faute in poore women, except they
had offended the lawe. Then my Lorde maior commaunded me to
warde. I asked him if suerties wold not serve me, and he made me short
answer, that he wold take none. Then was I had to the counter, and ther
remained xi. daies no frend admitted to speake with me. But in the
meane time ther was a priest sent to me which saide that he was com-   70
maunded of the bishop to examine me, and to geve me good councell,
which he did not, but first he asked me for what cause I was put in the
counter? And I told him I could not tel. Then he said, it was greate pity
that I shuld be there without cause, and concluded that he was very sory

---

Line 49. **papist:** Roman Catholic.

Line 52. **Lorde Maire:** William Laxton, October 1544–October 1545; Martin Bowes,
October 1545–October 1546. See Introduction, pages xxi–xxii.

Line 58. **chaunceller:** the church official to whom the bishop delegated his authority.

Line 67. **warde:** prison.

Line 67. **suerties:** sureties; personal guarantors.

Line 68. **counter:** the Counter; prison attached to the city court, under the jurisdiction of the
mayor.

Line 69. **xi. daies:** in Bale's edition, "xii. dayes." See page 31.

for me. Secondly he sayd, it was told him, that I should deny the sacrament of the alter. And I answered him agayne that, that I had said, I had
said. Thirdly he asked me, if I were shriven, I tolde him so that I might
have one of these .iii. that is to say, doctor Crome, sir Gillam, or Huntington, I was contented, bycause I knew them to be men of wisdome.
80   As for you or any other I will not dispraise, bycause I knowe ye not,
Then hee saide I would not have you thinke but that I or another that
shalbe brought you shalbe as honest as they. For if we were not, ye may
be sure, the kinge would not suffer us to preach. then I answered by the
sayng of Salomon. By communing with the wise, I may lerne wisdom:
But by talking with a fole, I shal take skathe, Prover .i. Fourthly he
asked me, if the host should fall, and a beast did eate it whether the
beast did receive God or no? I aunswered, Seinge ye have taken the
paines to aske this question I desire you also to assoile it your selfe. For I
wil not do it, bycause I perceive ye come to tempt me. And he said, it
90   was against the order of scoles that he which asked the question should
aunswere it. I told him I was but a woman and knew not the course of
scoles. Fifthly he asked me if I intended to receive the sacrament at Easter or no? I aunswered that els I were no Christen woman and there I
did rejoise, that the time was so nere at hand. And than he departed
thence with many faire wordes. And the .xxiii. day of March my cosine
Britaigne came into the Counter to me, and asked ther whether I might
be put to baile or no. Then went he immediatly unto my Lord mayor,
desiring of him to be so good unto me that I might be bailed. My Lorde
aunswered him, and said, that he would be glad to do the best that in
100 him lay. Howe be it he could not baile me without the consent of a spir-

---

Line 77. **shriven:** after confession, absolved of sin by a priest.

Line 78. **doctor Crome:** Dr. Edward Crome, prominent London Reformer and popular
preacher who publicly recanted 27 June 1546. **sir Gillam:** Sir William, otherwise unidentified.

Lines 78–79. **Huntington:** John Huntingdon, former priest, and an ardent Reformist
preacher.

Line 84. **wise, I:** emended from "wise.I".

Line 85. **skathe:** harm.

Line 90. **order of scoles:** rules of scholastic debate associated with Catholic scholarship.

Lines 95–96. **my cosine Britaigne:** Christopher Brittayn, a lawyer of the Middle Temple, one
of the Inns of Court.

ituall officer. So requiringe him to go and speake with the chauncellour
of London. For he saide, like as he could not commit me to pryson
without the consent of a spirituall officer, no more could he baile me
without consent of the same. So upon that, he went to the chauncelour,
requiring of him as he did afore of my lorde maiore. He aunswered him,
that the matter was so haynouse, that he durst not of him selfe do it.
without my Lord of London were made privy there unto. But hee said
he would speake unto my Lord in it. And bad him repair unto him the
next morowe and he shoulde well knowe my lordes pleasure and upon
the morow after, he came thither, and spake both with the chauncellor,   110
and with my Lord Bishopp of London my Lorde declared unto him,
that he was very well contented that I should come forth to a communication. And appointed me to apere before him the next day after, at
.iii. of the clock after none. More over he said unto him, that he
would ther should be at the examination, such lerned men, as I was
affectioned to, that they mighte see and allso make reporte that I was
handeled with no rigour. He aunswered him, that he knew no man that
I had mor affection, to than other. Than said the bishop Yes as I understand, shee is affectioned to Doctour Crome, Sir Gilliam, Whiteheade,
and Huntington; that they might heare the matter. For she did knowe   120
them to be lerned, and of a godly judgement. Also he required my
cosine Britain, that he should ernestly perswad me to utter, even the
verye bottome of my harte. And he sware by his fidelitye that no man
should take any advantage of my words. Neither yet would he lay ought
to my charge for anythinge that I should there speake. But if I said any
manner of thinge amis. He with other more wold be glad to reform me

---

Lines 100–101. **spirituall officer:** church official.

Line 107. **my Lord of London:** Edmund Bonner, bishop of London, 1540–1549, 1553–1559; active persecutor of Reformers.

Line 107. **privy:** aware.

Lines 112–13. **communication:** conference.

Line 119. **affectioned:** well disposed.

Line 119. **Sir Gilliam, Whiteheade:** emended from "Sir Gilliam Whiteheade". **Whiteheade:** David Whitehead (1492?–1571), Reformist disputant and tutor to Charles Brandon, duke of Suffolk.

therin, with moste Godly counsell. On the morowe after my lord of
London sent for me, at one of the clock, his hour beinge apointed at
thre. and as I came before him, he saide he was very sory of my trouble
and desired to know my opinion in such matters as were laid against
me. He required me also in any wise boldly to utter the secrets of my
hart, biddinge me not to fear in any point. For what so ever I did say in
his house no man should hurt me for it. I answered. For so much as
your Lordship appointed .iii. of the clocke and my frendes shall not
come in the hour, I desire you to pardon me of gevinge aunswere til
they come. Then said he, that he thought it mete to send for those iiii.
men which were afore named and apointed. Then I desired him not to
put them to the pain for it should not nede, bycause that .ii. gentell
men which were my frends were able inough to testifye that I shuld saie.
Anon after he went into his galery, with maister Spilman, and willed
him in any wise, that he should exhorte me to utter all that I thought.
In the meane while he commaunded his archdeacon to common with
me, who sayde unto me: maistres wherefore are ye accused and thus
troubled heare before the Byshoppe? To whome I aunswered agayne and
sayde. Syr, aske I praye you my accusers, for I knowe not as yet. Then
tooke he my boke out of my hande, and saide. Suche bookes as this,
hathe broughte you to the trouble ye are in. Beware (saith he) beware,
for he that made thys boke and was the authour therof, was an heretike
I warrant you, and burnte in Smithfielde. Then I asked him if he were
certain and sure, that it was true that hee hadde spoken. And he sayed
he knewe well the booke was of John frethes makinge. Than I asked
him, if he were not ashamed for to judg of the boke before he saw it
within, or yet knew the truth therof. I said also that such unadvised and
hastye judgment is a token apparent of a very slender witte. Then I

Line 136. **mete:** meet; fitting.

Line 140. **maister Spilman:** Francis Spylman, a witness of Askew's "Confession"; see page
177.

Line 142. **archdeacon:** John Wymesley, a Catholic author; he witnessed Askew's "Confession."

Line 151. **John frethe:** John Frith (1503–1533), Reformist theologian, author of *A Boke Made
by John Frith…Answering unto M. Mores Lettur* (1533); he was burned for heresy.

Line 154. **Rashe judgement reproach.:** margin.

opened the booke and shewed it him. He sayd he thought it had bene an other for he could find no fault therin. Then I desyred him, no more to be so unadvisedlye, rashe and swift in judgement, till he throughlye knewe the truthe, and so hee departed from me.

Immediatlye after came my cosen Bryttaine in with divers other as Maister Haule of Grayes Inne and such other like. Then my lord of London perswaded my cosen Brittain as he had done ofte before, which was that I should utter the bottome of my harte in any wise. My Lord said after that unto me that he would I should creadite the counsell of suche as were my frendes and well wyllers in this behalfe, whiche was, that I shoulde utter all thinges that burdened my conscience for he ensured me that I shoulde not nede to stande in doubt to say any thing. For like as he promysed them (he said) he promised me and woulde performe it. Which was, that neither he nor any man for him, should take me at advantag of any word I should speake. And therfore he bad me say my minde without feare. I answered him, that I had nought to say. For my conscience (I thanked God) was burdned with nothing.

Then brought he fourth this unsavery similitude. That if a man had a wound, no wise surgion would minister help unto it before he had seene it uncovered. In like case (sayeth he) can I geve you no good counsell, unlesse I know where with your conscience is burdened. I answered, that my conscience was clere in all thinges. And for to lay a plaister unto the whole skinne, it might appere much folye. Then ye drive me (saith he) to lay to your charge, your owne report which is this. Ye did say he that doth receave the sacrament by the handes of an ill priest or a sinner, he receiveth the devil and not God. To that I aunswered, that I never spake such wordes.

But as I said afore both to the quest and to my Lord mayer, so say I now againe that the wickednes of the priest shoulde not hurte me, but in spirit and faith I received no les, then the body and bloud of Christ. Then saied the bishop unto me, what saienge is this in Spirit? I will not take you at that advantage.

160
170
180

Line 160. **Maister Haule:** the chronicler Edward Hall (d. 1547).
Line 166. **ensured:** assured.
Line 177. **plaister:** plaster.

Then I aunswered my lord without fayth and spirite, I cannot
receyve him worthelye. Then he layed unto me that I shuld say, that the
sacrament remayning in the pixe, was but bread. I aunswered that I
190   never sayde so, but in dede the quest asked me such a question, wherunto I would not aunswere (I sayde) till such time as they had assoyld
me this question of mine, wherfore Steven was stoned to death? They
said they knew not. Then saide I again no more would I tell them what
it was. Then layde my lord unto me, that I had alleaged a certaine text
of the scripture, I aunswered that I alleged none other but Saint Paules
owne saying to the Athenianes in the .xvii. chapter in the Apostles actes
that god dwelleth not in temples made with hands. Then asked he me
what my fayth and beliefe was in that mater? I aunswered him I beleve
as the scriptur doth teach me. Then inquired he of me, what if, the
200   scripture do say that it is the body of Christ? I beleve, said I, as the scripture doth teache me. Then asked he againe what if the scripture do say
that it is not the body of Christ? My answer was stil, I beleve as the
scripture infourmeth me, And upon this argument he taried a great
while to have driven me to make him an aunswer to his mind. Howbeit
I would not, but concluded this with him that I beleve therein and in all
other thinges as christ and his holy Apostles did leave them. Then he
asked me, why I had so few wordes, And I aunswered, God hath geven
me the gift of knowledge, but not of utterance. And Salomon sayeth
that a woman of few wordes is a gift of God. Pro. xix.
210   Thirdlye my Lorde layed unto my charge that I should say that the
mass was superstitious, wicked, and no better then Idolatry.

I aunswered him no, I sayde not so. Howbeit I say the quest did aske
me whether private masse did releve soules departed or no? Unto
whome then I answered.

O Lorde what Idolatry is this? That we should rather beleve in private masses than in the healthsome death of the dere son of god. Then

---

Line 188. **shuld say:** did say.

Line 194. **alleaged:** quoted.

Line 199. **the:** emended from "te".

Line 204. **Howbeit:** however.

Line 216. **healthsome:** bestowing spiritual health.

said my Lord againe: What an answere was that? Though it were but
meane (sayed I): Yet it was good enough for the question. Then I toulde
my Lorde that there was a priest, which did here what I sayd there,
before my Lorde Mayer and them. With that the Chauncelor answered,   220
which was the same prieste. So she spake it in verye dede saith he before
my Lorde mayer and me: then were there certaine priestes, as Doctor
Standish and other which tempted me much to know my mind. And I
answered them alwayes thus. That I said to my lord of London, I have
sayde. And then Doctor Standish desyred my Lord, to bid me say my
mind, concerninge the same text of Saint Paules lerning, that I being a
woman, should enterprete the scriptures specialy where so many wise
lerned men wer. Then my lorde of London said he was informed that
one should ask of me if I would receive the sacramente at Easter, and I
made a mocke of it, then I desired that mine accuser might come forth,   230
which my Lorde would not. But he said againe unto me I sent one to
geve you good councell, and at the first word ye called him papist. That
I denied not, for I perceaved he was no lesse, yet made I him none
answere unto it. Then he rebuked me, and saide that I should reporte,
that there were bente againste me threscore priestes at Lincolne. In dede
(quod I) I sayd so. For my frendes tolde me, if I did com to Lincoln, the
priests wold assaulte me and put me to great trouble as therof they had
made their boast. And when I herd it I went thither in dede, not being
afrayed, because I knew my matter to be good. Moreover, I remained
there .ix. dayes, to se what would be said unto me. And as I was in the   240
minster, reading upon the bible, they resorted unto me by .ii. and by ,ii.
by .v. and by ,vi, minding to have spoken to me, yet went they their
wayes againe with out wordes speaking.
    Then my Lord asked, if there were not one that did speake unto me.
I told him yeas, that there was one of them at the laste, whiche did

---

Line 218. **meane**: unadorned.

Lines 222–23. **Doctor Standish**: John Standish (1507?–1570), Bishop Bonner's appointee as
rector of St. Andrew Undershaft. **D. Standish**: margin.

Line 223. **tempted**: emended from "t̄ēp̄ēted".

Line 240. **ix dayes**: in Bale's edition, "vi dayes." See page 56.

Line 241. **minster**: cathedral church.

speake to me in dede. And my Lord than asked me what he said? And I
told him, his wordes were of smal effect, that I did not now remembre
them. Then said my Lord there are many that read and know the scripture, and yet not follow it nor live therafter. I said againe, my Lord I
250 would wish that all men knew my conversation and livinge in all
poynts, for I am so sure of my selfe this houre that there are none able to
prove any dishonestie by me. If you know any that can do it, I pray you
bring them furth. Then my lorde went away and said he would entitle
sumwhat of my meaning. And so he wrote a greate circumstance. But
what it was I have not all in memory. For he wuld not suffer me to have
the copy therof. Only do I remembre this small porcion of it. Be it
knowen (sayeth he) of all men that I Anne Askew doo confesse this to
be my faith and beliefe, notwithstanding my reportes made afore to the
contrary. I beleve that they which are houseled at the handes of a priest
260 whether his conversation be good or not, do receive the body and bloud
of Christ in substance really. Also I do beleve that after the consecration
whether it be received or reserved, to be no lesse than the very body and
bloud of Christ, in substance. Finally I doo beleve in this and in all
other sacramentes of holly church in all poynts according to the old
catholike faith of the same. In witnes wherof I the said An have subscribed my name. There was sumwhat more in it, which because I had
not the copy I cannot now remembre. Then he redde it to me and asked
me if I did agre to it. And I said againe I beleve so much therof as the
holy scripture doth agre unto. wherfore I desire you, that ye will adde
270 that therunto. Then he aunswered that I shoulde not teach him what he
shoulde write. With that, he went forth into his great chamber, and

---

Line 252. **dishonestie:** unchastity.

Line 253. **entitle:** to write down under proper titles or headings.

Line 254. **circumstance:** detailed and circuitous narrative.

Line 259. **houseled:** received communion.

Line 260. **conversation:** behavior.

Line 262. **whether...reserved:** whether the consecrated elements are handed out or retained
for other purposes.

Line 270. **The tenor of Boners writing wherunto An Askew subscrybed.:** margin.

Line 271. **great chamber:** the Bishop's formal court at St. Paul's.

redde the same bill afore the audience, which enveygled and willed me to set to my hand saing also, that I had favour shewed me. Then said the Bishop I might thanke other and not my selfe, of the favour that I found at his hande. For he considered (he saide) that I had good frendes, and also that I was come of a worshipfull stocke. Then aunswered one Christofer, a servaunt to maister Dennie, rather ought ye (my Lord) to have done it in such case, for goddes sake than for mannes. Then my Lord sat downe and toke me the writings to set therto my hand: And I writte after this maner. I Anne Askew do beleve   280
all manner thinges conteined in the faith of the Catholike church.

> And for as much as mention here is made of the Writing of Boner, which this godly Ann sayd before she had not in memory, therfore I thought in this place to infer the same, both with the whol circumstance of Boner, and with the title therunto prefixed by the register, and also with her owne subscription: to the entent the reader seing the same subscription nether to agre with the time of the title above prefixed, nor with the subscription after the writing annexed, he might the better understand therby what credit is to be geven hereafter to such bishops and to such regesters. The tenor of Boners writing procedeth thus.   290

The true copy of the confession and beliefe of Anne Askew otherwise called Anne Kime made before the bishop of London the .xx. day of March in the yere of oure Lorde God after the computation of the church of England. 1544 and subscribed with her owne hand in the

---

Line 272. **enveygled:** inveigled; cajoled.

Line 276. **worshipfull stocke:** a family of distinguished character or rank.

Line 277. **maister Dennie:** Anthony Denny (1501–1549), Henry VIII's chief gentleman of the privy chamber, close adviser, and a Reformist sympathizer.

Line 281. **Catholike church:** "catholic" was a hotly contested term between Roman Catholics and Reformers. See Introduction, page xxxi.

Lines 282–90. **And...thus:** Foxe's headnote to his addition of the entry from Bishop Bonner's Register purporting to be Askew's signed confession of faith in the Roman Catholic doctrine of the mass. See Introduction, page xxxi.

Line 290. **writing:** emended from "wriing".

Lines 291–335. **The true copy...present:** A faithful transcript of the entry in Bishop Bonner's Register, although as was customary in the sixteenth century, Foxe's transcript includes variant spellings.

Lines 293–94. **yere...1544:** old style dating; equivalent to 20 March 1545. See Introduction, pages xx–xxi.

presence of the said B. and other whose names here after are resited, setforth and published at this present, to the entent the world may see,
what credence is now to be geven unto the same woman who in so short
a time hath most dampnably altered and changed her opinion and
beliefe and therfore rightfully in open court arrayned and condempned.

300   Be it knowen to all faithful people, that as touchinge the blessed sacrament of the altare, I do firventlye and undoubtedly beleve, that after the
words of consecratyon be spoken by the priest accordinge to the common usuage of this church of England there is present really the body
and bloud of our saviour Jesu Christ, whether the minister which doth
consecrate, be a good man or a bad man, and that also when so ever the
saide Sacramente is received, whether the receiver be a good man or a
bad man he doth receive it really and corporallye. And moreover I do
beleve, that whether the saide sacrament be then received of the minister or els reserved to be put into the pixe, or to be brought to anye per-
310   sonne that is impotent that is sicke, yet there is the very body and bloud
of our said savior, so that whether the minyster or the receiver be good
or bad, yea, whether the sacramente be received or reserved, always
there is the blessed body of Christ really.

   And this thing with al other thinges touching the sacrament and
other sacramentes of the churche, and all thinges els touchinge the
christen belefe. whyche are taught and declared in the kinges majesties
boke lately setforth, for the erudition of the christen people, I Anne
Askew, otherwise called Anne Kyme, doo trulye and perfectly beleve,
and so here presently confesse and knowledge. And here I do promise
320   that henceforth I shal never say or do any thing against the premisses, or
against any of them. In witnesse wherof I the saide Anne have sub-

---

Line 295. **B.:** "bysshop" in the Register.

Line 296. **this present:** this present time.

Line 301. **firventlye:** emended from "firvtlye".

Line 304. **which:** who; "that" in the Register.

Line 309. **pixe:** pyx; box in which the consecrated bread of the sacrament is kept.

Line 319. **knowledge:** acknowledge.

scribed my name unto these presentes, wrytten the xx. day of March in the yeare of our Lord God. 1544.

By me Anne Askew, otherwise called Anne Kime.

Edmund bishop of London.
Jhon bishop of Bedford.
Owen Ogelthorpe doctor of divinity.
Richard Smith doctor of divinity.
Jhon Rudde bacheler of divinity.
Wylliam Pie bacheler of devinity.   330
Jhon Wymesley Archdeacon of London.
Jhon Cooke.   Edward Halle.
Robert Jhon   Alexander Brette.
Fraunces Spilman.   Edmond Buttes.
   Wyth divers other mo being then present.

   Here maist thou note gentle reader in thys confessyon bothe in the bishop and his regester a double sleight of false conveyaunce. For although the confession purporteth the words of the bishops wryting. Wherunto she did set to her hand: yet by the title prefixed before maist thou see that both she was araigned and condemned before this was reg-   340
istred, and also that she is falsly reported to have put to her hand whyche in dede by this her owne booke appeareth not so to be, but after this manner and condition. I Anne Askew do beleve al manner thinges contained in the faith of the Catholike church, and not otherwise.

Line 322. **these presentes:** these statements in the document.

Line 328. **Richard Smith:** leading Catholic cleric, preacher, and author.

Line 329. **Jhon Rudde:** Dr. John Rudd; in the 1530s he was a chantry priest at All Hallows, Barking.

Line 332. **Jhon Cooke:** John Cook; possibly Dean Cook of the Court of Arches, a member of the London fraternity, the Name of Jesus in the Shrouds of St. Paul's.

Line 333. **Robert Jhon:** Robert Johnson, Bishop Bonner's registrar, and a member of the Name of Jesus in the Shrouds of St. Paul's.

Lines 336–44. **Here...otherwise:** Foxe's commentary on the discrepancy in dating. See Introduction, page xxxi.

Line 336. **Boner and his register reproved with an untruth.:** margin.

Line 337. **conveyaunce:** expression, utterance.

Then because I did adde unto it, the Catholike churche, he flonge
into his Chambre in a great fury. With that my cosen Bryttaine folowed
him: desiring him for Goddes sake to be good Lord unto me. He answeared that I was a woman, and that he was nothinge deceived in me.
Then my cosen Bryttaine desired him to take me as a woman, and not
350   to sette my weake womans wit, to his Lordshippes verye greate wisdome. Then went in unto him Doctor Weston, and saide, that the cause
whye I did wryte there, the Catholicke churche, was, that I understode
not the church wrytten afore. So with much a do, they perswaded my
Lorde to come out againe, and to take my name with the names of my
sureties, which were my cosen Brittayne and master Spilman of Graies
Inne. This being doone, we thoughte that I shuld have bene put to
Bayle immediatlye, according to the order of the lawe. Howe be it he
woulde not suffer it, but committed me from thence to prison again
until the next morowe. And than he willed me to appeare in the guild
360   Hall, and so I did. Notwithstanding they wold not put me to Bayle
there neither, but red the bishops wryting unto me as before, and so
commaunded me again to prison. Then were my sureties appoynted to
come before them on the next morow in Paules church, which did so in
dede. Notwithstanding they would once again have broken of with
them, because they wolde not be bound also for an other woman at
theyr pleasure, whome they knew not, nor yet what matter was layed
unto her charge. Notwythstanding at the last, after much a do and reasoning to and fro, they toke a bond of them of recognisance for my
forthe comming. And thus I was at the laste delivered. Wrytten by me
370   Anne Askewe.

Line 351. **Doctor Weston:** Hugh Weston, conservative rector of St. Botolph Bishopsgate.

Line 369. **forthe comming:** coming forward (when summoned by the court).

Foxe omits "The voyce of Anne Askewe out of the 54. Pslame." See page 72.

The latter Examination of the worthy servant of
God, mastres Anne Askew, the yonger doughter
of sir William Askew knight of Lincoln shire,
lately martired in Smithfeld, by the
wicked sinagoge of Antichrist.

I do perceive (dere frend in the Lord) that thou art not yet perswaded
throughly in the truth concerning the Lords supper, because Christe
said unto his Apostles. Take eat this is my body which is geven for you.
In geving forth the bread as an outward signe or token to be received at
the mouth, he minded them in perfect beleve to receive the body of his   10
whiche should dye for the people, or to thinke the death therof, the
only health and salvation of their soules.

The bread and the wine were left us, for a sacramental communion,
or a mutual participation, of the inestimable benefites of hys mooste
precious death and bloud sheding, and that we should in the end therof
be thanckfull together for that most necessary grace of our redemption.
For in the closing up therof, he said thus, thys do ye, in remembraunce
of me. Yea, so oft as ye shal eat it or drinke it. Luk .xi. and .i. Corinth.
xi. Els shuld we have bene forgetfull of that we oughte to have in dailye
remembraunce, and also bene altogether unthankful for it. Therfore it   20
is mete, that in our prayers we cal unto god to graft in our forheads, the
true mening of the holy ghost concerninge this communyon. For Sainct
Paule doth say that the letter sleieth: The sprite is it onely that geveth
life .ii. Corinthians .iii. Marke well the sixt chapiter of Jhon, wherall is
applied unto fayth. Note also the fourth chapiter of Saint Paules fyrste
Epistle to the Corinthians, and in the ende therof ye shall find that the
thinges which are sene are temporal, but they that are not sene are ever-
lastyng. Yea looke in the thirde chapiter to the Hebrues, and ye shal find
that Christ as a sonne and no servaunte, ruleth over hys house (whose

---

Line 5. **Antichrist:** the great opponent of Christ who would appear before the end of the
world (1 John 2:18); Reformers' derogatory term for the Roman Catholic papacy.

Line 6. **1546:** margin.

Line 10. **minded:** reminded, exhorted.

Line 12. **health:** spiritual well-being, salvation.

30   house are we, and not the deade temple) if we hold fast the confidence
and rejoysing of that hope to the end. Wherfore as saithe the holy
Ghost. To day if you shall heare hys voyce, harden not your hartes. &c.
Psal. cxiiii.

The summe of my examination, before
the kinges counsel at Grenewich.

Your request, as concerning my prison fellowes, I am not able to satisfy:
Because I hard not their examinations: But the effect of mine, was this.
I beinge before the Councell, was asked of master Kyme. I answeared,
that my Lord Chauncellor knew already my mind in that matter. They
40   with that answer were not contented: but said, it was the kings pleasure,
that I should open the matter to them. I answered them plainly that I
wold not so do. But if it were the kings pleasure to hear me, I would
shew him the truth. Then they sayed it was not mete for the kinge with
me to be troubled. I answered, that Salomon was reckened the wisest
king, that ever lived: yet misliked he not to heare two poore comon
women: much more his grace a simple woman, and his faithful subject.
So in conclusion I made them none other aunswer in that matter. Then
my Lord chauncelour asked me of my opinion in the sacrament. My
answer was this: I beleve, that so oft as I in a christian congregation, do
50   receive the bread in remembraunce of Christes death, and with thankes
geving according to his holye institution, I receive there with the frutes
also of his moste glorious passyon. The bishop of Winchester bad me
make a direct answer. I said, I wold not sing a newe songe to the Lord in
a straunge land. Than the byshop said, I spake in parables, I answeared
it was best for him. For if I shewe the open truthe (quoth I) ye wil not
accept it. Then he sayd I was a Parate. I told him again, I was ready to

---

Lines 28–33. **Yea looke...Psal. cxiiii:** the Psalm number is incorrect; Bale's edition gives the
correct Vulgate reference to Psalm 94. The words of Heb. 3:7–8 are based on Ps. 95:7–8 in the
King James version. **whose...temple:** Christians are a spiritual community of believers; see
Heb. 3:6.

Line 38. **master Kyme:** Thomas Kyme, Askew's husband. See Introduction, page xix.

Line 41. **open:** reveal, disclose.

Line 44. **Salomon:** see 1 Kings 3:16 ff.

Line 56. **Parate:** parrot.

suffer all thinges at his hands not only hys rebukes, but all that shoulde
folowe besydes, yea and all that gladly. Then had I dyvers rebukes of the
councel, because I would not expresse my minde in al thinges as they
woulde have me. But they wer not in the mean time unanswered for all   60
that, which now to rehers were to muche. For I was with them there
about v. hours. Then the clarke of the counsell conveyed me from
thence to my lady Garnish. The next day I was brought again before the
councel. Then would they nedes know of me, what I saide to the sacrament. I answeared, that I already had said that I could say. Then after
divers wordes, they bad me go by. Then came my Lord Lisle, my Lord
of Essex, and the Bishop of Winchester, requiringe me earnestlye that I
should confesse the sacrament to be flesh bloud and bone. Then said I
to my lord Parr and my Lorde Lisle, that it was great shame for them to
councell contrarye to theyr knowledge. Wherunto in few words they   70
did saye, that they would gladly all thinges were well. Then the bishop
said, he wold speake with me familierly. I sayde, so did Judas whan he
unfrendly betrayed Christ. Then desyred the byshop to speake with me
alone. But that I refused. He asked me why? I said: that in the mouthe
of two or thre witnesses, every matter shoulde stand, after Christes and
Paules doctryne. Mathew xviii. ii. Corinth. xiii. Then my Lord
Chauncelor began to examine me again of the Sacrament. Then I asked
him how longe he would hault on bothe sides? Then woulde he neades
know where I found that, I said in the scripture .iii. Regum .xviii. Then
he went hys way. Then the Bishop said I should be brent: I answered   80
that I had searched all the scryptures, yet coulde I never finde, that
eyther Christe or his Apostles putte anye creature to death. Well well

---

Line 63. **my lady Garnish:** "garnish" is slang for the money jailors extorted from new prisoners (earliest *OED* citation: 1592); thus "my lady Garnish" is Askew's ironic term for prison.

Lines 66–67. **Lord Lisle:** John Dudley, viscount Lisle (1502?–1553), a privy councillor and later, duke of Northumberland. **my Lord of Essex:** William Parr (1513–71), earl of Essex, brother of Queen Katherine Parr and a privy councillor.

Line 69. **my lord Parr:** the earl of Essex.

Line 78. **hault...sides:** waver between two opinions, a common reference to 1 Kings 18:20.

Line 80. **brent:** burned at the stake.

said I, God will laugh your threatninges to skorne. Psalme .ii. Then was
I commaunded to stande aside. Then came to me Doctor Cox, and
Doctor Robinson. In conclusion we coulde not agree. Then they made
me a bil of the sacrament: willing me to set my hand therunto but I
would not. Then on the sonday I was sore sicke, thinkinge no les then
to die. Therfore I desired to speake with Latimer, it wold not be. Then
was I sent to Newgate in my extremity of sicknes. For in al my life afore
90   was I never in such pain. Thus the lord strengthen you in the truth,
pray, pray, pray.

The confession of me Anne Askew for the time I was
in Newgate concerning my beliefe.

I find in the scriptures (sayth she) that christe toke the breade and gave
it to his disciples, saing, take, eate, this is my body which shalbe broken
for you, meaning in substance his own very body, the bread being therof
an only sign or sacrament. For after like manner of speaking he said, he
wold breake down the temple, and in iii. dayes build it up againe signi-
fieng his owne body by the temple as Sainct Jhon declareth it. Jhon .ii.
100   and not the stony temple it selfe. So that the breade is but a remembraunce of his death or a sacrament of thankes geving for it, whereby we
are knit unto him by a communion of christen love. Although ther be
many that cannot perceive the true meaning therof, for that vale that
Moses put over his face befor the children of Israel, that they shoulde
not see the clerenesse therof. Exo. xxiiii. and .ii. Corin. iii. I perceive the
same vail remaineth to this day. But whan God shall take it away, then
shall these blinde men see. For it is plainlye expressed in the hystory of

---

Line 84. **stande aside**: in Bale's edition, Paget's interrogation appeared at this point in the text.
See page 99 and Introduction, page xxviii.

Lines 84–85. **Doctor Cox**: Richard Cox (1500–1581), humanist scholar and Reformer in
Katherine Parr's circle. **Doctor Robinson**: probably Thomas Robinson or Robertson (fl.
1520–1561), archdeacon of Leicester in the diocese of Lincoln.

Line 86. **bil**: formal written document.

Line 88. **Latimer**: Hugh Latimer (1485?–1555), Reformist preacher, closely associated with
Katherine Parr's circle, especially the duchess of Suffolk.

Line 89. **Newgate**: prison for those charged with criminal offences in the city of London.

Line 92. **Askew**: emended from "Akew".

Bel in the bible, that God dwelleth in no thinge materyall. O kynge (saith Daniel) be not deceived. Daniel .xiiii. for God wil be in nothing that is made with handes of men. Act. vii. Oh, what stifnecked people are these, that wil alwaies resist the holye ghost? But as their fathers have done: so doo they, because they have stony harts. Wrytten by me Anne Askew that neither wishe death, nor yet fear his might: and as meary, as one that is bound towardes heaven. Truth is laide in prison. Luk .xxi. The law is turned to Wormwood. Amos .vi. And there can no right judgement go forth. Esay .lix. Oh forgeve us al our sinnes, and receive us gratiouslye. As for the works of our hands, we wil no more cal upon them. For it is thou Lord that art our God. Thou shewest ever mercy unto the fatherles. Oh if they would doo this (saithe the Lorde) I shoulde heale their sores, yea withal my harte woulde I love them. O Ephraim, what have I to do with Idols any more: who so is wyse, shal understand this. And he that is rightly enstructed, wil regard it. For the wais of the Lord are righteous. Such as are godly, wil walk in them. And as for the wicked, they wil stomble at them. Ose. xiiii. Salomon (saith S. Steven) builded an house for the God of Jacob. Howbeit, the hiest of al, dwelleth not in temples made with hands: As saith the prophet Esaye .lxvi. Heaven is my seat, and thearth is my fotestole. What house wil ye build for me? saith the lord, or what place is it that I shal rest in? hath not my hand made al things? Act. vii. Woman beleve me (saith Christe to the Samaritane) the time is at hand, that ye shall neither in thys mountain nor yet at Jerusalem worship the father. Ye worship ye wot not what, but we know what we worship. For salvation commeth of the Jewes. But the hour cometh, and is now, when the true worshippers shal worship the father in sprite and verity Jhon iii. Laboure not (saith Christ) for the meat that pearisheth, but for that that endureth into the life everlasting which the sonne of manne shal geve you. For him God the father hath sealed. Jhon vii.

Line 110. **stifnecked:** proud.
Line 121. **Ephraim:** see Hos. 14:8.
Line 134. **Jhon iii:** as in Bale's edition, the correct chapter is John 4.
Line 137. **Jhon vii:** as in Bale's edition, the correct chapter is John 6.

The summe of the condemnation of me
Anne Askew at the Guild Hal.

140 They said to me ther that I was an hereticke, and condempned by the
law, if I would stande in mine opinyon. I answeared that I was no
hereticke, neyther yet deserved I any death by the lawe of God. But as
concerning the faith whiche I uttered and wrote to the counsel I would
not (I said) deny it, because I knew it true. Then woulde they neades
know if I wold deny the Sacrament to be Christes body and bloude of
Christ: yea. For the same sonne of God, that was borne of the virgin
Mary, is now glorious in heaven, and wil come againe from thence at
the latter day like as he went up. Act. i. And as for that ye cal youre
God, it is a peace of breade: for a more profe therof (marke it whan ye
150 list.) Let it lie in the boxe but iii. monethes, and it wil be mouldy, and so
turn to nothinge that is good. Wherupon I am perswaded, that it can
not be god. After that they willed me to have a priest: And then I
smiled. Then they asked me, if it were not good? I saide, I woulde confesse my fautes unto god. For I was sure that he would heare me with
favor. And so we were condempned with a quest. My belefe whiche I
wrote to the councel was this. That the Sacramentall bread was left us to
be received with thankes geving, in remembraunce of Christes deathe,
the onlye remeady of oure soules to recover. And that therby we also
receive the whole benefytes and frutes of his most glorious passion.
160 Then woulde they neades know whether the bread in the boxe were
God or no. I sayd: god is a spirit, and wil be worshipped in spirit and
truthe. Jhon iiii. Then they demaunded. Wil you plainly deny Christ to
be in the Sacrament? I answeared that I beleve faythfully the eternal
sonne of God not to dwell there. In witnesse wherof I recited again the
history of Bel, and the xix. chapiter of Daniell, the vii and xvii. of the

---

Line 148. **latter day:** Day of Judgment.

Line 153. **The belefe of Anne Askew concerning the sacraments.:** margin.

Line 155. **with a quest:** in Bale's edition, "without a quest" (page 112). See Introduction,
page xxvi.

Line 160. **bread in the boxe:** communion wafer in the pyx.

Line 165. **xix chapiter:** as in Bale's edition, the correct chapter is Daniel 9.

Actes, and the xxiiii. of Mathew, concluding thus. I neither wish deathe, nor yet feare his might, god hathe the prayse therof wyth thanckes.

My letter sent to the Lord Chaunceler.

The Lord God, by whom al creatures have theyr beinge, blesse you with the lighte of his knowledge. Amen. My duty to your lordship remem- 170
bred &c. It might please you to accept this my bold sute, as the sute of one, which upon due considerations is moved to the same and hopeth to obtain. My request to your lordship is only, that it may please the same to be a meane for me to the kinges majestye, that hys grace may be certefied of these few lines whiche I have wrytten concerninge my belefe. Which whan it shalbe truly conferred with the hard judgement geven me for the same, I think his grace shall wel perceive me to be wayed in an uneven pair of balaunces. But I remit my matter and cause to almightye God, whyche rightlye judgeth all seacreates. And thus I commend your Lordshippe to the governaunce of hym and felowship of 180
al saintes. Amen.

By your handmaid Anne Askew.

My faith briefly wrytten to the kings grace. — *asking for pardon*

I Anne Askew of good memorye, although God hathe geven me the breade of adversytye and the water of trouble, yet not so muche as my sinnes have deserved, desire thys to be known to your grace. that forasmuch as I am by the law condempned for an evil doer: Here I take heaven and earth to record, that I shall die in my innocency. And according to that I have said first, and wil say last, I utterly abhor and detest al heresies. And as concerninge the supper of the Lord, I beleve so 190
much as Christ hath said therin. Which he confirmed with his most blessed bloud. I beleve also so much as he willed me to follow and beleve, and so muche as the catholike church of him doth teach. For I wil not forsake the commaundement of hys holy lippes. But loke what

---

Line 168. **Lord Chaunceler**: Sir Thomas Wriothesley (1505–1550), lord chancellor who became first earl of Southampton in 1547; he was a prominent conservative determined to stop the Reformers.

Line 176. **conferred**: compared.

[handwritten: these words are from God]

God hath charged me with his mouth, that have I shut up in my hart, and thus briefly I ende, for lack of learning Anne Askew.

[handwritten: FOR LACK OF HENRYS LEARNING OR ANNES?]

The effect of my examination and handling, sence my departure from Newgate.

On Tuesdaye I was sente from Newgate to the signe of the crown, wheras Master Rich and the bishop of London withal their power and flattering words, went about to perswade me from God. But I did not esteme their glosing pretences. Then came there to me Nicolas Shaxton, and councelled me to recante as he had done. Then I said to him, that it had bene good for him, never to have ben born with many other like words. Then master Riche sent me to the tower, where I remained til iii. a clock. Then came Rich and one of the counsell, charging me upon my obedience, to shew unto them if I knew man or woman of my sect. My aunswer was, that I knew non. Then they asked me of my lady of Suffolk, my lady Sussex, my Lady of Hertford, my Lady Denny and my lady Fizwilliams. I said, if I should pronounce any thing against them, that I were not able to prove it. Then said they unto me, that the king was infourmed, that I could name, if I would a great nombre of my sect. Then I answered, that the king was as wel deceived in that behalf, as dissembled with in other matters. Then commaunded they me to shew

---

Line 199. **signe of the crown:** an inn identified by the sign over its door.

Line 200. **Master Rich:** Richard Rich (1496–1567), member of the conservative court faction; see Introduction, page xxvii.

Line 202. **Nicolas Shaxton:** Nicholas Shaxton (1485?–1556), former bishop of Salisbury, condemned for heresy on the same day as Askew; see Introduction, pages xxii–xxiii.

Line 205. **tower:** the Tower of London.

Line 207. **my sect:** Reformers.

Lines 208–9. **my lady of Suffolk:** Catherine Brandon, duchess of Suffolk (1519/20–1580), a Reformist patron and friend of Queen Katherine Parr. **my lady Sussex:** Anne Radcliffe, countess of Sussex. **my Lady of Hertford:** Anne Stanhope, countess of Hertford (1497–1587), one of Katherine Parr's circle and wife of Edward Seymour, afterwards Protector Somerset. **my Lady Denny:** Joan Denny, wife of Henry VIII's privy councillor, Sir Anthony Denny.

Lines 209–10. **my lady Fizwilliams:** possibly Jane Ormond, third wife and widow of Sir William FitzWilliam (d. 1534), a member of Henry VIII's Privy Council, and grandfather of Anne Cooke Bacon.

Line 214. **with in:** emended from "within".

howe I was maintained in the counter, and who willed me to sticke by my opinion. I sayd that there was no creature that therin did strenghthen me. And as for the helpe that I had in the counter, it was by the meanes of my maid. For as she went abrode in the streates, she made mone to the prentises, and they by her did send me monye. But who they were I never knew. Then they said, that ther wer divers gentle women, that gave me mony. But I knew not their names. Then they said that there were divers Ladies, which had sent me mony. I answeared, that there was a man in a blew cote, which delivered me x. shillings, and said that my lady of Hertford sent it me. And another in a violet coat did geve me viii. shyllings, and said that my lady Denny sent it me. Whether it wer true or no, I cannot tel. For I am not sure who sent it me, but as the maid did say. Then they said, there were of the councel that did maintain me. And I said, no. Then they did put me on the racke, because I confessed no ladies or Gentle women to be of my opinion, and theron they kept me a longe time. And because I lay stil and did not cry, my Lord chauncellour and master Rich, toke paines to racke me with their owne handes, till I was nigh dead. Then the liefetenante caused me to be loused from the rack. Incontinently I swounded, and then they recovered me again. After that I sate ii. long hours reasoning with my Lord chancellor upon the bare flour, wheras he with many flattering wordes, perswaded me to leave my opinion. But my lord God (I thanke his everlasting goodnesse) gave me grace to persever and wil doo (I hope) to the very end. Then was I brought to an house, and laid in a bed with as weary and painfull bones, as ever had

220

230

Line 219. **prentises:** apprentices.

Line 229. **racke:** an instrument of torture, a frame with a roller at each end to which the victim's wrists and ankles were tied; the joints were stretched by rotating the rollers.

Line 231. **Wrisley and Rich racking Anne Askewe.:** margin.

Lines 232–33. **liefetenante:** the lieutenant of the Tower, Sir Anthony Knevet. See Textual Introduction, page liv.

Line 233. **Incontinently:** immediately.

Line 234. **swounded:** swooned.

Line 235. **reasoning:** holding a discussion.

240 pacient Job I thanke my Lord God therof. Then my Lord Chancellor sent me word if I wold leave my opinion, I shuld want nothing. If I wold not, I shuld forth to Newgate, and so be burned, I sent him again word, that I wold rather die, than to breake my faith. Thus the Lord open the eies of their blinde hartes, that the truthe may take place. Farewel dere frend, and pray pray, pray.

Anne Askewes answer unto Jhon Lassels letter.

Oh frend most dearly beloved in God I mervell not a little, what shoulde move you to judge in me so slender a faith, as to feare death, which is thend of al misery. In the Lord I desyre you, not to beleve of 250 suche wickednes. For I doubt it not, but God wil perform his work in me, like as he hath begon: I understand the councel is not a little displeased: that it should be reported abrode, that I was racked in the towre. They say nowe that they did there, was but to feare me, wherby I perceived, they are ashamed of their uncomelye doinges, and feare much least the kinges majesty shuld have information there of. Wherof they would no man to noyse it. Wel, their crueltye God forgeve them. Your hart in Christ Jesu. Farewel and praie.

I have red the processe, which is reported of them that know not the truth, to be my recantation. But as sure as the Lorde lyveth. I never 260 ment thing les than to recant. Not withstanding this I confesse, that in my first troubles, I was examined of the bishoppe of London about the sacrament, yet had they no graunt of my mouth, but this: that I beleved there in, as the word of God did binde me to beleve. More had they never of me. Then he made a copye which is now in print, and required

---

Line 246. **Jhon Lassels:** John Lassells; a Reformer from Nottinghamshire and an attendant of the King's Chamber, he was condemned with Askew. See page 192.

Line 253. **feare:** frighten.

Line 254. **uncomelye:** improper.

Line 256. **noyse:** report.

Line 258. **processe:** proceedings.

Line 261. **troubles, I:** emended from "troubles. I".

me to set therunto my hand. But I refused it. Then my ii. sureties did
wil me in no wise to sticke ther at. For it was no great matter, they
sayde.

Then wyth much a doo, at the laste I wrote thus: I Anne Askewe do
beleve thys, if Gods word do agre to the same, and the true catholique
church. Then the byshop, beyng in great displeasure with me, because I   270
made doubtes in my writing, commaunded me to pryson, wher I was a
whyle. But afterwardes by the meanes of frendes, I came out againe.
Here is the truth of that matter. And as concernynge the thyng that ye
covet moste to knowe, resorte to the vi. of John, and be ruled alwayes
therby. Thus fare ye well. Quod Anne Askewe.

The confession of the faith whiche Anne Askewe
made in Newgate, before she suffred.

I Anne Askewe, of good memory, although my mercifull father hath
geven me the bread of adversytie, and the water of trouble: yet not so
muche as my synnes have deserved: confesse my selfe here a synner   280
before the throne of hys heavenly majestie, desyryng his forgevenes and
mercy. And for so muche as I am by the lawe unrightuously condempned for an evyl doer, concerning opinions, I take the same moste mercifull God of myne, whiche hathe made bothe heaven and earth, to
recorde, that I holde no opynions contrarie to his mooste holye worde.
And I trust in my mercyfull Lorde, whiche is the gever of all grace, that
he wyll graciously assiste me against all evyll opinions, whiche are contrary to his blessed veritie. For I take hym to wytnesse, that I have done
and wyll doo unto my lyves ende, utterly abhorre them, to the utter-
moste of my power. But this is the heresye whiche they reporte me to   290
holde, that after the priest hath spoken the wordes of consecration,
there remayneth bread styll.

But they both saye, and also teache it for a necessarye artycle of
faythe, that after those wordes be once spoken, there remayneth noo

---

Line 265. **sureties**: guarantors.
Line 277. **suffred**: suffered death.
Line 290. **The matter and cause why Anne Askewe suffered death.**: margin.

bread, but even the selfe same body, that hong upon the crosse on good fryday, both flesh, bloud and bone. To this belefe of theirs saye I naye: For then were our common Crede false, which sayeth that he sytteth on the ryghte hande of God the father almyghtie: And from thence shall come to judge the quicke and dead. Lo, this is the heresie that I holde.

300   And for it must suffer the death. But as touchyng the holy and blessed supper of the Lorde, I beleve it to be a moste necessary remembraunce of his glorious sufferynges and death. Moreover, I beleve as muche therin, as my eternall and onely redemer, Jesus Christe would I should beleve. Finally I beleve all those scriptures to be true, whome he hath confyrmed with his moste precious bloud. Yea, and as S. Paule sayth, those scriptures are sufficient for our learning and salvation, that Christe hath left here with us. So that I beleve, we nede no unwrytten verities to rule his churche with. Therfore looke what he hathe sayde unto me with his owne mouthe, in his holy Gospell, that have I with

310   Gods grace closed up in my harte. And my full trust is (as David sayth) that it shalbe a lanterne to my footesteppes. Psalm .xxviii. Ther be some do saye, that I denie the *Euchariste* or sacrament of thankes geving. But those people do untruely reporte of me. For I both saye and beleve it, that if it were ordered, lyke as Christe instituted it, and lefte it, a moste syngular comfort it were unto us all. But as concerning your masse, as it is nowe used in our dayes, I do saye and beleve it, to be the mooste abhominable ydoll that is in the worlde. For my God wyll not bee eaten with teeth, neither yet dyeth he agayne. And upon these wordes, that I have nowe spoken, wyll I suffer death. O Lorde, I have mo enemies

320   nowe then there be heares on my head. Yet Lorde, let them never overcome me with vayn words, but fyght thou Lorde in my stede, for on the

---

Line 297. **common Crede:** the Apostles' Creed, a statement of Christian belief.

Line 306. **Scripture sufficient to our salvation:** margin.

Line 311. **Psalm xxviii:** as in Bale's edition, the correct Vulgate reference is Psalm 118 (Ps. 119 in the King James version; see verse 105).

Line 317. **The masse abhominable Idol.:** margin.

Line 320. **heares:** hairs.

Line 320. **The praier of Anne Askewe.:** margin.

cast I my care. With all the spight they can imagine, they fall upon me, whiche am thy poore creature. Yet swete Lorde, lett me not sett by them whiche are against thee. For in thee is my whole delyght. And Lord I hartely desyre of thee, that thou wylt of thy moste mercifull goodnes forgeve them that violence, whiche they doo and have done unto me. Open also thou ther blynde hartes, that they may hereafter do that thyng in thy syght, whiche is only acceptable before thee. And to set fourth thy veritie aryght, without al vayne phantasies of synfull men. So be it. O Lorde so be it. 330

By me Anne Askewe.

Hetherto we have intreated of this good woman, now it remaineth that we touch somwhat as touching her end and martyrdom. She beyng borne of such stock and kynred, that she might have lyved in great wealth and prosperitie, if she wold rather have folowed the world then Christ, but now she was so tormented, that she could neither live long in so great distres, neither yet by the adversaries be suffred to die in secret. Wherfor the daie of her execution was appointed, and she brought into Smithfielde in a chayre, because she could not go on her feete, by meanes of her great tormentes, when she was brought unto the 340 stake, she was tied by the middle with a chaine, that helde up her body, when all thinges were thus prepared to the fire, the kinges letters of pardon were brought, wherby to offer her safe garde of her life if she would recant, which she would neither receave, neither yet vouchsafe once to loke upon. Shaxton also was there present who openly that day recanting his opinions, went about with a long oration to cause her also to

---

Line 322. **care. With:** emended from "care with".

Foxe omits the "The Balade whych Anne Askewe made and sange whan she was in Newgate." See pages 149–50.

Lines 332–76. **Hetherto...June:** a translation of the concluding paragraph on Askew in Foxe's Latin edition (199). His account of Askew's execution may come from eyewitnesses. See Textual Introduction, page liv.

Line 333. **touching:** emended from "touhing".

Line 339. **in a chayre:** a detail also in Louth's account. See Introduction, page xxxvii.

Line 340. **Anne Askewe refused the kinges pardon:** margin; **the:** emended from "tht".

Lines 341–45. **she was tied...upon:** Foxe was apparently the first to publish these details.

turne, against whome she stoutly resisted. Thus she being troubled so
many maner of waies, and having passed through so many torments,
having now ended the long course of her agonies, being compassed in
350 with flames of fire, as a blessed sacrifice unto God, she slept in the
Lorde, in An. 1546. leaving behind her a singular example of Christen
constancie for all men to folowe.

The description of Smythfielde with the order and maner of certayne of the Councell, sytting there at the burnyng of Anne Askewe and Lacels with the others.

John Lasselles, John Adams, and Nicolas Belenian.

There was at the same tyme also burnt together with her one Nicolas
Belenian priest of Shropshyre, John Adams a tayler, and John Lasselles
360 Gentleman of the Courte and housholde of kynge Henry. There is a
certaine appologetical, or defensive Epistle extant, whiche this man
briefly wrote, beyng in pryson, touchyng the Sacrament of the body
and bloud, wherein it doth bothe confute the errour of them whiche
not beyng contented with the spyritual receavyng of the Sacrament wyll
leave no substaunce of bread therein, and also doth put of the synister
interpretation of many thereupon. It happened well for them, that they
died together with Anne Askewe. For albeit that of them selves they
were strong and stout menne, yet through the example and praier of
her, thei being the more boldned, receyved occasion of more greater
370 comforte, in that so painfull and doolefull kynde of death, not only
beholdyng her invincible constancie, but also oftentimes stirred up
through her perswasions, they did set apart all kynde of feare. Thus they
confirming one another with mutuall exhortations, taried lookyng for
the tormenter and fyre, whiche at the last flamyng round about them,
consumed their blessed bodies in happie martyrdome, in the yeare of
our salvation 1546. about the moneth of June.

After line 356 is the woodcut printed on page 164 of the present edition.

Line 357. **Nicolas Belenian**: unidentified; no other accounts of the execution name Belenian.

Line 376. **June**: the date was 16 July 1546.

Appendix 1

IN ANNÆ ASKEVÆ CONSTANTISSIMÆ
fœminae & martyris bustum, Epitaphium Sapphicum, I.F.

Lictor incæstis manibus cruente,
Membra quid frustra eculeis fatigas,
Vique uirtutem laceras puellæ
    Te melioris?

Fortius istis pietas nitescit   5
Pressa tormentis, quatitur nec ullis
Veritas uinclis: citius sed ipsa
    Lassa fatiscunt.

Instat immani rabidus furore
Carnifex: ruptis iacet illa neruis   10
Fœmina in neruis, socias ut edat
    Relligionis.

Exprimit nullum tamen illa nomen,
Machinam uincit mulier tacendo.
Stant, stupent illi, furiunt trahendo: 15
    Proficiunt nil.

Artubus luxis resoluta cedunt
Ossa iuncturis, nihil in pudico
Corpore infractum est. Superat tyrannos
    Pars tamen una.   20

Sola enim nullis potuit moueri
Lingua rupturis: socias periclo
Dum suo soluit, iubet & quietam
    Stertere in aurem.

Ergo quæ nullis alias reuinci   25
Quiuit harpastris, moribunda tandem
Soluitur flammis, cineres coronat
    Vita perennis.

Sola nequaquam potitur brabeio
Hæc tamen: partes ueniunt coronæ,   30
Martyres unà: Opifex, Lasellus:
    Belenianus.

Appendix 1. This Latin Epitaph appeared at the end of Askew's *Examinations* in John Foxe's *Rerum in Ecclesia Gestarum Commentarii.* See Textual Introduction, page liii.

Title. **Epitaphium Sapphicum:** Epitaph in Sapphic verse; Sapphic stanzas are composed of three eleven-syllable lines (–˘– – –˘˘–˘– –) and one five-syllable line(–˘˘– –). I.F.: John Foxe.

EPITAPH IN SAPPHIC VERSE
upon the tomb of the most steadfast woman and martyr
ANNE ASKEW. J. F.

O warder, whose wicked hands are drenched in blood, why
do you vainly stretch her limbs on the rack and violently
tear apart a virtuous girl better far than you?

Her piety shines forth the brighter for being subjected
to torture; nor does she waver in truth through any fear   5
of chains: rather do these sooner wear out and fall apart.

The executioner comes forth, seething with ruthless fury:
her tendons untied, the woman lies tied up to make her
betray her partners in religion.

But she divulges no name, and by her silence the woman proves   10
stronger than the machine. They stand dumbstruck, and are
driven mad by the delay: yet they achieve nothing.

Her limbs are forced apart; her bones are broken, severed
from their joints; nothing in that chaste body is left intact.
Still one part of her defeats the tyrants.   15

For her tongue alone could not be moved by any suffering:
in rescuing her companions from her own peril, she bids
them slumber with untroubled ears.

So she who could not otherwise be overcome by instruments
of torture is at last dissolved by death in the flames,   20
and her ashes are blessed with life everlasting.

Yet she is by no means alone in winning the heavenly prize:
sharing the martyr's crown in company with her are a craftsman,
Lassels, and Belenian.

Epitaph in Sapphic Verse: Translation by G.P. Goold. J.F.: [by] John Foxe.

Appendix 2

A Ballad of *Anne Askew*, Intituled:
I am a Woman poore and Blind.

I am a Woman poore and blinde
and little knowledge remaines in me,
Long have I sought and faine would I finde,
what hearbs in my garden were best to be.

A garden I have which is unknowne,   5
that God of his goodnes gave unto me:
I meane my owne body wherein I would have sowne
the seede of Christs true veritie.

My spirit within me is vexed sore,
my flesh striveth against the same: 10
My sorrows do increase daily more and more,
my conscience suffereth most bitter paine:

I with my selfe being thus at strife,
would faine have bin at peace and rest:
Musing and studying in my mortall life,   15
what thing I might doe to please God best,

With whole intent and one accord,
unto a Gardner that I did know:
I went and desired him for the love of the Lord,
true seedes in my garden for to sow.   20

Then this proud Gardner seing me so blinde,
he thought on me to worke his will:
And flattered me with words so kind,
to have me continue in blindnesse still.

Appendix 2. This ballad about Askew is mentioned by Thomas Nashe in 1596. It was entered in the Stationers' Register on 14 December 1624. See Introduction, page xxxix.
Line 18. **Gardner:** an allusion to Stephen Gardiner, bishop of Winchester.

195

He fed me then with lyes and mockes,   25
for veniall sinnes he bad me goe,
To give my money to stones and stockes,
which was starke lyes and nothing so.

With stinking meate then was I fed,
for to keepe me from my salvation.   30
I had tren-talies of Masse, and Buls of lead,
not one word spoken of Christs passion.

In me was sowne all kinde of fained seedes,
with Popish ceremonies many a one,
Masses of Requiem with other Jugling deeds,   35
till Gods spirit out of my garden was gone.

Then was I commanded full straigtly,
If of my salvation I would be sure:
To build some Chappell, or some Chauntry,
to be prayd for whilst the world endure.   40

Beware of new learning, saith he, it is lies,
which is the thing I most abhorre:
Medele not with it in any manner of wise,
but doe as your fathers have done before.

My trust I did put then in the Diviles workes,   45
thinking them sufficient my soule to save.
Being worse then either Jewes or Turkes,
thus Christ of his merrits I did deprave.

Line 27. **stones and stockes:** gods of wood and stone.

Line 31. **tren-talies:** trentals; sets of thirty requiem masses. **Buls of lead:** the leaden seals attached to the pope's edicts.

Line 35. **Jugling:** cheating or deceiving.

Line 39. **Chauntry:** chantry; a chapel or altar in a church, endowed to ensure a daily mass sung for the souls of the dead.

Line 47. **Being...Turkes:** non-Christians, assumed to be incapable of salvation.

Line 48. **deprave:** emended from "derpave"; often used for or confused with "deprive" (*OED*).

I might liken my selfe with a wofull heart,
unto the dumbeman in Luke the eleven: 50
From whome Christ caused the Divell to depart
but shortly after he tooke the other seaven.

My time thus good Lord so wickedly spent,
alas shall I die the sooner therefore:
No, Lord, I finde written in thy Testament,   55
that thou hast mercy enough in store.

For such sinners as the Scripture saith,
that will gladly repent and follow thy word:
Which I will not deny whilst I have breath,
for Prison, fire, Faggot, nor firce sword.   60

Strength me good Lord in thy truth to stand,
for the bloudy Butchers have me at their wil
With ther slaughter knives ready drawn in ther hand
my simple carkas to devour and kill.

O Lord forgive me mine offence,   65
for I have offended thee very sore:
Take therefore my sinfull body from hence,
and then shal I vild wretch offend thee no more

I would with all Christians and faithfull friends
to keepe them from this Gardners hands,   70
For he will bring them soone unto their ends,
with cruell torments of fierce firebrands.

I dare not presume for him to pray,
because the truth of him was well knowne:
And since that time he hath gone astray,   75
and much pestilent seed abroad he hath sowne

Line 50. **eleven**: emended from "elven".
Line 60. **firce**: fierce.
Line 68. **vild**: vile.

Because that now I have no space,
the cause of my death truely to show:
I trust hereafter by Gods holy grace,
that all faithfull men shall it plainely know.   80

To thee O Lord I bequeath my spirit,
which art the workemaster of the same:
It is thine, Lord therefore take it of right,
my carkas on earth I leave, from whence it came

Although to ashes it be now burned,   85
I know thou canst raise it againe,
In the same likenesse that thou it formed,
in Heaven with thee evermore to remaine.

Imprinted at London for T.P.

Line 88. **in**: emended from "it".

Imprint. The basetext, the copy at the Central Library, Manchester, England, is torn so that the bottom of the initials is missing.

23299545R00167

Made in the USA
Middletown, DE
20 August 2015